The Depression
of the Nineties

Contributions in Economics and
Economic History

The Depression of the Nineties
An Economic History

Charles Hoffmann

CONTRIBUTIONS IN
ECONOMICS AND ECONOMIC HISTORY
NUMBER 2

Greenwood Publishing Corporation
WESTPORT, CONNECTICUT

Library of Congress Catalog Card Number: 78–90790
SBN: 8371–1855–7

Greenwood Publishing Corporation
51 Riverside Avenue, Westport, Connecticut   06880

Greenwood Publishing Ltd.
42 Hanway Street, London, Wl, England

Printed in the United States of America

*To the memory of
my mother and father, who made it
possible for me to see the light,
And to my sons, Richard and Brian,
who hopefully will see it
more clearly.*

Contents

Tables

Figures

Acknowledgments

Most written products are the result of conscious intellectual cooperation as well as influences which have long receded from consciousness. This work is no exception. Although I must be held responsible for the finished product, there are many debts owed to those who have aided me along the way.

In perusing the statistics and documents of the period, I found the custodians of such material very helpful. At the National Bureau of Economic Research, staff members generously provided useful economic series and analyses. The staff of the Columbia University Library, especially those in the School of Business Library which I made most use of, always gave me conscientious assistance. Mrs. Ruth B. Oakley, of the Queens College Library, always smilingly fulfilled my requests. For this help I am grateful.

To Professor Henry David, Human Resources Project, Columbia University, I owe two debts. It was he who first stimulated my interest in the economic history of the United States as an undergraduate. More recently, when this dissertation was being completed, he generously gave of his time and energy to read the typescript and to make both editorial and substantive comments. Any stylistic merit that appears owes much to him.

Mr. Robert Smuts, a staff member of the Human Resources Project, also made valuable suggestions and criticisms. My friend, Dr. Saul Benison, carefully read through the typescript more than once and I benefited greatly from his suggestions on form and content. He, too, helped me to make the finished product more readable. Mr. Matthew Simon, a fellow student at Columbia University writing a dissertation on the balance of payments of the United States, conscientiously provided me with much bibliographical and statistical information. He readily made available the fruits of his research which are an important part of the chapter on the balance of payments during the depression.

Dr. George Garvy, of the Federal Reserve Bank of New York, read through the entire typescript at an early stage of preparation and offered many worthwhile suggestions. Professor Carter Goodrich, my faculty adviser, helped me through the trials leading up to the dissertation defense. He and the other members of the Dissertation Committee made criticisms helpful to me in molding a better product. Professor Albert G. Hart, another member of the Committee, offered many valuable suggestions which led to a more informed view of the depression. Despite his late arrival on the scene (I did not have the benefit of his assistance until October, 1953), he was able to help clarify certain key elements in the depression.

My wife, Shirley, proved an indispensable partner, especially in the hectic days of the dissertation's completion. Besides her moral support she provided invaluable assistance in completing the final draft and in finishing many figures with meticulous care. Without her sympathetic and loving support, the task would have been longer and more complicated.

December, 1953   CHARLES HOFFMANN

* * *

I am grateful to my friends Saul Benison, of the National Foundation, William Hamovitch and the late Matthew Simon, both of Queens College of the City University of New York, and Herbert Cohen of Greenwood Publishing Corporation, for the encouragement in publishing this work which they so generously provided.

Mitchell Blazer assisted me greatly with his work on figures, tables, notes, bibliography, and proofreading; Mrs. Elsie Scevola's typing of parts of the manuscript expedited its processing; my secretary, Miss Marianne O'Brien, not only cheerfully carried the monotonous burden of typing and proofreading but also contributed effective ideas on figure and table design and gave helpful editorial suggestions; my son, Richard, helped in the indexing of authors. Their efforts lightened my burden considerably and for this I express my gratitude.

February, 1969   C. H.

Prefatory Note

This study was written some fifteen years ago and was an attempt to view the depression of the nineties through the newly fashioned macroeconomic frame which economists were using for current business-cycle forecasting and policy prescription. Income-output flow analysis, an instrument which had been forged by Keynes, is apt for dissecting the economy when in the throes of cyclical crises. Despite the incompleteness of the statistical data essential to effective use of income-flow analysis for the nineties, such an approach to the problem of the nature and causes of the depression appears to yield more productive results than the usual paths trod by the historian.

The results of the study, therefore, are far from definitive, due to the incompleteness of the data. Not only were certain crucial aggregates not available, but most of those which existed (sometimes in preliminary form) were on an annual basis, complicating the task of determining turning points in the cycle. Nevertheless, sufficient suitable material was uncovered to allow a meaningful description and causal analysis of the depression. This work was such an attempt and its tentative results are a preliminary offering to students of the period.

Publishing this work now affords an interesting opportunity to see how much a research product requires modification in a period when scholarly inquiry and information expand at a swift and increasing pace. We review this development with two aims in mind: (1) to take partial measure of the refined, extended, and new information unearthed or constructed during the last fifteen years; (2) to discern the extent to which these data affect the findings of this study and thus impose a more complete explanation of the depression.

In Chapter 1 the problem of the depression of the nineties is introduced first by placing the depression in the broad perspective of the sweeping quantitative changes in the economy from 1869 to 1913. The major events of the depression are dealt with specifically in Chapter 2 so that the reader can sense the social processes at work during this period of crisis.

The heart of the study, starting with preliminary Gross National Product (GNP) figures, involves a very rough approximation of the major components of GNP: gross private domestic investment, consumption expenditures on goods and services, net foreign investment, and government expenditures on goods and services. These major indicators of economic activity are causally related to monetary and price factors in the depression with great attention given, wherever possible, to the points in time when economic activity turned down or began to expand again.

The attempt to piece together in jigsaw fashion the major output variables which measure the course of economic activity yields an incomplete picture, many pieces of which are missing, but the main outlines and characteristics are clear and cast light on the meaning and nature of the depression. To the extent that data uncovered and published since 1953 fill out the picture, our view of the depression may have to be modified in major or minor ways.

The GNP figures presented in the body of the work are preliminary and incomplete. They were working figures for those putting the new national income tool to use in measuring the broad advance of a rapidly growing industrial order and were eventually refined, as more data were assimilated, into a full series running back well into the nineteenth century.

Since annual data on gross private domestic investment were not available in the early 1950's, the measure of fluctuations in investment had to be gleaned from a variety of sources. (Major investment areas—railroads, manufacturing, agriculture, mining, communications, and other transportation—are surveyed in Chapter 3.) Annual data on producer-durable output afford a quantitative basis for inferring changes in investment in equipment in various activities—farming, railroads, shipping, business administration, electrical output, and so on. Building construction indicators of various sorts are supplemented by a most valuable monthly index of overall building activity which makes possible inferences about exactly when building investment declined and what causal role building played in shaping the depression. Various annual and quarterly data on railroad investment—railroad mileage construction, and purchases of locomotives, freight and passenger cars—contribute further to grasping the role of investment before and during the economic contraction. General quantitative information on investment in mining and street railways helps to add important details to the investment picture. Incomplete though this investment picture is, it provides some basis for assessing investment's function in shaping the timing and intensity of the economic contraction.

The impact of consumption on the depression and vice versa is suggested by annual data on the value of output destined for domestic consumption in Chapter 4. Of course, this variable is not congruent with consumption expenditures on goods and services since services and inventory changes are excluded. Moreover, annual data do not throw light on downturns and upturns in economic activity. Yet, these detailed data tell a wide-ranging story of what probably happened to the consumption of perishable, semidurable, and durable goods during the depression years. The fluctuations in the consumption of cigars and cigarettes, newspapers and magazines, fuel and lighting products, clothing and shoes, dry goods and house furnishings, are noted along with the ups and downs in the use of furniture, floor coverings, china and house utensils, musical instruments, jewelry, and pleasure craft.

Data on net foreign investment are incomplete, though solid statistics on merchandise exports and imports and certain services are available. Crude reconstruction of capital flows and the level of foreign investment and United States investment abroad is undertaken and assumptions and estimates on investment income are made in Chapter 5. A total approximate balance of payments is used to throw some light on how the economy was affected by its economic transactions with the rest of the world.

Government expenditures are not complete; the totals used in Chapter 6 for purposes of generalizing the impact of government fiscal operations on the economy are the expenditures only of the federal government. During the nineties this represented about half of total government expenditures (states, cities, and so on).

Within this frame of changes in economic activity, as measured by crude surrogates for major national output components, data on prices of factors of production and on monetary variables such as currency, deposits, and loans are injected in Chapters 6 and 7.

This incomplete statistical configuration is the basis for analyzing the depression of the nineties. To the extent that certain important quantitative changes have been identified and rough orders of magnitude and directions of change of others sensed, the depression, its characteristics, and its principal causal links can more effectively be described and analyzed.

Efforts in the last fifteen years to refine, extend, and construct new statistical data on the United States economy during the latter part of the nineteenth century have generally produced excellent results that can be put to good use in comprehending the depression of the nineties. The performance of the economy can now be described in much fuller quantitative detail, both horizontally and vertically. More series on more aspects of economic activity can now be seen in broader and deeper statistical dimensions. Overall economic performance can now be viewed broadly as it is in today's economy: national output and its components are traced back, on an annual basis, to 1889. The performance of industries and sectors of the economy are more thoroughly chronicled. And yet, despite this signal advance in quantifying the anatomy and physiology of economic life, there are still important gaps in data and the shape of most of the data makes impossible the kind of precise analysis of the business cycle which the student of contemporary cyclic phenomena takes for granted.

Fifteen years ago the only annual data on national output were preliminary GNP figures, an array of data on commodity output destined for domestic consumption, and various indexes of sectoral output. Today the national output picture is richer in its principal macroeconomic components: refined GNP and Net National Product figures; gross private domestic investment broken down into new construction and equipment and inventory changes; consumption expenditures on goods and services; net exports, including a complete series on the balance of payments; and total expenditures for all governmental units. These annual data are almost all available in current as well as constant prices and provide a set of variables with which to analyze the economy's accomplishments and a framework within which to evaluate data on sectoral and industry performance.[1]

Other macroeconomic data, developed and refined in recent years, reflect aspects of total economic activity implicit in the national income statistics: national productivity rates, employment, man-hours, hours worked, worker employment rates, prices, and so on. Together with national income data, these statistics provide the economic historian and economist with a treasure of material with which to focus on formerly unanswerable historical questions.

While these macroeconomic statistical data have been generated at a rapid rate since the early 1950's, a parallel growth of quantitative material for industries and economic sectors has also taken place. In some instances, these latter data have become the building blocks for constructing the global statistics for total output, investment, consumption, and the like. Whether or not these data have performed such a role, they have all contributed to the progressive filling out of the economic structure with hard quantitative measurement of that structure in action.

Some examples of this kind of statistical advance help to outline the shape of developing sources for economic description and analysis of the past. In sectoral contexts, data on commodity output (for five-year spans), farm gross product and investment (on a decennial basis), and share of service income (again for every ten years) have been gathered. For industries, annual time series have been constructed for oil wells drilled, gross residential building capital formation, building construction in Ohio, nonfarm dwelling construction, and the like. Other miscellaneous data for selected years of the nineteenth century include: interregional income differentials, employee compensation in specific occupations, new price indices, unemployment and related series during the nineties, and refined series on monetary variables (money supply, loans, and so on).

And yet, even with the unearthing of these rich statistical mines which can be so much more fruitfully exploited by the historian and the economist, shortcomings of the data beyond problems of reliability and accuracy frustrate the student of past economic activity, especially if he casts an inquiring eye on the business cycle. Because so many of the series newly at hand are for a five- or ten-year span they cannot be utilized at all to answer questions about a particular cycle, unless there is a fortuitous dovetailing in time of cycle and series. Even when the series are on an annual basis, their usefulness is limited in tracing finely the movements of the business cycle. For only monthly or quarterly series make possible clear-cut identification of the downturn or upturn in a particular economic activity or in the economy as a whole. Thus, none of the significant additions to our statistical measurement of economic activity during the nineties throw light directly on turning points, since none of the series is on a monthly or quarterly basis. Our vastly improved quantitative measurement of the economy each year of the nineties, which opens the way to a fuller understanding of the depression, is lacking in this important detail. We must depend, therefore, upon old building construction and railroad rolling stock series, on a monthly and quarterly basis, respectively, to give us a tentative answer to the question of the depression's turning points.

How do these new data affect the findings of fifteen years ago presented in the chapters that follow? They certainly fill out in greater detail the partial delineation of the economy's fluctuating output of goods and services. Some tentative estimates are bolstered; other provisional generalizations must be modified by this more recent information and its interpretation. In the main, the conclusions are upheld, subject to refinements imposed by the authority of newer, more informed data.

I

The broad quantitative framework of the economy in the period 1869 to 1913, presented in Chapter 1, can be effectively filled in and extended with more annual data on output and other important indicators of economic performance. GNP and its components are available for 1869, 1879, 1889, and then on an annual basis. Balance-of-payments data have been fashioned into extensive classifications for visible and invisible transactions as well as capital and gold flows so that a complete annual series now covers the entire period. Similarly, other series on employment, prices, productivity, and the like contribute to a more ramifying quantification of the process of industrialization and development. These recently constructed measures of the United States' economic growth do not throw into question the generalizations of Chapter 1; rather, they offer a richer choice of economic variables with which to describe and analyze that growth. Interestingly, refinements of the GNP data depicted in Figure 2 of Chapter 1 do not change the overall framework of the depression in any appreciable way. Figure 1 traces fluctuations in newer real GNP from 1890 through 1902. Clearly, the broad contours of the period remain the same as those traced in Figure 2. The depths of the two depression troughs are fundamentally the same—below 90 percent of capacity—and the depressed state of the economy throughout the nineties (after 1892) is unmistakable in either chart. The reattainment of full-capacity output is not realized until after the turn of the century.

The data in Table 1, from which the GNP figures in Figure 1 are derived, reveal the extent of overall real economic fluctuations extending from before the depression period until total output and its components regained the heights of capacity performance in 1901 and 1902. GNP's severe real contraction was compounded of a seemingly moderate decline in the consumption of goods and services (which, given high unemploy-

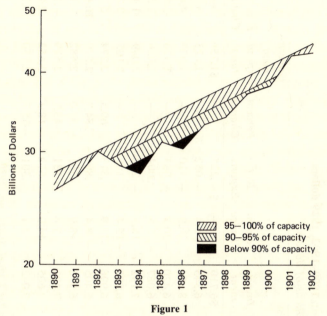

Figure 1
GNP, 1890-1902, Compared to Capacity

ment and reduced working hours, probably meant sharp real declines for millions of families), very sharp drops in real investment, improvements in net exports, and a mild upward trend in government purchases of goods and services.

Table 2 details these overall fluctuations in current values, no account being taken of price changes, and thus, given the money illusion, these variations reflect deeper changes in declining national output and its components and shallower rises in these data. Such changes have to be refined by the economist to reach the true measure of economic variations, but the social and psychological impact of actual dollar changes should not be lost in the economist's pursuit of a methodological imperative.

Table 1

National Output, 1890–1902, 1929 dollars

(billions of dollars)

Year	Gross National Product	Percent Change	Consumption	Percent Change	Investment	Percent Change	Net Exports	Percent Change	Government Expenditures	Percent Change
1890	$26.196	—	$17.955	—	$6.710	—	$ −.225	—	$1.756	—
1891	27.365	4.5	19.247	7.2	6.345	− 5.4	−.052	—	1.825	3.9
1892	30.010	9.7	20.157	4.7	8.054	26.9	−.110	—	1.909	4.6
1893	28.569	−4.8	20.256	.5	6.420	−20.3	−.083	—	1.976	3.5
1894	27.756	−2.8	19.659	−2.9	6.067	− 5.5	.004	—	2.026	2.5
1895	31.082	12.0	22.119	2.5	7.192	18.5	−.278	—	2.049	1.1
1896	30.444	−2.1	22.056	− .3	6.088	−15.4	.195	—	2.105	2.7
1897	33.327	9.5	23.794	7.9	6.996	14.9	.313	60.5	2.224	5.7
1898	34.068	2.2	24.193	1.7	6.405	− 8.4	.891	184.7	2.579	16.0
1899	37.172	9.1	27.053	2.8	6.976	8.9	.561	−37.0	2.582	.1
1900	38.197	2.8	27.296	.9	7.491	7.4	.831	48.1	2.579	−.1
1901	42.587	1.5	30.651	2.3	8.605	14.9	.679	−18.3	2.652	2.8
1902	43.004	.98	30.911	.8	9.042	5.1	.301	−55.7	2.750	3.7

Source: John W. Kendrick, *Productivity Trends in the United States*, pp. 293ff.
Note: Figures are based on the U.S. Commerce Department concept of output.

Table 2

National Output, 1890–1902, Current Dollars

(billions of dollars)

Year	Gross National Product	Percent Change	Consumption	Percent Change	Investment	Percent Change	Net Exports	Percent Change	Government Expenditures	Percent Change
1890	$13.129	—	$ 9.512	—	$3.071	—	$ −.115	—	$ .661	—
1891	13.530	3.1	10.068	5.8	2.794	− 9.0	−.026	—	.694	5.0
1892	14.273	5.5	10.166	1.0	3.438	23.0	−.053	—	.722	4.0
1893	13.849	−3.0	10.447	2.8	2.687	−21.8	−.041	—	.756	4.7
1894	12.619	−8.9	9.417	−9.9	2.447	− 8.9	.002	—	.753	− .4
1895	13.928	10.4	10.370	10.1	2.911	19.0	−.126	—	.773	2.7
1896	13.295	−4.5	10.028	−3.3	2.382	−18.2	.086	—	.799	3.4
1897	14.617	9.9	10.851	8.2	2.783	16.8	.139	61.6	.844	5.6
1898	15.388	5.3	11.315	4.3	2.631	− 5.5	.408	193.5	1.034	22.5
1899	17.356	12.8	12.797	13.1	3.195	21.4	.266	−35.8	1.098	6.2
1900	18.684	7.7	13.630	6.5	3.518	10.1	.412	54.9	1.124	2.4
1901	20.668	10.6	15.191	11.5	3.995	13.6	.334	18.9	1.148	2.1
1902	21.554	4.3	15.913	4.8	4.251	6.4	.153	−54.2	1.237	7.8

Source: Kendrick, *Productivity Trends*, pp. 296ff.
Note: Figures are based on the U.S. Commerce Department concept of output.

II

The annals of the depression—Chapter 2—are based primarily on contemporary data and account for and focus on the important events and short-run movements which help us to perceive the depression as a social process first, before its abstract quantitative measures are set forth and analyzed. Its details could be extended by the many new data made available, but too extensive reliance on secondary analysis would transform the chapter into something it was not intended to be. One interesting point on the estimate of unemployment in 1893 deserves mention. Our figure of about 2.5 million appears to be on the low side, if Lebergott's estimate of 3.3 million is accepted as more authoritative.[2]

III

Chapter 3, paradoxically, is the least successful of the chapters on major GNP components in reconstructing the total and subtotals for the investment component, though most successful in pinpointing the role that specific sectors of investment played in overall contraction and in the turning points of the business cycle. The latter success arises from the existence of monthly and quarterly data on building construction and railroad construction and purchases of equipment and rails at the time this monograph was first put together. From these limited but invaluable less-than-annual series and certain indirect indicators of investment, the central part played by investment in shaping the amplitude and duration of the depression seems established in the unrevised version.

The additional data now available support these earlier findings. Unfortunately, since they are all on an annual basis, no new light is cast on turning points, but it seems clear that the added series do not throw doubt on the inferences based on the monthly and quarterly data set down fifteen years ago.

Table 3

**Gross Private Domestic Investment,
1890–1902, 1929 prices**

(billions of dollars)

Year	Total	Percent Change	New Construction & Equipment	Percent Change	Change in Business Inventories	Percent Change
1890	$6.710	—	$6.231	—	$ .479	—
1891	6.345	− 5.4	5.907	− 5.2	.438	− 8.6
1892	8.054	26.9	7.488	26.8	.566	29.2
1893	6.420	−20.3	6.219	−16.9	.201	−64.5
1894	6.067	− 5.5	5.887	− 5.3	.180	−10.4
1895	7.192	18.5	6.404	8.8	.788	337.8
1896	6.088	−15.4	5.734	−10.5	.354	−55.1
1897	6.996	14.9	6.197	8.1	.799	125.7
1898	6.405	− 8.4	5.847	5.6	.558	−30.2
1899	6.976	8.9	5.859	.2	1.117	100.2
1900	7.491	7.4	6.768	15.5	.723	−35.3
1901	8.605	14.9	7.470	10.4	1.135	57.0
1902	9.042	5.1	8.410	12.6	.632	−44.3

Source: Kendrick, *Productivity Trends*, p. 293.

Tables 3 and 4 provide the broad measures of investment and its two components: new construction and equipment and changes in inventories. The changes are again projected in real terms as well as in dollars of current value to yield the more refined measure of what happened as well as the psychological reality of change in current values.

The substance of Chapter 3 seems justified: investment was a volatile variable which had a major causal impact on total econ-

Table 4
Gross Private Domestic Investment,
1890–1902, Current Dollars
(billions of dollars)

Year	Total	Percent Change	New Construction & Equipment	Percent Change	Change in Business Inventories	Percent Change
1890	$3.071	—	$2.788	—	$.283	—
1891	2.794	− 9.0	2.537	− 9.0	.257	− 9.2
1892	3.438	23.0	3.128	23.3	.310	20.6
1893	2.687	−21.8	2.574	−17.7	.113	−63.5
1894	2.447	− 8.9	2.356	− 8.5	.091	−19.5
1895	2.911	19.0	2.508	6.5	.403	342.9
1896	2.382	−18.2	2.209	−11.9	.173	−57.1
1897	2.783	16.8	2.392	8.3	.391	126.0
1898	2.631	− 5.5	2.347	− 1.9	.284	−27.4
1899	3.195	21.4	2.583	10.1	.612	115.5
1900	3.518	10.1	3.092	19.7	.426	−30.4
1901	3.995	13.6	3.337	7.9	.658	54.5
1902	4.251	6.4	3.860	15.7	.391	−40.6

Source: Kendrick, *Productivity Trends,* p. 296.

omic activity and because of investment's low level the economy was kept from achieving capacity performance from 1893 until 1901 or 1902. The 1892 level was not achieved again until 1900 in current dollar terms and 1901 in real terms. Only the sharp increase in 1901 and the continued, if less marked, increase in 1902 lifted investment close to its capacity level. The severe declines in investment in 1893, 1894, and 1896 are a major explanation for the deep economic contraction. Declines in construction and equipment, already inferred from the incomplete data of fifteen years ago, were accompanied by sharper drops in accumulations of inventories in the same years, the decline for 1893–1894 reaching a staggering 75 percent and that for 1896 a whopping 55 percent.

The data in Chapter 3 document the dragging effect that contraction in building and railroad construction and railroad purchases of rails and equipment imposed on the economy. The various series in Table 5 on residential construction detail one aspect of building construction, reflected in Long's monthly series on building permits which appears in the chapter. The different series in Table 5 show declines in real terms ranging from 21 to 30 percent for 1893–1894 and from 10 to 83 percent for 1896 and in current dollars ranging from 22 to 30 percent for 1893–1894 and from 10 to 16 percent for 1896. It is important to note that these declines occurred within a broader framework from 1890 to 1902 in which, excepting the series on expenditures for new private nonhousekeeping residential facilities, the peaks of 1890 or 1892 in construction were never attained again throughout the period until 1902. The nineties were a deeply depressed period for building construction and thus it was a major factor retarding general economic activity.

In sum, then, Chapter 3's main point—that investment deficiencies stemming principally from weakness in building and railroad investment impeded general economic growth and precipitated cyclical decline—is substantiated by the new statistical series now available. In this context, the shrinking of European investment abroad (particularly British, as the world's industrial economies were experiencing cyclical contraction through 1894), occurring at a time when the attractiveness of and need for railroad expansion had waned and when domestic construction was in a protracted cyclical decline, contributed significantly to the long and deep economic malaise of the nineties.

Table 5

Residential Construction, 1890–1902

	1890	1891	1892	1893	1894	1895	1896	1897	1898	1899	1900	1901	1902
1. New private nonfarm dwelling units started (thousands)	$328	298	381	267	265	309	257	292	262	282	189	275	240
Percent change	—	-9.1	27.8	-29.9	-.8	16.6	-16.8	13.6	-10.3	7.6	-33.0	45.5	-12.7
2. Expenditures for (1) millions of current dollars	$790	612	763	583	594	679	606	643	574	608	433	610	572
Percent change	—	-22.5	24.7	-23.6	1.9	14.3	-10.8	6.1	10.7	5.9	28.8	40.9	-6.3
3. Expenditures for (1) millions of 1929 dollars	$2,015	1,615	2,073	1,589	1,678	1,946	1,726	1,869	1,599	1,579	1,067	1,521	1,378
Percent change	—	-19.9	28.4	-23.3	5.6	16.0	-11.3	8.3	-14.4	-1.3	-32.4	4.25	-9.4
4. Expenditures for new private nonhousekeeping residential facilities, millions of current dollars	—	13	9	9	7	7	10	17	12	10	11	38	51
Percent change	—	—	-30.8	—	-22.2	—	42.9	70.0	-29.4	-16.7	10.0	245.4	34.2
millions of 1929 dollars	—	35	25	25	20	20	29	50	34	26	27	95	124
Percent change	—	—	28.6	—	-20.0	—	45.0	72.4	-32.0	-23.5	3.8	251.9	30.5
5. Gross capital formation: housekeeping residential real estate, millions of current dollars	$875	694	843	662	672	756	683	719	646	679	503	683	648
Percent change	—	-20.7	21.5	21.5	1.5	12.5	-9.7	5.3	-10.2	5.1	-25.9	35.8	-5.1
millions of 1929 dollars	$2,232	1,831	2,290	1,804	1,898	2,167	1,945	2,090	1,800	1,763	1,239	1,703	1,561
Percent change	—	-18.0	25.0	-21.2	5.2	14.2	-10.2	7.5	-13.9	-2.1	-29.7	37.4	-8.3
6. Net capital formation: housekeeping residential real estate, millions of current dollars	$681	493	636	444	452	529	444	474	382	386	186	364	310
Percent change	—	-27.6	29.0	-30.2	1.8	17.0	-16.1	6.8	-19.4	1.0	-51.8	95.7	-14.8
millions of 1929 dollars	$1,736	1,301	1,727	1,210	1,277	1,515	1,264	1,379	1,063	1,003	459	908	748
Percent change	—	-25.1	32.7	-29.9	5.5	18.6	-82.6	9.1	-22.9	-5.6	-54.2	97.8	-17.6

Source: Leo Grebler, D. M. Blank, and L. Winnick, *Capital Formation in Residential Real Estate*, pp. 332ff.

IV

The data in Chapter 4 are a very rough first approximation to consumption during the depression and have to be qualified both in terms of conceptual shortcomings and the totals now available for expenditures on consumer goods and services during the nineties. (See Tables 1 and 2 above.) The statistical series presented in the chapter on durable, semidurable, and perishable goods derive from Shaw's data on commodity output destined for domestic consumption—a concept patently short of the category, Consumption of Goods and Services. It seems quite clear, given the modest drop in overall consumption in 1894 and the imperceptible decline in 1896, that the new data show that the analysis of consumption in Chapter 4 exaggerates the general contraction in consumption.

A careful analysis of the conceptual difference between Shaw's Commodity Output Destined for Domestic Consumption and Consumption of Goods and Services uncovers the shortcomings of the series first employed. To construct value of consumer goods and services requires adding to and perhaps subtracting from Shaw's series. Since food is excluded, that very significant (and quite stable) component of consumption must be counted. For many families, food was a major part of total consumption so that its stability of output and use would keep the average decline in consumption from being very great. In addition, all imported goods which reach ultimate consumers must be aggregated. Another required major addition to Shaw's series is the value of services performed for consumers. Each one of these salient categories, probably behaving quite differently during a depression and a period of rapid industrialization, could have a determining impact on the sum of consumer goods and services. Furthermore, though Shaw's series is labeled as "destined" for domestic consumption, some leakage to exports is possible. For the period under review, the probability of this being of any moment is not great, but the conceptual consequences should be considered. Generally, under almost all possibilities of such leakages, the results under conditions of declining output (say, 1893, 1894, and 1896), with exports of such commodities occurring in both or only one of the years being compared, would be greater contraction in consumption than Shaw's series record. Of course, when two years (say, 1892 and 1893 or 1893 and 1894) are compared, assuming export leakages for both years, if the leakage is greater for the first than for the second the decline in Shaw's data will be moderated.

The data in Tables 1 and 2 reveal real declines in consumption of about 3 percent for 1894 and .3 percent for 1896, while the contractions in current value were about 10 and 3 percent, respectively. The disparity between these recent (and more conceptually sound) series and the data dissected in Chapter 4 calls for some analytic (and speculative) reconciliation since the latter data show consumption declines for the three deep depression years ranging up to 20 percent for major categories and considerably higher for specific categories such as musical instruments, floor coverings, and the like. Clearly, the exclusion of food from Shaw's perishables category gives any measure of consumption based on his series a downward bias in years of declining commodity consumption since food is undoubtedly an item for which most people do not reduce expenditures except in the most dire circumstances. Although the roles of consumer services and imported consumer goods in the aggregate of consumption expenditures are not as clear-cut as that of food, their omission from the consumption total may render that aggregate unreliable and grossly inaccurate. During the depression, services and imports may very well have fluctuated in much the same way as perishables, semidurables, and durables. Consumer services were most probably income elastic. Many people per-

formed most of their own services or did without some (for example, education). Imports of consumer goods were subject to
several forces. Two readily identifiable ones were the trend toward industrialization, with domestic products displacing some
consumer imports, and the fact that consumer imports were
generally "luxury" goods and thus were mainly purchased by
more affluent people. For many of them, however, bad times
would cause some retrenchment in luxury goods.

Whatever the quantitative dimensions of these various
conceptual considerations, the fact of total consumption
expenditures for the depression years declining only moderately
demands that the data in Chapter 4 be used *only* as reasonably
accurate measures of commodity output of perishables, semidurables, and durables. This means that to the extent that overall consumption declined moderately the drops in commodity
consumption were very much sharper than total consumption
(offset at least by stability in overall food consumption). The
generalizations about per capita consumption likewise must be
seen only as relating to commodity output, which fell sharply
below capacity levels. So far as generalizations about the groups
that suffered the depression's effects most acutely, they remain
valid since unemployment or disability reduced these groups'
income sharply and visited poverty levels of consumption on
them for varying periods of time. With millions of families
suffering the loss of their breadwinners in 1893 and 1894, the
reduction for them in consumption of goods and services must
have been pinching whatever the actual decline in overall
consumption.

V

The economic relationships between the United States and
the rest of the world greatly affected internal economic change,
both cyclical and secular. Chapter 5 attempts to identify tenta-

tively the most significant of these relationships quantitatively as a basis for assessing their impact on a rapidly expanding economy in the throes of severe cyclical stress. The data presented in Chapter 5 vary from complete and reliable (for gold flows and balance of trade) to incomplete and quite provisional (for certain invisibles and capital flows) so that the total balance-of-payments picture is sketched together with variable reliability. Fortunately, in the past fifteen years, hard work on the balance of payments has come to fruition and a consistent and complete set of data for major categories makes possible more firm generalization.[3]

That more definitive set of balance payments data is reproduced in Table 6 on a fiscal-year basis. The balance-of-trade statistics have remained basically unchanged since this type of information began to be accurately recorded. (Seeming discrepancies for annual totals are due to fiscal-calendar year differences.) The shipping balance is a considerably refined version built from revision of the older data in the light of new information and clearer conceptualization. Certain individual years are now considerably different from earlier totals, though the negative impact of the series is clear. The passenger balance statistics likewise differ from the specifics of older research and publication with the order of magnitude changing though not the negative sign. The financial balance is a new total erected from refined interest and dividend payments to which bankers' commissions rightfully have been added. The new totals are greater than the older ones, but many of the variations in the category conform to the pattern revealed in Chapter 5. The resulting fluctuations in the balance of payments on current account during the nineties can be seen in a clearer pattern than what the statistics in Chapter 5 suggest. With the exception of the fiscal year 1894 (July 1, 1893, through June 30, 1894— from the monetary panic in the summer of 1893 to the trough of the first phase of the depression), during the 1890–1896 period the current account was unbalanced—a condition to be expected of the economy until appreciable capital exports were generated. The favorable balance in current account during fiscal 1894 was a consequence of the deep contraction of the economy which led to further declines in imports, shipping costs, interest and dividend payments, and bankers' commissions (as many foreign investors in United States enterprise reduced further investment and even repatriated their claims). The pattern of imbalance in current account was consistently made possible by continuous, growing foreign investment in the United States economy. When such investment did not quite cover the current account deficit, gold movement completed the overall balance. During the depression, the flow of foreign investment into the United States economy was determined by the availability of investment funds (as already noted, western European economies were in cyclical contraction), expectations of capital gains, vicissitudes of the stock market (gains were realized; bargains were seized), changes in interest rates, considerations of confidence in the United States remaining on a gold standard, and the like.

The long-established accurate series on gold flows, in addition to the newly completed more exact data on current account transactions, yield a firmer set of figures on net international capital movements and on the net accumulating balance of the United States' international indebtedness. These data in Table 6 supersede earlier series and estimates which were both incomplete and open to question. The data now available give a consistent series that throws light on important questions raised during the depression. The extent of net repatriation of foreign investment—often put forth by certain contemporaries as a very large continuing amount and a major consequence of a misbegotten silver policy—is put in proper perspective. With the exception of the fiscal year 1894, foreign investment in the United States continued—though at a reduced level—for the fiscal years 1890 through 1896. This was a period when several important factors were interacting and net foreign investment was a more complex phenomenon than contemporaries and later analysts with large axes to grind would have had us think. A major part of the thrust of industrialization gathering momentum during the nineties was clearly aimed at penetrating foreign markets, a growing commitment requiring rising capital exports. The well of investment funds for foreign investment in the United States was drying up somewhat from 1890 through 1895 as Europe experienced economic contraction. Expectations for gain in United States railroads and other industries grew gloomier as the nineties unfolded. Confidence in our remaining on the gold standard was certainly undermined somewhat by legislation and indecisive policy. Yet, despite the conjuncture of these negative factors, foreigners continued to invest in the economy. The net attractiveness of such investment in the face of these negative forces is a phenomenon which has been obscured. Its reality is a factor that must modify considerably the conventional and somewhat diabolical view of the depression and the decade.

VI

The role that money played in the depression of the nineties was defined in widely differing ways by contemporaries and, even today, from our vantage point of more extensive data, more refined theoretical concepts, and greater understanding of the way banking and monetary mechanisms function, a definitive view of money's causal path in the cyclical contraction still eludes us. In Chapter 6, we present the basic statistical series on the supply of money and its components, as well as related data, including fiscal operations of the federal government. Our view is that the depression's severity owed much to monetary and

Table 6

United States Balance of Payments and Net International Indebtedness, Fiscal Years 1890–1900

(*millions of dollars*)

	1890	1891	1892	1893	1894	1895	1896	1897	1898	1899	1900
Balance of trade	$36.9	$53.0	$215.7	$−12.3	$231.2	$68.6	$95.8	$278.9	$610.7	$523.8	$536.6
Shipping balance (Freight, insurance, etc.)	−27.7	−23.9	−20.8	−21.6	−15.8	−21.2	−19.7	−20.4	−15.3	−17.1	−20.0
Passenger balance (tourism, remittances, etc.)	−91.3	−99.5	−101.5	−73.4	−74.4	−111.0	−100.2	−90.9	−90.9	−103.3	−126.1
Financial balance	−129.5	−138.5	−147.7	−143.5	−116.7	−130.6	−126.4	−131.2	−136.3	−128.5	−119.3
Net bankers' commissions	−4.7	−4.8	−4.8	−4.8	−3.7	−4.2	−4.4	−4.4	−3.7	−4.1	−5.0
Net interest and dividends	−124.8	−133.7	−142.9	−138.7	−113.0	−126.4	−122.0	−126.8	−132.6	−124.4	−114.3
Balance of payments on current account	−211.6	−208.9	−54.3	−250.8	24.3	−194.2	−150.5	36.4	359.3	274.9	271.2
Net gold movements	5.2	69.8	0.6	87.9	4.5	30.1	78.9	−44.7	−105.0	−51.4	3.7
Net silver movements	13.8	4.6	12.9	17.5	37.2	27.1	31.8	31.4	24.2	25.6	21.5
Net international capital movements	192.6	134.5	40.8	145.4	−66.0	137.0	39.8	−23.1	−278.5	−249.1	−296.4
Net accumulating balance of international indebtedness	2,906.5	3,041.0	3,081.8	3,227.2	3,161.2	3,298.2	3,338.0	3,314.9	3,036.4	2,787.3	2,490.9

Source: Matthew Simon, "The United States Balance of Payments, 1861–1900," in *Trends in the American Economy in the Nineteenth Century*, Studies in Income and Wealth, National Bureau of Economic Research, 24: 702–705.

banking conditions and dysfunction, but that the economic contraction was shaped mainly by fundamental changes in real and financial investment opportunities.

Changes in the supply of money affected business decisions at important junctures of the business cycle and even after contraction set in. Early in the nineties, the supply of money grew at a slower than average rate and in the latter part of 1892 gold outflows and declines in bank reserves restricted the availability of funds. As economic contraction set in, gold holdings, bank reserves, and deposits declined. During the banking panic in the summer of 1893, bank suspensions and failures stimulated hoarding and reduced the effective supply of money greatly, forcing many enterprises to curtail or stop production even when market conditions did not exact such retrenchment. This undoubtedly intensified the downward movement of the economy.

After the trough in 1894, economic expansion was paralleled by increases in bank reserves and the money supply. This continued into 1895. Later in that year, however, increases in gold outflows, declines in bank reserves, and contraction in the supply of money helped push the economy into another cyclical retreat.

The data offered in Chapter 6 have been added to and presented in an insightful analytic framework in the monumental work of Milton Friedman and Anna J. Schwartz. Their perception of the place of money in economic events is provocatively different from that of many other economists and they seriously question the efficacy of attempts at short-run control of the business cycle with either monetary or fiscal tools. Instead, they project an important role for the supply of money over time: it must grow at a steady rate of about 5 percent a year, otherwise economic activity will be adversely affected.[4]

For Friedman and Schwartz, the intensity of the depression

of the nineties was an inevitable result of monetary mismanagement. The monetary stock grew inadequately from 1891 to 1897—at a rate of 2 percent a year— and was actually down 5 percent from 1892 to 1896. (Inevitably, after the fact of depression, the average rate of growth of money supply for the period will be down. Is the lower rate cause or effect?) The silver policy engendered a loss of confidence in the government's determination to maintain the gold standard and a series of "flights" from the dollar ensued. Financing adverse capital flows put added strain on prices and income. Gold exports reduced the money supply. The attempt to uphold fixed exchange parity in an atmosphere of uncertainty and low confidence led to rapid fluctuations in short-term balances with consequent economic disturbances. Given this situation, two alternatives existed: declines in domestic prices and a drop or a reduced rate of increase in money income; or abandonment of the gold standard and depreciation of the dollar. These two students of the period hold that under the circumstances either early acceptance of a silver standard or commitment to a gold standard would have had much better results than the equivocal situation in which there were doubts about what would happen to the standard and as a consequence wide fluctuations in the money supply occurred with disruptive results.[5]

Whether one accepts this analysis or not, Friedman and Schwartz have thrown new light on monetary factors in the depression and their analysis and data ought to be put to effective use. This writer views with skepticism the heavy weight placed on annual increases in money supply at a roughly fixed rate as the major monetary means to economic stability. Such monetary growth may be a necessary—but is not a sufficient—condition for stability. Even under circumstances of monetary adequacy, other economic factors play determining roles leading to fluctuations in economic activity.

Table 7

Currency, Deposits, Bank Reserves, and Treasury
Balances in the United States, 1890–1900

(millions of dollars)

| Year, End of June | Currency Held By Public | Per cent Change | Deposits Adjusted | | | | Vault Cash | Per cent Change | Treasury Cash | Per cent Change | U.S. Gov't Deposits | Per cent Change |
			Commercial Banks	Per cent Change	Mutual Savings Banks	Per cent Change						
1890	$ 888	—	$3,020	—	$1,373	—	$478	—	$245	—	$31	—
1891	921	3.7	3,098	2.6	1,427	3.9	512	7.1	173	−29.4	26	−16.1
1892	929	.9	3,541	14.3	1,517	6.3	600	17.2	147	−15.0	14	−46.2
1893	985	6.0	3,203	−9.5	1,546	1.9	529	−11.8	138	−6.1	14	0.0
1894	883	−10.4	3,341	4.3	1,571	1.6	686	29.7	142	2.9	14	0.0
1895	881	−.2	3,596	7.6	1,650	5.0	621	−9.5	215	51.4	15	7.1
1896	832	−5.6	3,434	−4.5	1,693	2.6	567	−8.7	288	34.0	17	13.3
1897	873	4.9	3,609	5.1	1,784	5.4	651	14.8	261	−9.4	16	−5.6
1898	1,017	16.5	4,120	14.2	1,869	4.8	704	8.1	231	−11.5	49	206.3
1899	1,068	5.0	4,966	20.5	1,999	7.0	738	4.8	273	18.2	76	55.1
1900	1,191	11.5	5,187	4.4	2,128	6.5	763	3.4	280	2.6	99	30.3

Source: Milton Friedman and Anna J. Schwartz, A Monetary History of the United States: 1867–1960, National Bureau of Economic Research Study, pp. 705, 735, 749.

Yet our findings in Chapter 6 need qualification and modified emphasis in the light of the Friedman-Schwartz statistics and analysis. Table 7 provides some of the principal monetary series essential for our modified analysis. They are more refined than our data and call for review of the material in Chapter 6.

The series in Table 7 establish generally the low rate of growth in the determinants and components of the money supply during the depression and years immediately preceding and reflect also an appreciable decline in the money supply and its base during the cyclical contractions. These annual data, when seen in the context of quarterly data analyzed in Chapter 6, give us a more solid basis for understanding how money behaved and why during this period of severe economic dislocation.

Vault cash, comprised of specie and legal tender money, was the basic reserve under the National Banking System and its quantity was the critical factor in the size of the total money supply. This reserve could be augmented by inflows from currency held by the public, Treasury cash, and gold, either imported, produced domestically, or held by the public. (Outflows to these uses reduced reserves.) Currency held by the public from 1890 through 1893 (the sharp increase in June, 1893, occurred during the banking panic and reflects stepped-up hoarding at a time when deposits were functioning ineffectively and there was a premium on cash) remained high and thus did not add to reserves as gold flowed abroad. The decline in Treasury cash from 1890 through 1894 was an aspect of the same money-tightening phenomenon as the Treasury had to redeem silver certificates and loans in gold for hoarding and export, and to finance deficits begun in 1893. This reduced its cash holdings as well as deposits and dried up another source of bank reserves. The gold stock also declined in fluctuating fashion each year starting from 1890, the loss exceeding $200 million by 1896. (See Table 6 above and the data in Chapter 6.) Given these major contractions in the source of reserves, with no central bank to moderate the impacts, the sharp declines in vault cash in 1893, 1895, and 1896 and their negative effects on the economy are readily understandable. The increase each year in national bank notes offset the negative impact of declines in currency held by the public for the other years. For example, in June, 1894, national bank notes reached a high of $200 million at the same time as vault cash reached its peak of $686 million prior to its sharp decline in 1895 and 1896.

The severe drops in reserves (vault cash) for 1893, 1895, and 1896 were not equaled by the decline in deposits of commercial banks, a major portion of the money supply, which amounted to just under 10 percent in 1893 and under 5 percent in 1896, with the total in 1895 up about 7.5 percent over 1894. These lesser declines and actual increase occurred because, though commercial bank deposits had to be backed by vault cash, the existence of excess reserves made it possible for the 25 percent reserve ratio to be maintained without reducing deposits. Once excess reserves vanished, deposits had to contract. (Mutual savings bank deposits followed a continuous upward trend during the nineties at an average rate of over 4 percent a year, responding to tighter money conditions in 1893, 1894, and 1896 with reduced proportions of increase rather than actual declines. Institutional as well as market conditions insulated these deposits from the sharper impacts on commercial bank deposits.)

These data document the constraining effects of tight money on an economy whose other markets were signaling a halt to the advance of output in 1892 and from late in 1894 through 1895. Together with the material in Chapter 6 on monetary forces at work, they give us a more complete view of how the monetary veil shaped itself to the contortions of the economic body.

The information in Chapter 6 on the fiscal accounts of the

United States government and the quantitative impression of these operations on the fluctuating private economy adds to our understanding of the depression. But though we take the measure of the government's receipts, expenditures, surplus or deficit, and changing debt in monthly, quarterly, and annual spans, this seemingly complete picture falls short of *total* government accounts since the fiscal operations of state, local, and other governmental units were not earlier quantified. Thus annual federal receipts and expenditures during the nineties were on the order of $300–600 million for each category. On the expenditure side, for example, these represented just under 50 percent of the total expenditures of all governmental units. (For the 1890's, leaving 1898 out because of the war, federal expenditures ranged from 44.9 percent of the total in 1899 to 50.7 percent in 1893. Only in 1892 and 1893 did the federal amount exceed 50 percent of the total.)

Comparing the total of government expenditures in Table 2 above with Table 7 completes our measure of the role of all governments in total output. The deficits of the federal government in 1893 through 1896 were modest, ranging from just under $30 million in 1895 to slightly in excess of $59 million in 1894, and could not have stimulated the economy very greatly. The almost uninterrupted upward trend in all government expenditures at an annual rate between 3 and 5.5 percent from 1891 through 1897 was a countercyclical force of minor impact even if the multiplier effect is considered. (Assuming for illustration a multiplier of 5, the increase in government expenditures of $34 million in 1893 and $26 million in 1896 would have generated incomes of $170 and $130 million, respectively.) In 1894, total government expenditures declined slightly, removing the scant upward countercyclical pressure in the worst year of the depression.

The absence of data on total government receipts and thus on overall surplus or deficit does not impede our analysis significantly since realistic assumptions can easily and securely be made and gaps reconstructed. Differences between local and state government expenditures (which we have) and receipts were not likely to be great in either direction since conventional wisdom and politics did not suffer deficits in state and local fiscal affairs and other than random surpluses would vanish as soon as the citizenry and their political representatives were aware of any windfall—a most unlikely depression occurrence.

Thus the imcomplete data on fiscal operations in Chapter 6 have now been mainly if not fully rounded out. The result is a clearer, if basically unchanged, picture.

VII

Chapter 7, which deals with a variety of prices including interest and wage rates, can be added to by including or substituting new, extended, or recast price indices. But, for the most part, the series used adequately reflect the main economic changes. Adding series not earlier available would fill out the view and can be done if a particular phase of price change is to be analyzed in depth. Such series can be reviewed in certain of the works cited at the end of this preface.[6]

For one area of Chapter 7, wage rates and earnings, additional and refined statistical data developed by Rees and Jacobs enhance our information and analysis of this aspect of the depression period. In their presentation of wages in manufacturing, they deal perforce with the cost of living, paralleling and refining the work of Douglas and Hansen but also adding new components of cost of living.

The data in Table 8 provide us with information beyond that found in Douglas' work. The decline of 12.8 percent in average annual earnings in all manufacturing from 1892 to 1894 was considerably sharper than Douglas' 9.5 percent decline for all industries excluding farm labor. This greater decline in earnings in manufacturing is consistent with other data, indicating the very considerable contraction in manufacturing output. The decline in average days in operation of over 8 percent from 1892 to 1894 is only a rough indicator of the falling off in employment. Average hours worked per day waned by just over 1 percent. (Of course, both of these series omit the fact of unemployment.) The resulting shrinkage in average hourly and daily earnings of 4.8 percent (1892 to 1895) for both categories compares with Douglas' decline in all manufacturing of only 1.5 percent for the same years.

It should be kept in mind that money wages did not rise to any appreciable degree throughout the nineties. As Table 8 shows, by 1900 average annual earnings had risen by less than 2 percent. This almost imperceptible rise overshadowed the greater increases in average hourly and daily earnings (4.9 and 4.2 percent, respectively), because the average days in operation and the average hours worked per day ebbed over the decade by 1.7 and 1.3 percent, respectively. While real wages rose 1890 to 1900, the steadiness of average annual money earnings, except for cyclical declines, attests to the general softness of demand for labor during the nineties.

The differences between the Rees-Jacobs and Douglas data suggest that if the newly devised data are more accurate, the impact of the depression on earnings in manufacturing was much more severe than we thought. This situation is for workers who retained their jobs and does not take into account changes in the cost of living. (This last consideration would apply equally to both sets of data so working out the real earnings is not necessary for this comparison.)

The Rees-Jacobs data on rents in New York, Chicago, Philadelphia, Boston, Cincinnati, and St. Louis fill in a gap in our cost-of-living information for the depression years. Their indices

Table 8
Average Days in Operation Per Year, Hours Per Day, and Annual, Daily, and Hourly Earnings, All Manufacturing, 1890–1900

Year	Average Annual Earnings	Percent Change	Average Days in Operation Per Year	Percent Change	Average Daily Earnings	Percent Change	Average Hours Per Day	Percent Change	Average Hourly Earnings (cents)	Percent Change
1890	$425	—	294	—	$1.44	—	10.02	—	14.4	—
1891	429	.9	297	1.0	1.45	.7	10.01	− .1	14.4	0.0
1892	431	.5	296	− .3	1.46	.7	10.04	.3	14.5	.7
1893	410	−4.9	271	−8.4	1.51	3.4	9.99	− .5	15.1	4.1
1894	376	−8.3	272	.4	1.38	−8.6	9.92	− .7	13.9	−7.9
1895	392	4.3	284	4.4	1.38	0.0	9.97	.5	13.8	− .7
1896	393	.3	274	−3.5	1.43	3.6	9.96	− .1	14.4	4.3
1897	395	.5	284	3.6	1.39	−2.8	9.94	− .2	14.0	−2.8
1898	394	.3	288	1.4	1.37	−1.4	9.97	.3	13.7	−2.1
1899	420	6.6	290	.7	1.45	5.8	9.94	− .3	14.6	6.6
1900	432	2.9	289	− .3	1.50	3.4	9.89	− .5	15.1	3.4

Source: Albert Rees, Real Wages in Manufacturing, 1890–1914, p. 33.
(a) Per full-time equivalent worker.

for these six cities, based on advertised rents, reveal a varying pattern of rent changes for each city. In New York, rents remained the same from 1891 through 1894, rising by just over 1 percent in 1895, then declining in 1896 over 3 percent, and rising in 1897 by over 1 percent. In Chicago, rents rose in 1893 by over 3 percent and then dropped by over 7 percent in 1894 and an additional 4.5 percent in 1895, 3 more in 1896, and over 5 percent in 1897. Tenants' rents in Philadelphia remained the same in 1893, then dropped by 3 percent in 1894, and another percent in 1895. In 1896, rents rebounded by over 4 percent then fell by 4 percent. In St. Louis, rents rose in 1894 and 1896, while those in Boston dropped in 1894 and rose slightly in 1896. The data for Cincinnati start in 1895 and show a rise for 1896 exceeding 3 percent.

These varied changes in rents reflect the local, sheltered nature of housing with the market following these rather than national patterns. For many families, then, the depression impact on their levels of living so far as rent is concerned was intensified or eased by the happenstance of their residence.[7]

VIII

Our reassessment of the basic findings of this monograph, in the light of the new material cited, does not throw them into question but rather reinforces them. To some extent, generalizations need qualification or are extended by the greater detail now available. The shape, severity, and determining factors of the depression remain much the same today as they emerged, tentatively, some fifteen years ago.

The duration and timing of the depression stand up, for the most part, under our more informed scrutiny. The new and the old data support the cyclical framework with one exception. The data are consistent with a peak of economic activity in January, 1893, contraction until the trough was reached in June,

1894, then upturn and expansion until a second peak was attained in December, 1895. The end to the subsequent contraction, however, is not as clearly discernible. Rendigs Fels makes a case for October, 1896, as the trough month rather than June, 1897, the NBER trough and the one this writer had accepted. Certainly the evidence is mixed; Fels chooses the earlier date because at that time roughly 50 percent of series that conform well to the business cycle were rising. The "expansion" from the earlier date was not robust and, not until late in 1897, spurred on by fine crops in the United States (while poor crops eventuated abroad), did the economy move ahead at a steady pace. Although Fels's dating of the trough may be questioned, even if one accepts it as correct, the shape of the depression is only slightly modified at its last trough.[8]

The severity of the depression is borne out by the old and new statistical data. GNP declined, at its worst, about 10 percent and in terms of unused capacity the depression was a deep one. The decline in investment and its major components was characteristically severe, as in all major depressions. Unemployment, by the new estimates, was about 20 percent of the labor force at its worst or over 3 million. (Lebergott's figures on unemployment are higher than ours made in 1953.) Average money wages declined more cyclically, and were generally lower than the first approximation presented in this monograph. However the general decline in consumption suggested in our analysis of the domestic output of consumer goods is exaggerated. The newly available series on consumption of goods and services is evidence that overall consumption fell only moderately in the worst depression year. Still, for the middle of the nineties, consumption remained at low levels in per capita and capacity terms and for millions of families levels of living ebbed greatly.

In assessing which factors mainly determined the shape and

severity of the depression we find more continuous and extensive data to support this study's main findings. The decline of investment opportunities, principally in the two major areas of railroads and building construction, is more amply documented now even if the findings on cyclical turning points remain unchanged. Investment, in the form of expenditures on plant, equipment, and inventories, is now measured annually. More extensive annual data on building construction, conforming to the generalizations supported in this study, chronicle the generally retarded state of building in the middle nineties. But the monograph's reliance on monthly and quarterly data on building and railroad investment to pinpoint the leading downturns in investment remains unchallenged.

The role of foreign investment in the United States is now clearer: annual data trace the ups and downs in the net capital inflow which stimulated investment in general. The tentative finding that despite the disarray of the banking panic in 1893, the widely proclaimed lack of confidence in our monetary standard, and the dogmatic assertions that the net capital flow was outward, net foreign capital continued to flow in except for the period of greatest monetary dislocation (though at reduced rates due to the cyclical contraction in western European economies) is consistent with the newly constructed balance-of-payments series. These data reveal that only in the period July, 1893, through June, 1894, was there a small net outflow of capital.

The fuller monetary information at hand draws more sharply the relationship between gold flows, bank reserves, and the money supply. Our generalizations on monetary developments have to be more clearly focused on money market tightness and cyclical turning points. The tightening of credit late in 1892 and 1895 contributed to the downturns—the direction of real economic contraction was reinforced by the relative short supply of money. The banking panic in the summer of 1893 reduced significantly the effective amount of money and tumbled economic activity more than nonmonetary factors required.

The picture of government fiscal operations, incompletely drawn in the earlier study from federal receipts and expenditures, now includes totals from all governmental units. The result does not defy our earlier appraisal of the minor expansionary impact of the federal government's deficits on total economic activity.

Continued development of new and refined statistical series and their insightful application to the problem of the depression will enhance our understanding of that important episode in the nation's economic development. The probability is high that such data and analysis will inform our view with greater detail on specific economic series within the framework of overall activity rather than overturn the general causal relations that have been uncovered.

NOTES

1. See John W. Kendrick, *Productivity Trends in the United States,* and Simon Kuznets, *Capital in the American Economy.*

2. Stanley Lebergott, *Manpower in Economic Growth,* pp. 180 ff.

3. See Conference on Research in Income and Wealth, *Trends in the American Economy in the Nineteenth Century,* pp. 629–715; Oskar Morgenstern, *International Financial Transactions and Business Cycles;* and *Historical Statistics to 1957,* pp. 557–566.

4. See Milton Friedman and Anna J. Schwartz, *A Monetary History of the United States 1867–1960.*

5. Ibid., pp. 97, 104–105, 111, 119, 134.

6. For an example, see Conference on Research in Income and Wealth, *op. cit., Output, Employment, and Productivity in the United States after 1800,* and *Output, Input, and Productivity Measurement;* L. Grebler, D. M. Blank, L. Winnick, *Capital Formation in Residential Real Estate;* S. Kuznets, *Capital in the American Economy;* A. Rees, *Real Wages in Manufacturing, 1890–1914;* and *Historical Statistics to 1957.*

7. Rees, *Real Wages in Manufacturing,* pp. 96 ff.

8. R. Fels, *American Business Cycles,* pp. 204–208.

Selected Bibliography

Conference on Research in Income and Wealth, *Output, Employment, and Productivity in the United States after 1800.* New York: National Bureau of Economic Research, 1966. Distributed by Columbia University Press.

Conference on Research in Income and Wealth. *Output, Input, and Productivity Measurement.* Studies in Income and Wealth, vol. 25. National Bureau of Economic Research Report. Princeton: Princeton University Press, 1961.

Conference on Research in Income and Wealth. *Trends in the American Economy in the Nineteenth Century.* Studies in Income and Wealth, vol. 24. National Bureau of Economic Research Report. Princeton: Princeton University Press, 1960.

FELS, RENDIGS. *American Business Cycles 1865–1897.* Chapel Hill: University of North Carolina Press, 1959.

FRIEDMAN, MILTON, and ANNA J. SCHWARTZ. *A Monetary History of the United States 1867–1960.* National Bureau of Economic Research Study. Princeton: Princeton University Press, 1963.

GREBLER, LEO.; BLANK, D. M.; and WINNICK, L. *Capital Formation in Residential Real Estate: Trends and Prospects.* National Bureau of Economic Research Study. Princeton: Princeton University Press, 1956.

KENDRICK, JOHN W. *Productivity Trends in the United States.* National Bureau of Economic Research Study. Princeton: Princeton University Press, 1961.

KUZNETS, SIMON (assisted by Elizabeth Jenks). *Capital in the American Economy: Its Formation and Financing.* National Bureau of Economic Research Study. Princeton: Princeton University Press, 1961.

LEBERGOTT, STANLEY. *Manpower in Economic Growth: The American Record Since 1800.* New York: McGraw-Hill, 1964.

LONG, CLARENCE D. *The Labor Force Under Changing Income and Employment.* National Bureau of Economic Research Study, General Series, no. 65. Princeton: Princeton University Press, 1958.

MORGENSTERN, OSKAR. *International Financial Transactions and Business Cycles.* National Bureau of Economic Research Study. Princeton: Princeton University Press, 1959.

REES, ALBERT (Assisted by DONALD P. JACOBS). *Real Wages in Manufacturing, 1890–1914.* National Bureau of Economic Research Study. Princeton: Princeton University Press, 1961.

SIMON, MATTHEW. "Cyclical Fluctuations and the International Capital Movements of the United States, 1865–1897." Ph.D. dissertation, Columbia University, 1955.

THOMAS, BRINLEY. *Migration and Economic Growth.* National Institute of Economic and Social Research, Economic and Social Studies 12. Cambridge, England: Cambridge University Press, 1954.

U.S., Bureau of the Census. *Historical Statistics of the United States, Colonial Times to 1957.* Washington, D.C.: Government Printing Office, 1960.

U.S., Bureau of the Census. *Historical Statistics of the United States, Continuation to 1962 and Revisions.* Washington, D.C.: Government Printing Office, 1965.

The Depression
of the Nineties

Introduction

The main purpose of this study is to explain the principal forces generating the depressed level of economic activity in the 1890s. To the extent that a more meaningful economic view of the depressed middle nineties emerges, a better understanding of an important period in the social and economic development of the United States is possible.

The period from 1893 to 1897 is here treated as one "depression."[1] This is merely definitional and does not imply a controversy over whether or not there were two "cycles" (by National Bureau of Economic Research definition), starting with the peak in January, 1893, and running to a trough in June, 1894; a second trough occuring in June, 1897, after which economic activity rose steadily to reach a new peak in December, 1899. This peak, however, was far below the levels of capacity implicit in the 1892 peak and in the projected annual growth of capacity for the economy. The 1899 and 1901–1902 peaks were submerged ones at about 95 percent of potential capacity. Thus, while recovery started in 1897, it did not reach full capacity until the 1907 peak.

This depression merits the keen interest of economic historians. It occurred at a time when the economy was rapidly

3

taking on its modern industrial-manufacturing shape. In this context, it affords an excellent opportunity to relate, in a dynamic framework, cyclical to secular development.

The depression, moreover, was among the most severe in this country's economic history. Whether we use a simple index such as bank clearings,[2] or composite indices constructed around basic areas of economic activity,[3] the result is to place this depression among the five most severe contractions since the Civil War. Most important indices, taken singly or in composite, clearly demonstrate that the depression was indeed quite severe.[4]

Where a more systematic attempt is made to measure the amplitude and duration of business cycles, the severe nature of the depression is still borne out. Burns and Mitchell, in their monumental work, compare the fluctuations of seven series to see how they vary in each depression from "average" behavior over the entire period of fourteen cycles surveyed by the National Bureau of Economic Research (NBER). For the most part, these series fluctuated more sharply during the 1893–1897 depression than for the "average."[5] The severe nature of this depression, suggested in these various indices, is given fuller meaning and specificity in this volume.

Specifically, the task of this work is to inspect an important period in the economic history of the United States, to set forth its main characteristics, to evaluate the severity of the economic contraction, and to explain the nature of the depression in terms of important economic variables and the broader trend developments of the economy. As we have said, the period from 1893 to 1897 is taken as a depressed one. The first "depression," by NBER definition from early in 1893 to the end of 1894, is not followed by a complete recovery. In numerous respects, the peak of December, 1895, is not as high as the peak of January, 1893. Recovery in 1897 is not robust and full capacity is not

reached for some years. Nonagricultural unemployment remains
at a high level until 1899, dipping below 10 percent that year
for the first time since 1893.[6] The downward trend of prices is
not reversed until after the second "depression" has taken hold.
Thus the entire period emerges as essentially a depressed one.[7]

A description of the major economic determinants of the period and how they interacted with one another should throw
light on the nature of the depression. The definition of these
major determinants and their description necessarily occupy the
major portion of this study. Our aim is to identify the economic
forces that were the major factors in shaping the depression and
perhaps to see in what ways the depression affected the force
and direction of economic development, and vice versa.

Both data available to contemporaries and those gathered
since have been utilized.[8] The different ways now used to look
at economic activity provide today's student with an advantage
over earlier observers. The contemporary economic historian
will usually look at his subject in a dynamic frame of reference:
he will take into account interactions between different sectors
of the economy. He will not search out a single cause, but will
carefully review the complex set of economic relationships that
are involved in economic activity. He will scrutinize the changes
in the major components of national income or product to take
the measure of economic fluctuations. He will focus on the investment factor with new insights derived from Keynes' work
and its aftermath. In his analytic and descriptive endeavors he
will, consciously or not, be applying many of the new concepts
and emphases which are now part of informed economic
thought.

This is a historical rather than a statistical study. The study of
a single depression is historical: it can only lead to valid statements about the nature of that one depression. A statistical
study would have to analyze the entire universe of depressions

before useful inferences about the nature of depressions could validly be drawn. Historical studies are the basis of statistical inference.[9]

The manner in which the depression is approached also implies a theoretical framework. The use of such analytic categories as consumption, investment, monetary factors, prices, and so on, brings the investigator of the depression to this problem with a set of tools that he considers well suited to it. Naturally it means that he will look at his problem in a certain way.[10] There is, however, no commitment on the author's part to use such categories in a rigid way or as a means of confirming any particular hypothesis; the approach is intended to be broad and flexible. Specific emphasis on different aspects of the approach should be determined by the nature of the problem, the data, and the way in which the investigation develops.

Our first step is to place the depression in a broad, historical frame of reference. The structural changes in process at the time of the depression are brought into focus by examining the major changes in the economy over the period 1869–1913. The forty-five-year period is taken because it affords an opportunity to see the sweep of such important changes as rapid technological advance, the diminution of the relative importance of agriculture, the development of large industrial combinations, the beginning of significant United States investment abroad, the slackening in railroad building, and so on. To see the depression in the context of the nineties alone is likely to obscure the important secular changes which contributed to the nature of the depression. The years 1890 and 1900 are too close to the depression to allow a framework of change inclusive of secular forces. The period chosen is more ideally suited to that end. Structural changes that are traced are related to manpower and the natural and technical resources of the economy as well as the United States' involvement in the world economy.

After viewing the broad sweep of economic change in the United States, we present the historical background and general nature of the period 1893–1897 through recounting the main events of the depression. Once the annals of the depression are clearly depicted, the later task of analyzing sectors of the economy proceeds with the chronological order of events already available as a frame of reference.

After the dynamic course of economic development is charted and the events of the depression are outlined, the significant changes during the depression are dealt with. First, the various forms of investment are analyzed for clues as to the nature of major changes in that area and their relationship to changes in other areas. Here as elsewhere quantitative measurements are employed together with qualitative information. In like manner consumption, international economic relationships, monetary factors (including the rate of government spending), and prices are examined.

In the final chapter, the major forces which shaped the depression from 1893–1897 are summarized. The descriptive analysis of the different sectors of the economy makes it possible to see which forces within each sector of the economy were more influential than others. In this way, the characteristics of the depression are set forth. Such a description and analysis of the depression within the framework of significant economic change aims at clarifying the nature of the depression and its effect on economic development. In tracing the interaction of economic institutions under great stress and dislocation the more subtle long-run changes are often seen in microcosm. Viewing the depression from 1893 to 1897 in this manner not only provides insight into its dynamics but also helps show the impact the depression had on the transformation of the economy into its modern, manufacturing-industrial form.

NOTES

1. See A. R. Eckler, "A Measure of the Severity of Depressions, 1873–1932," *Review of Economic Statistics* 15 (May, 1933):79.

2. J. B. Hubbard, "Business Volumes During Periods of Decline and Recovery," *Review of Economic Statistics* (November, 1930), pp. 181–185. Hubbard's mechanical index shows that the drop in clearings from 1893 to the trough was the sharpest in the period 1883 through 1929.

3. Eckler's composite index of six series (railway operating revenues, value of total merchandise imports, pig-iron production, anthracite and bituminous coal production, cotton comsumption, and clearings for selected cities) ranks the decline from 1892 to 1894 as the fourth most severe in the period surveyed. See Eckler, "A Measure of the Severity of Depressions, 1873–1932," pp. 75–81. Other indices such as unemployment and output also show sharp declines. Cf. A. G. Hart, *Money, Debt and Economic Activity,* pp. 259–263, where the decline in employment and output for the depression is gauged at over 20 percent. See the Appendix to Chapter 2 below for unemployment estimates, most of which also indicate that the depression was severe.

4. See C. D. Long, *Building Cycles and the Theory of Investment,* pp. 213 ff., where the sharp decline in construction is noted. C. D. Bremer, *American Bank Failures,* pp. 25–28, 32, compares the great number of bank failures and the vast amount of resources involved to other depression periods.

5. A. F. Burns and W. C. Mitchell, *Measuring Business Cycles,* chap. 12. See Chart 74 in particular.

6. Paul H. Douglas and Aaron Director, *The Problem of Unemployment,* p. 26.

7. U.S. Bureau of the Census, *Historical Statistics of the United States, 1789–1945* pp. 231–233. Some indices, such as pig-iron production, pass the 1893 peak late in 1895 but then shortly thereafter decline sharply again. See ibid., p. 333.

8. See the bibliographical note for an evaluation of materials available to the author.

9. Cf. R. A. Gordon, "Business Cycles in the Interwar Period: The 'Quantitative-Historical' Approach," *American Economic Review* (May, 1949): 47–63.

10. Cf. Felix Kaufmann, *Methodology of the Social Sciences,* pp. 182–188.

I

The Economic Setting for
the Depression:
the Process of Economic Growth,
1869–1913

In the economic development of the United States during most of the nineteenth century, financial panics, occuring about once a decade, were usually symptomatic of more complex economic dislocations than the mere disruption of stock exchanges and banking institutions. Such panics as that of 1893 usually ushered in a period of economic instability disrupting the everyday activities of most people. The depressions associated with the panics were violent economic disorders arising from the conflicting interests and developments of a ramified market economy adjusting, often painfully, to the many changes in the technology and administration of the nation's business.

The depression from 1893 to 1897, which began with a disturbing financial panic that spread rapidly throughout the economy, was one of the worst depressions since the Civil War. Within the period 1869–1913, which we take as the broader framework of our analysis, this depression was rivaled in intensity only by that of the seventies.[1] As the series traced in Figures 2 through 7 show, the depression was both long and deep. One unusual characteristic of the depression was that it had two phases with two distinct bottoms, each as deep as that of 1908. It was, therefore, a long depressed period running for many years after 1892. Recovery is noticeable by 1897, but not until 1901–1902 did the economy again approach capacity output.

This severe depression occurred when the economy was in the process of fundamental transformation from an agricultural-industrial economy to one in which, although large-scale agriculture still was a salient feature, the outstanding characteristic was a manufacturing-industrial complex. Study of the depression, therefore, affords an excellent opportunity to see this momentous transformation, which generated sharp pressures on different sectors of the economy. In analyzing the economic contraction, we shall see the nature of the depression and its role in this transformation in sharper focus. In the last decades of the nineteenth century, the economy was undergoing many ramifying changes, some of which were both the stimuli giving added impetus to and the responses springing from industrialization. The ramifications of these often swift changes in technology and business organization were felt throughout the economy and even extended abroad. These changes were both apparent and subtle. They were of a deep social character affecting widely the ways by which people made their livings and carried on their lives.

To comprehend more freely why the depression of the nineties was so severe and to understand what forces shaped it, we must see the economy in process of change. The significant changes and their effects on the economy during the depression period are essential parts of the historical framework within which our analysis must proceed. By taking the measure of the nature, rate, and interrelationships of economic growth in the period from the Civil War to World War I we will be in a better position to assess the fluctuations of the major variables in the depression of the nineties.[2] We are concerned in this chapter with seeing short-run business-cycle fluctuations in the context of secular developments of a rapidly industrializing society.

Wealth and Output

A telescoped picture of the economic growth is reflected in the changes in wealth from 1880 to 1912 as shown in Table 9. While such wealth increased in 1912 to a level almost five times that of 1880, growth was at different rates for various sectors of the economy. Rates of growth for agriculture, transportation, and other industries, though they increased appreciably, lagged behind the overall growth. Growth was most rapid in manufacturing and related industries, the rate of increase in manufacturing and mining being almost double that for the economy. As with most statistics, those on wealth show the significant role manufacturing was playing in the nation's rapid industrialization.

Although the data in Table 9 help us to see overall economic growth roughly from 1880 to 1912, they do not give us any clues as to the contour of rates of growth year by year. Rates of growth for the decades from 1880 to 1912 indicate that wealth during the eighties increased by 80 percent, whereas in the nineties it rose only by 48 percent. The rate of increase from 1900 to 1910 of about 60 percent reversed the decline of the nineties.[3] These rates, however, do not give us more than a very crude notion of the nature of sectoral changes wrought by the very rapid reproduction of wealth throughout the economy. A

Table 9

**Value of Real Estate Improvements and Equipment,
by Major Business Categories, Selected Dates, 1880–1912,
1929 Prices**

(*billions of dollars*)

		June 1		December 31, 1912
Category	1880	1890	1900	1912
Agriculture	$5.530	$7.490	$9.980	$15.810
Electric light and power	0	.141	.804	3.730
Mining and manufacturing	2.250	5.850	10.580	21.840
Transportation	9.200	16.120	24.200	39.400
Communication	.200	.446	1.220	2.480
Other industries	5.300	10.400	12.890	19.860
Total	22.480	40.450	59.670	103.100

Source: Simon Kuznets, *National Product Since 1869*, p. 231.

more meaningful analysis must await the appraisal of additional data of a more detailed and refined nature.

A more complete picture of changes in economic activity is mirrored in the annual data traced in Figure 2. The variations in the economy depicted in Table 9 take on more shape as we trace the growth in certain macroeconomic indicators of economic activity. The overall changes in growth rates, as well as the year-to-year nuances and the cyclical reactions of the economy, are more meaningfully seen in juxtaposition. Thus the unfolding pattern of economic development from 1869 to 1913 can be used to advantage in analyzing the depression. Figures 2 through 7 delineate the secular and cyclical changes in major series of economic activity, the interrelating of which gives a more realistic, dynamic notion of the principal economic forces constantly shaping the next period of production, distribution, and consumption.

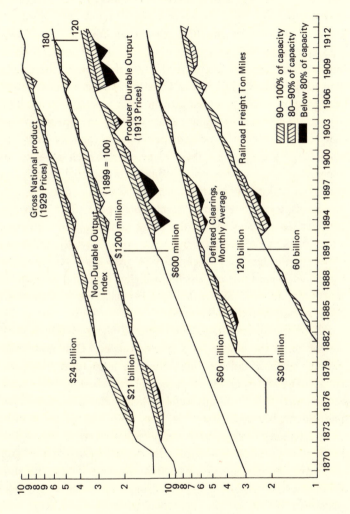

Figure 2
Indicators of Physical Volume, 1869-1913

In the ratio charts that follow, the different rates at which growth proceeds by decades or longer periods are seen at a glance. The potential growth is seen in the lines linking peaks, a high peak representing a level of output that is technologically and economically capable of further development at the rate indicated by former high peaks. Thus levels of economic activity falling below these potential growth lines represent proportions of a continuously expanding capacity level. In depressions, activity is usually over 5 percent below such capacity lines and, when activity falls to less than 90 percent of such capacity, the depression is of great severity. Using such potential growth lines reveals situations in which new peak levels do not reach the projected growth line from a former high peak. Such peaks are considered "submerged" in the sense that they are recoveries which surpass earlier levels but have not achieved possible levels due to the tendency of capacity to grow each year. In other words, each year makes possible a higher economic capacity so that maintaining a certain level of capacity requires increased levels of output and employment.

All of the series[4] traced in Figure 2 show clearly that the depression in the nineties was long and severe. Only nondurable output and GNP failed to fall below the 80 percent of capacity mark.[5] The different series show that for most of the decade economic activity was appreciably below the potential growth line. Even when recovery set in from 1897 on, the levels of activity attained failed to reach the potential growth line. So, both in terms of duration and amplitude, the depression was of great intensity. Comparing levels of activity in the nineties with those in the seventies—another period of severe depression—emphasizes this fact.

Although the seventies and the nineties were mostly depressed periods, economic activity in the eighties was at levels closer to growing capacity. From 1900 to 1913, too, most series showed a relatively high level of stability close to capacity, though producer durable output fell far below capacity from 1907 to 1913. During the eighties economic activity exhibited the least instability and the closest conformity to potential growth for 1869–1913 as a whole. While the economy was rapidly being transformed into an industrial-manufacturing order, it was experiencing frequent and wide fluctuations symptomatic of continuous sectoral changes as factors of production were channeled into the new streams of industry.

Further analysis of Figure 2 discloses the different rates of economic growth in this framework of overall expansion. GNP increased over the entire period at an annual rate of about 4 percent, a rate lower than that of any of the other series. This relatively modest growth in GNP resulted mainly from the lag in agricultural growth over the period. Railroad freight ton-miles carried grew roughly at an average rate of 13 percent a year, followed by producer durable goods, while nondurable output lagged behind outside clearings. These different rates of growth attest to the rapid growth of manufacturing and allied industries. On the other hand, growth of nondurable output more nearly approximates overall economic growth including the nonmanufacturing sectors of the economy.

Two significant characteristics of economic growth in the time span from 1869 to 1913 were the protracted periods of depressed activity and the rather rapid growth. As Figure 2 illustrates, only in the eighties was the economy's capacity approximated for any length of time. In the seventies and nineties activity dropped to deeply submerged levels—falling as low as 75 percent of capacity. The recovery of the nineties did not thrust the economy to capacity levels until sometime between 1899 and 1907. Thus the depression starting in 1893 persisted almost a decade until resource and manpower limits were approximated. The summary impression of the period 1869–1913 should be clear: economic activity proceeded to higher levels in spurts; in the periods between spurts, levels of output were greatly depressed. In some sectors of the economy, these depressed levels reached below the 75 percent of capacity mark. Such deep troughs were not prolonged, but even the recoveries that followed the contractions did not always lift the economy to its full capacity.

As wealth and output grew apace, that portion of the labor force engaged in manufacturing and railroading also increased, though at a more modest rate. While population over 14 years of age increased almost 2 percent each year, the number of wage earners in manufacturing and railroading rose at a slightly higher pace from 1889 to 1913. The more rapid rise in wealth and output than in the population and labor force implied a solid increase in productivity as new technology and industrialization made their impact felt. As the economy adjusted to the ever-rising demand of manufacturing and allied industries, the economy's resources and labor were more and more attracted to these expanding areas of activity.[6]

Distribution of labor among different occupational pursuits changed continuously as the demands of new manufacturing activities were transmitted through the market mechanism. The absolute and relative increase in working force made possible an important influx into manufacturing, construction, transportation, mining, and tertiary occupations. The use of child labor in manufacturing also increased. At the same time, agricultural workers increased in number by over a third from 1869 to 1913, though relatively there was a decline from about half the gainful workers to less than a third. This change in the composition of the labor force is a salient aspect of the transformation of the economy into its modern industrial form.[7]

In this period of growing wealth and output, in which the importance of new and more concentrated capital was manifest, the distribution of product changed somewhat. According to King's estimates, services income (labor and entrepreneurial services) declined as a proportion of income payments from 78.5 percent in the seventies to 75.8 percent in the decade after 1900. Within the service income classification, entrepreneurial income rose from 26.4 percent to 28.8 percent of income payments in the same period. Thus employee compensation declined from 50 percent to 47.1 percent. At the same time, property income (dividends, interest, and rent) increased from 23.6 percent to 24.2 percent. Dividend and interest income held its own while rental incomes rose from 7.8 percent to 8.3 percent of income payments. Thus the quickening of economic expansion through industrialization rewarded direct property ownership and entrepreneurial skills more proportionately than labor and corporation owners and creditors.[8]

Commodity Output

The overall indices which we have surveyed testify to the rapid, wave-like development of the economy from 1869 to 1913. To give more detail to this overall economic growth, a review and analysis of the different types of commodities produced and their growth is helpful. Figures 3 and 4 trace such growth in commodity output.[9]

The varying tempos of economic growth for the different types of commodities are disclosed in Figures 3 and 4. Five of the seven series charted show overall growth rates to 1913 more rapid than that of GNP, as shown in Figure 2. The rate of growth of consumer perishable output was slightly less than that of GNP while that of nondurables was less by a greater amount. In the rapid development of manufacturing output, these comparisons verify the obvious: output of manufactured goods grew more rapidly than total output.

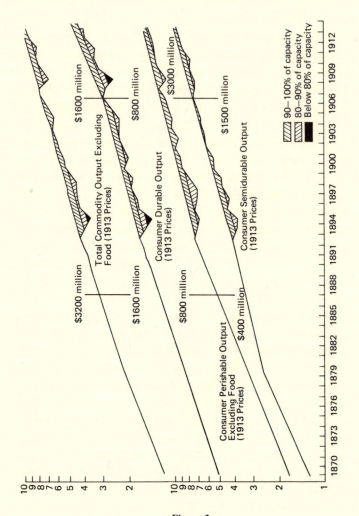

Figure 3
Finished Commodity and Consumer Goods Output, 1869-1913

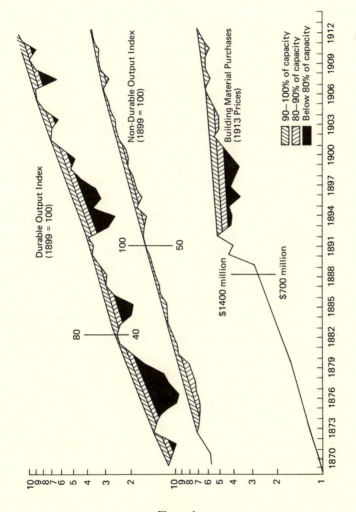

Figure 4
Manufacturing Output and Building Material Purchases, 1869-1913

The growth of total commodity output excluding food closely paralleled that of GNP from 1869 to 1913. For the later part of this period, when comparison of annual data is possible, the growth pattern was very similar. On the basis of the annual data from 1889 to 1913, the cyclical pattern differed only in amplitude of fluctuation. Both series showed the same cyclical reactions but total commodity output fell off more sharply in each cyclical downturn. In the nineties contraction of total commodity output reached just below 80 percent of capacity at the 1894 trough. In the next trough, output was about 85 percent of capacity. Contraction of GNP never reached as low as 85 percent of capacity, but it too shows the double-trough pattern of the depression of the nineties. The relatively dampened fluctuations of total commodity output excluding food, measuring as it does all types of finished commodities, reflect the averaging forces of wide and narrow oscillations of different types of commodities.

Of all finished commodities, durable output grew most rapidly and appeared most sensitive to the business cycle. In the nineties, the output of durables fell off more quickly and to a greater extent than the output of other finished commodities with the exception of construction materials.[10] In both troughs of the depression of the nineties, durable output fell below 70 percent of capacity, as illustrated by the dark areas of the troughs in Figure 4. The same characteristic sensitivity to business conditions is portrayed in the sharp dips in the eighties and seventies. Thus even in the contraction of the eighties, when economic activity declined relatively slightly, output of durables fell off sharply.

Output of construction material did not exhibit a consistent pattern of growth over the period. From 1890 to 1902, output fluctuated at severely depressed levels, with the 1902 level approximating that of 1892 but still only representing 90 percent of capacity. The declines in the nineties were very severe ones

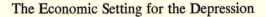
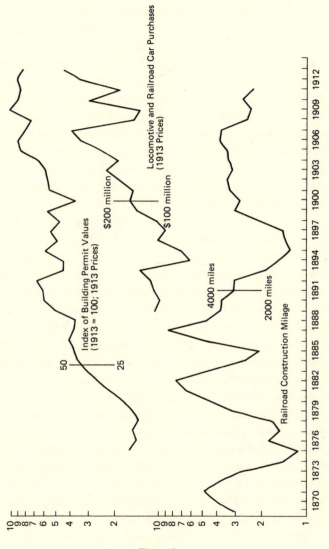

Figure 5
Selected Investment Indicators, 1869-1913

—the level at each of the two troughs being about 60 percent of capacity—as building construction was in one of its "long building cycle" contractions. These data on material output are corroborated by the Index of Building Permit Values (in constant dollars) traced in Figure 5 where building activity falls to 65 percent of capacity in the two depression troughs. In the 1907–1908 contraction, however, output of building materials did not fall below 90 percent of capacity. The data on building permit values in Figure 5 indicate that the contraction was more severe, with construction falling below 80 percent of capacity. Using either series or both, it is clear that the 1907–1908 decline was more modest than that of the nineties. The eighties were also a period of relative stability for building, according to the data reflected in Figure 5, with activity falling below 85 percent of capacity in the 1887–1888 period, conforming to the pause in overall economic activity as mirrored in GNP. While the data on the seventies are incomplete, there is little doubt that it too was a period of severely depressed building activity. Thus, for the period 1869 to 1913, reactions of building construction activity to the business cycle were strong or weak, depending upon which phase of the "building cycle" was in process. A concomitant contraction in both cycles led to intensification of both sets of contractions.[11]

While output of durables and construction materials grew rather rapidly, compared to the growth of the entire economy, consumer durable and semidurable output expanded less rapidly. Overall growth of each of these latter classifications from 1869 to 1913 was at a rate close to that of GNP. The growth rate of consumer durables was slightly more elevated than that of GNP, while the rate of semidurable growth was about the same. By comparison with the fluctuations of producer durables and construction materials, those of consumer durables and semidurables were much less wide in amplitude. At depression troughs, as in 1894 for example, output for both classifications reached lows at about 80 percent of capacity. As the period 1869–1913 came to a close, the rates of growth of the two diverged, as did their sensitivity to the business cycle. Output of consumer durables grew more sharply from 1908 on than in the previous period. The cyclical decline from 1907–1908 led to a level of output slightly over 75 percent of capacity. After the depression of the nineties, output of consumer semidurables grew at a slightly retarded pace. Cyclical fluctuations were not deep, output never falling below the 90 percent of capacity mark.

At the other extreme of rates of growth are the nondurables —one series on all nondurables, the other on consumer perishables. The output of these commodities failed to grow at as swift a rate as total output. From 1869 to 1913, the output of all nondurables did not yield to business contraction as much as did most other activities. Only at the trough of depression periods did such output recede to levels below 90 percent of capacity. Consumer perishables fared similarly: only in the severest period of the contraction of the nineties did output fall below the 90 percent of capacity mark. In subsequent contractions, resistance to depressive forces shows up strongly. The consumption of cigars, cigarettes, newspapers, toilet articles, and the like remained relatively stable over the years and did not grow at rates approximating those of more sensitive economic activities. Growth here was at a moderate, stable pace.

Thus, in the growth of commodity output from 1869 to 1913, a period of significant expansion and development of basic and allied industry, those commodities most essential to rapid industrialization grew at the swiftest rates. The finished products which provided the sinews of mass-production techniques were accumulated more rapidly than those products which satisfied consumers' wants directly. The output of these primary commodities was also most responsive to changes in business conditions; in periods of economic contractions they usually declined sharply. Among consumer goods, sensitivity was greatest among those products which most resembled producers' goods; that is, consumer durables, the purchase of which was most easily postponable, showed sharp declines in output during depressions. On the score of growth rate, however, consumer durables did not increase at faster rates than other consumer goods.

These traits of growth and sensitivity to the business cycle, widely accepted today as inherent in our economy, apparently developed early in the industrialization of the economy. From 1869 to 1913, the relationships among different kinds of goods fell into a definite pattern: consumer-goods output grew relatively slowly but resisted, for the most part, the effects of economic contraction; producer-goods industries expanded output at a swift pace but suffered sharper declines when total economic activity declined; building construction grew more in line with its own long cycles so that rates of growth and contractions were a function of more protracted economic forces as well as of the business cycle. The period under review was one of rapid but unstable growth in which capacities were far from fully reached except in certain brief spurts.

Investment Growth

Our analysis of the broad outlines of economic growth and the expansion of finished commodity output has in effect gauged the impact of a second industrial revolution on the United States economy. The rapid increase in all kinds of manufactured goods, in different proportions for different types, was a consequence of powerful stimuli attracting profit-seekers in areas where expansion promised quick and high returns. In the period from 1880 to 1912, net capital formation (net construction and equipment) increased by over $117 billion (in 1919 prices).[12] While the data on the degree to which capital formation grew in different areas of the economy are fragmentary, there are indications as to which areas of investment provided the major thrust to this large amount of capital formation.

Figure 5 shows fluctuations in some of the more important investment fields during the period.[13] The series illustrates oscillations and growth in two major areas of investment—railroading and building construction—which gave sustenance to the development of basic manufacturing and mining industries. These series help to fill out our view of economic growth from 1869 to 1913, though many important investment data for other important industries are necessarily omitted.

A cursory glance at the statistics of locomotive and railroad-car output, railroad construction, and building construction readily discloses the violent fluctuations in these activities. These very great oscillations in output are a key to the rapid economic growth and the severe cyclical disturbances characteristic of this entire period. Although other investment factors must have played an important role in economic growth and development, it seems incontrovertible that building and railroad investment were major forces in determining the timing and intensity of the phases of business cycles during the period.

Building construction, an activity related not only to the expansion of industrial plant but also to the process of urbanization, which was a concomitant of industrialization, showed a very sharp growth from the late seventies to 1912. It was a growth from a low plateau during the period 1875–1879. During the eighties, growth was sharp and almost uninterrupted, save for the downward drop from 1887 to 1888. This continuous and sharp advance during the eighties must have been a significant factor in that decade's relative prosperity and in the limited extent of economic contractions. The decline of the nineties was very sharp and prolonged, with the lowest point reached in 1900 after the rest of the economy was well on the way to recovery. The double trough in the nineties was below 65 percent of capacity. The trough in 1900 was below 50 percent of capacity. This precipitate drop in building activity as well as the long lag in its recovery are important factors in explaining the severity of the depression of the nineties and the dragging nature of its recovery. Despite this sharp contraction, however, the number of dwelling units increased by about 25 percent in the nineties.[14] By the turn of the century, sharply increased activity—part of the "building-cycle" expansion—helped push the economy upward at a swifter pace.

Railroad expansion was, like building activity, both a stimulus and response to the ramifying growth of manufacturing. Railroad investment—in the form of purchases of rolling stock, track, and equipment as well as new construction—was usually accompanied by local investment along the route and also at the cities linked together. The sharp increase in freight ton-miles carried by United States railroads, traced in Figure 2, is a rough indicator of the tremendous upsurge in the output of goods and the vast development of market networks throughout the country and across the seas. The relative stability in economic growth during the eighties is reflected in these ton-mile data. The contraction of the nineties is mirrored in the decline in freight tonnage to levels slightly above 80 percent of railroad-carrying capacity. This relatively sharp decline, when viewed against the most modest contractions in the eighties and later, suggests that railroads suffered greatly in the nineties and also contributed to the economic malaise of that depressed period. The railroads' investment plans ought to reflect these unfavorable events.

Analysis of railroad investment series—locomotive and railroad-car output and construction—bears out this expectation.

At the end of the eighties—a period of vast railroad expansion—output of rolling stock was still rising sharply and this growth continued, after 1890, to a peak in 1893. From that point until 1907, rolling stock declined sharply below capacity, sinking rapidly to a level about 40 percent of capacity in 1894. While output rose sharply after that, with a setback in 1897, each contraction in output was substantial and the 1908 decline was even more precipitate than that of 1894. Interestingly enough, the 1908–1909 and 1911 declines were both sharper than those in 1894 and 1897 and trace a double trough, as did those of 1894 and 1897. The volatile nature of this aspect of railroad investment, in which heavy and expensive equipment was involved, must have been a significant determinant of levels of activity in machinery and steel industries and thus of total output.

Although railroad construction does not follow the growth trend that most other major series do, its violent fluctuations parallel those of other investment series. After the eighties—the peak years of widespread and oscillating railroad construction—this investment activity settled to a much lower average. The downward drift of such investment is a natural development of a saturated market. Starting in the nineties, railroad construction consisted more in the replacement of old sections rather than the opening up of new areas in any significant and sustained manner. The sensitivity of railroad construction to the business cycle is apparent. In the depressed seventies, construction was curtailed tremendously for almost the entire decade. Even the relatively mild contraction starting in 1882 precipitated a sharp drop in railroad construction. This cycle sensitivity appeared again in the nineties when the decline was even more precipitate than that of the seventies. Once 1892 construction levels were regained at the end of the decade, construction oscillated cyclically from a much lower level than in previous decades.

Both building and railroad investment experienced violent

fluctuations in this period of great industrial expansion. Other areas of investment likewise had sharp upward and downward movements. The durables output index, in Figure 4, encompassing as it does all durable output including consumer and producer goods, gives us only an average notion of what probably happened to investment in manufacturing. Here too, despite the averaging effect, the fluctuations are quite sharp, though not as sharp as the extremes in building activity or railroad investments. For the seventies, output fell to levels about 60 percent of capacity. In the relatively stable eighties, the decline from 1882 to 1885 set output back as far as the 75 percent of capacity mark. The two troughs of the nineties were less marked than those of the seventies but more so than that in the eighties. The 1908 and 1911 declines, the former reaching as low as 65 percent of capacity, paralleled the contractions which occurred in the nineties, though the recovery in between troughs was more marked, even though it did not exceed 90 percent of capacity. Manufacturing investment could hardly have oscillated less than manufacturing output of durables. It, too, must have been a major force for economic instability as well as economic growth.

Price Changes

The phenomena of economic growth and cyclical instability from 1889 to 1913 interacted in a set of developing market relationships. The changes traced above were real ones, measured quantitatively; we abstracted out price changes. But since the incentives propelling economic activity upward were pecuniary and since, implicitly, cyclical reactions reflected changing profit considerations, changes in prices must be sketched to obtain a fuller view of economic development.

Figure 6 traces price movements representing major areas of economic activity for both producers and consumers.[15] In the

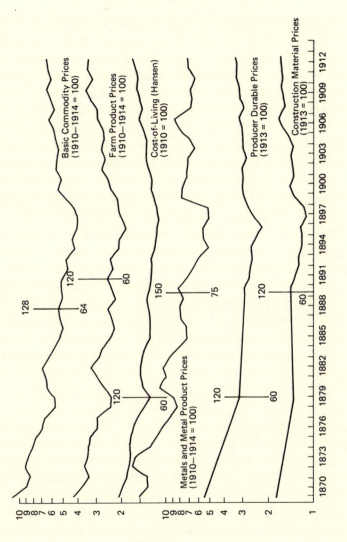

Figure 6
Price Series, 1869-1913

forty-five-year span from 1869, all prices went through a secular decline and then reversed the trend. By 1913, price levels had roughly recovered to the levels of the early seventies. In these price series are veiled the technological as well as the disparate growth factors at play during the period.

The decline of prices from 1869 to the troughs in 1896 or 1897 was a long and substantial one. All series except metals were at higher levels in 1869 than at any subsequent year until World War I. But all series did not decline to the same degree. Prices of metals declined most—about 67 percent. The decline from the peak of 1872 to the 1897 bottom was more marked—over 70 percent. Prices of producer durables declined most of all the other series—about 60 percent from 1869 to 1896. These declines, especially in the earlier years of the period, were mainly due to major continuing technological improvements in metal and producer durable industries, as well as in manufacturing as a whole. By the nineties, the decline in producer durable prices was less steep than those of farm products and basic wholesale commodities. Metal prices, however, dropped by most of all—38 percent from 1890 to 1897. The drop in producer durable prices from 1889 to 1896 amounted to 25 percent, while the contractions in farm product and wholesale commodity prices from their predepression peaks to troughs in 1896 and 1897 were about 27 percent.

In this secular price decline, prices of farm products and basic wholesale commodities dropped by 56 percent and 60 percent respectively. This occurred while corn output increased 160 percent, wheat output almost doubled, and the number of cattle increased by 40 percent. In the same period, GNP increased by about 200 percent. The more rapid decline in farm prices was not due to increased output in agriculture alone, or to the world agricultural market situation, but rather to these factors as well as the important changes in composition of GNP.

Vis-à-vis agricultural output, industrial output's rise was not fast enough to raise the relative value of farm output. Basic wholesale commodity output probably followed a pattern similar to agricultural products. The sharp declines in these basic commodities were a result of increased output in these areas as well as the more but not sufficiently rapid growth of finished commodities.[16]

While producer durable and metal prices were declining sharply as producer durable output more than quadrupled from 1869 to 1896, prices of construction materials fell off by 37 percent. From 1869 to 1897, output of construction materials increased by 200 percent.[17] Prices of construction materials dropped the least sharply of all the series charted. The price decline was arrested and even slightly reversed in the eighties, a period of relatively stable general economic activity with construction activity increasing sharply. The failure of construction material prices to fall as much as producer durable and metal prices was probably related to the sharper increase of their output. Even in the eighties, output of producer durables and metals increased more than that of construction materials. The relative drag on construction-material prices was probably also the result of market conditions in which construction, being localized and subject to less labor-cost flexibility, did not respond to the competitive forces of a national market as did producer durable metal products, basic commodity, and farm product prices. Once local market conditions were depressed, in a general economic contraction, the price rigidity probably intensified the decline in construction activity. From 1889 to 1897, prices of construction materials fell off only about 21 percent—much less than that of the other prices.

As these producer prices were declining, the cost of living (measured mainly by consumer food prices) was also falling off. The decline from 1869 to 1897 amounted to about 46 percent. The narrower amplitude of cost-of-living fluctuation is a characteristic of retail as opposed to wholesale prices. The decline of the cost-of-living index in the nineties was also less marked than that of all the other series, amounting only to 17 percent. Since the other series declined by at least 25 percent, except for construction materials, this was a marked difference.

Since there is no workable series on wage-rate fluctuations, we cannot compare such declines with the cost of living. It is certain, nevertheless, that workers' real incomes rose in the period, as did output. From the data above, showing changes in the proportion of national income going to employee compensation, it follows that since employee compensation declined as a proportion of total income the relationship of the decline in cost of living to wage income was one which did not increase real wage income at a rate as fast as other real incomes.

In the upswing of prices after 1897 to 1913, there was not much divergence among the series. Construction-material prices and the cost of living rose by 49 percent; those of metal products about 40 percent; and prices of producer durables rose by 52 percent. Prices of basic commodities rose by almost 60 percent. Of all prices, those of farm products increased most—by 79 percent.

From 1869 to the depression of the nineties, basic and farm commodities sold in generally unfavorable market conditions; the terms of trade within the economy were going against these areas of economic activity, lagging behind finished commodity growth. Relative competitive conditions also worked against the producers of basic commodities. By the end of the century, new higher levels of industrial output and income existed alongside conditions of relatively retarded basic commodity growth, and in some areas of agriculture a standstill in output came to pass. In these circumstances of robust demand, competitive market relationships with relatively restricted supply led to a relatively sharp increase in prices. Prices of metal products fluctuated relatively little after 1899: while other prices were rising gradually, those of metals were lower in 1913 than in 1899. This was an inevitable consequence of combination in some areas of metal production as well as market technological progress. For producer goods and construction materials, output increased considerably, though at retarded rates: increases were less sharp than for basic commodities. The characteristic of more marked price fluctuations for basic commodities as against relatively dampened price fluctuations for manufactured goods whose prices are more easily administered was becoming institutionalized. During the nineties, many producers of durables saw the advantages of combination to prevent future sharp price declines and to protect, generally, their capital investment.

Changing Economic Relationships

In concentrating on significant quantitative growth in economic series from 1869 to 1913, we have, perforce, glossed over and omitted consideration of patterns of change occurring concurrently. We must now complete our picture of an industrializing economy in process of development by sketching very briefly certain important modifications in certain economic relationships.

As manufacturing expanded, many related activities also grew. The extraction of mineral resources was very closely related to this manufacturing growth and much of the economy's capital formation went into mining activities. Mining output increased more than manufacturing from 1869 to 1913: bituminous and anthracite coal production swelled thirteenfold in that period; petroleum production mushroomed from almost nothing to almost 250 million barrels in 1913. Pig-iron production soared over seventeenfold.[18]

This phenomenal growth of mining was not experienced by other sectors of the economy. A summary of these developments in each sector of the economy is presented in Table 10. These data on proportions of national income going to different industrial sectors depict changes in the structure of the economy. The economy's growth was most prominent in manufacturing, mining, and the miscellaneous category (including the important financial sector). Other sectors were stable or declined in the proportion of income shared. The most significant relative declines were in agriculture and services.

Such changes in wealth and income, in the context of manufacturing development, led to further changes in the size and nature of economic units interacting on the various markets. From 1869 to 1913, the number of manufacturing establishments increased by only 6.5 percent, while the value of product almost quadrupled.[19] The size of units also increased sharply. Manufacturing units grew extremely large in response not only to technological but also to business factors. One economic historian emphasizes this: "The really significant development in the field of industrial organization . . . was the appearance of the trusts, during the middle and late eighties and the early nineties, when prices fell below all previous low levels and consequently margins between costs of production and the amount received for staple manufactures were reduced to a minimum." In response to such changed market conditions and production techniques, the trusts "sought primarily to stabilize and economize processes of production" and they modified considerably business relationships with the many economic units dealing in the trusts's wares—glass, petroleum, sugar, wallpaper, printpaper, nails, and so on.[20]

The combination movement was a response to unfavorable competitive conditions and formal and informal agreements were entered into to maintain prices and stabilize production—

Table 10

National Income and Aggregate Payments, Percentage Distribution by Industries, 1869–1913

(based on values in current prices)

Period	Agriculture	Mining	Manufacturing	Construction	Transportation & Other Public Utilities	Trade	Service	Government	Finance & Miscellaneous
Average of:									
1869–1879	20.5%	1.8%	13.9%	5.5%	11.9%	15.7%	14.7%	4.4%	11.7%
1879–1889	16.1	2.1	16.6	5.5	11.9	16.6	13.6	4.9	12.8
1889–1899	17.1	2.5	18.2	4.9	10.7	16.8	11.8	6.0	12.0
1904–1913	17.0	3.3	18.9	4.3	11.0	15.0	8.9	5.4	16.2

Source: U.S., Bureau of the Census, *Historical Statistics*, p. 13.
Note: The figures are based on Martin's estimates of aggregate payments.

to minimize uncertainty and risk. The development of combinations arose from certain conditions: not too many units, stabilized technology, excess productive capacity or the possibility of its developing rapidly. As manufacturing markets grew and capitalization swelled, the threat of losses forced entrepreneurs to seek control of the market. Those economic activities which could not readily organize such combinations, therefore, found that their relative bargaining power was seriously reduced.[21]

From 1880 to 1910, the combination movement extended through much of manufacturing industry. Thirteen combinations arose in local brewing, flour milling, petroleum oil, matches, and so on. In the nineties, almost 160 combinations were effected, 79 occurring in 1899. In 1900, as many combinations emerged as in the entire decade of the eighties; in 1901, the United States Steel Corporation was formed. The more than 180 combinations arising from 1880 to 1901 controlled over 2,000 plants. Only 63 of these combinations were organized before 1897.[22]

Farmers, not being in a position to set up trusts or marketing agreements, had attempted for some time, in the face of adverse price and market conditions, to exercise some collective control over economic conditions. From 1880 to 1910, the number of farms increased by about 60 percent and tenant ownerships increased from 25 percent of all farms to 37 percent.[23] The Grange, a social organization, had become an association concerned with economic problems. In the eighties, regional farmers' associations such as the Southern Alliance achieved some success in getting state legislatures to pass favorable acts against the abuses of middlemen and rail carriers. The People's party in the 1892 election was a symbol of the farmer's strategy—economic relief through political power. But once farm prices started rising, the impetus to political and economic action abated. The farmer remained an individual economic unit whose output failed to affect the vast competitive market in which he dealt to any great degree.[24]

As for the individual worker, his bargaining power was, in most cases, very weak. The flow of workers from the farms and from abroad was a steady pressure on the labor market. Except for skilled workers in building trades, printing, and transportation, and workers in mining, workers were, for the most part, unorganized. The rise of the Knights of Labor—an organization of skilled and unskilled alike—was meteoric but short-lived. The AFL did not become a major force until the turn of the century. Juxtaposed alongside large business units, the individual farmer, worker, and small businessman were hardly market equals.[25]

International Economic Relations

We have only alluded here and there, in our analysis, to the outside world. Although most people considered the nation economically independent, the national economy was linked in many crucial ways to the economics of the Old World. Not only was the United States economy dependent on foreign capital in its growth, but the farmer also depended upon the world markets and industry produced more and more for export. The United States economy, willy-nilly, was greatly affected by the economies of western Europe, and we in turn had impacts on their economic activities.

Table 11 below shows changes in exports and imports in the period under review.[26] Our trade transactions with the rest of the world are a microcosm of what was happening in the United States. The rapid increase in exports of manufactured goods as well as the rise in imports of crude materials and semimanufactures indicate the impact of industrialization on international trade relationships. At the same time, exports of crude materials and foodstuffs demonstrate how dependent our country was on

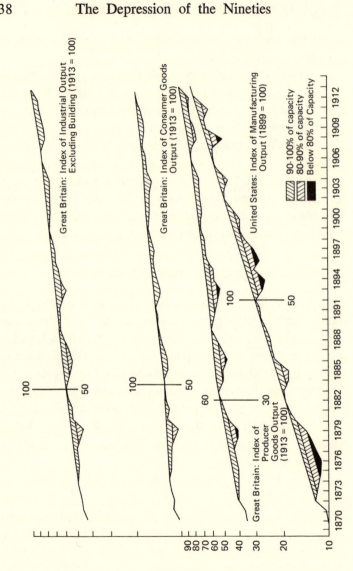

Figure 7
Manufacturing Output in Great Britain and the United States, 1869-1913

world trade. Changes in terms of trade had significant effects on national markets and on the economy as a whole.

The implicit interdependence between the United States economics of western Europe, and we in turn had impacts on rhythms of economic growth and fluctuation are suggested in Figure 7 which traces growth and fluctuations for all British activity (except building) and for activity in British producer-goods and consumer-goods industries. These areas of activity are compared to growth and fluctuations in United States manufacturing as a whole.[27]

Figure 7 indicates that economic growth in the United States from 1869 to 1913 was much more rapid than that in Great Britain and presumably in the other industrial economies of western Europe. The index of manufactures in the United States increased at a rate slightly faster than GNP, about the same as nondurables and at a slightly slower pace than durables. It is broadly representative of United States series and comparable to the British series. But though economic growth in the United States was more rapid than that abroad, there was much less amplitude to British fluctuations. Only in the British series on producer goods industries output does activity drop appreciably below the 90 percent of capacity mark. For the other two series, contractions just below the 90 percent of capacity mark occurred only at the worst troughs. In United States manufactures series, the declines reached below the 80 percent of capacity level, as they did for producer durables, durables, and clearings. In extreme contractions of durables and clearings, the declines fell below the 70 percent of capacity level at the deepest troughs. Thus European economic growth was much slower than that in the United States, but it occurred with greater relative stability during the period surveyed.

The British series also show that their deepest depressed periods occurred at about the same time as those in the United

Table 11
Value of Merchandise Exports and
Imports, by Economic Classes,
Selected Years, 1869–1913
(*millions of dollars*)

Fiscal Year	Total Exports	Crude Materials	Crude Foodstuffs	Manufactured Foodstuffs	Semi Manufactures	Finished Manufactures
1869	$ 275	$145	$ 23	$ 44	$ 14	$ 47
1880	324	243	266	193	29	93
1890	846	309	132	225	46	133
1900	1,371	340	226	320	163	332
1910	1,710	574	110	259	268	499
1913	2,429	740	132	321	409	776

Fiscal Year	Total Imports	Crude Materials	Crude Foodstuffs	Manufactured Foodstuffs	Semi Manufactures	Finished Manufactures	Excess [a] of Imports
1869	$ 418	$ 50	$ 53	$ 95	$ 63	$167	$ 94 [b]
1880	668	142	100	118	111	197	168
1890	789	180	128	133	117	231	69
1900	850	232	98	133	134	203	545
1910	1,557	573	145	162	285	368	188
1913	1,613	649	212	194	349	408	692

Source: Historical Statistics, pp. 244, 246–247.
   (a) Exports and imports as tabulated do not yield excess of exports figure since re-exports are included in excess figure but not in export total tabulated above.
   (b) Excess of imports.

States, with the exception of the eighties. In that decade, the pattern was reversed: British economic contraction was longer and relatively deeper than the decline in the United States where railroad and building construction, illustrated in Figure 5, were powerful forces sustaining the high levels of activity. In the seventies, the British contraction started later, the trough coming after that in the United States. The recovery to 90 percent of capacity was achieved in one year after the trough of 1879. The contraction of the nineties started much earlier in Great Britain than in the United States and the trough was reached in 1893 just as the United States economy was beginning its deep downturn.[28] (There was no double bottom in Britain.) Then, as the United States economy progressed through the depression of the nineties, the British economy reached 90 percent of capacity for many activities by 1894, with that level being reached for producer goods in 1898. Its upward movement (with a suggestion of a double bottom in producer goods decline in 1897), reaching a capacity peak in 1899, occurred as the United States economy was straining to attain 90 percent of capacity. After 1900, the economic movements of both economies were more synchronized though the drop in 1908 was more precipitate in the United States.

These analyses of the timing and severity raise the question of the causal relationships between depressions in Europe and in the United States. Without answering the question of whether United States depressions "caused" those in Europe or vice versa, it is clear that economic contraction in Europe at least meant a falling off in European investment and purchases in the United States. This was undoubtedly true during the nineties, when British contraction preceded the United States decline. Once the trough of European cycles had been reached, investment and purchases abroad increased again, though the British expansion apparently did not immediately buoy up the United

States economy. During European contractions, imports of manufactures from the United States declined at the same time as United States imports from Europe also fell off. Usually the decline in United States imports was more marked than that of United States manufactures exports.[29]

Summary

As the United States economy was being transformed into an industrial order with large-scale agriculture from 1869 to 1913, it experienced a series of sharp depressions sometimes followed by complete and sometimes by incomplete recoveries. Such incomplete recoveries occurred in 1895, 1899, and 1910. For many years, economic activity was far below capacity levels. Yet, in this period of sharp economic fluctuations, the economy also grew at relatively high rates—much higher than those in European economies. With the exception of the eighties, the amplitude of business-cycle fluctuations in the United States was wider than in western Europe. As the economy was rapidly transformed into an industrial order, new wealth and income relationships were being established through changing market structures. The period was characterized by a pronounced secular decline in prices to 1896 and 1897, with the rates of decline reflecting changed proportions in national income and different rates of growth in the output of various products. The market, at the end of the century, brought together the individual farmer, worker, or businessman, for the most part unorganized, and the powerful corporation or its more highly developed business form, the trust or combination. It was in this framework of far-reaching economic changes that the depression of the nineties took place.

NOTES
1. See A. F. Burns and W. C. Mitchell, *Measuring Business Cycles,* p. 78, for a listing of economic contractions and expansions during the

period. For a ranking of the contractions in the period, see J. B. Hubbard, "Business Volumes During Period of Decline and Recovery," *Review of Economic Statistics* 12 (November, 1938): 131–135; A. R. Eckler, "A Measure of the Severity of the Depressions, 1873–1932," ibid., 15 (May, 1923): 75–81.

2. Most of the data in this chapter are broad series of aggregates taken from U.S. Bureau of the Census, *Historical Statistics of the United States, 1789–1945* (hereafter cited as *Historical Statistics*) and other standard works dealing with historical series. For the most part, they have been used as published. These data are employed with the realization that the classifications as well as their measurements are often very rough ones in which questions of comparability, reliability, and precision arise. We use them to give us a broad sweep of economic growth without imputing a spurious precision to any of them. Thus, if it appears that we accept them at face value, that is only a literary license which should not carry with it the implication that they are any more than useful benchmarks.

3. These wealth data are not as inclusive as Kuznets' reproducible wealth figures, but the latter are not broken down by categories. The difference in rates using reproducible wealth is only a few percentage points for each decade; this does not affect our generalizations. See Simon Kuznets, *National Product Since 1869*, p. 228.

4. The series in Figure 2 are taken from the following sources: Gross National Product: Simon Kuznets, "Annual Estimates of National Product, 1869–1949," Capital Requirements Study (unpublished preliminary memorandum of National Bureau of Economic Research, 1951), pp. 9, 27; Nondurable Output Index: Edwin Frickey, *Production in the United States, 1860–1914*, pp. 64, 117; Producer Durable Output: William H. Shaw, *Value of Commodity Output Since 1869*, pp. 61–62, 294; Deflated Bank Clearings Outside New York City: Frederick E. Macaulay, *Some Theoretical Problems Suggested by the Movements of Interest Rates, Bond Yields and Stock Prices in the United States Since 1856*, pp. 255 ff.; and Railroad Freight-Ton Miles: *Historical Statistics*, pp. 200, 203.

5. Nondurable output characteristically falls off less than most manufacturing since it includes the least dispensable of goods, including processed food and other perishables.

6. Data on population are from *Historical Statistics*, p. 28, while those on labor-force changes are from Paul H. Douglas, *Real Wages in the United States, 1890–1926*, p. 440. Population increase arose from increases in native-born and large-scale immigration. In the middle nineties, immigration slackened off, due to the depression. See *Historical Statistics*, pp. 33–34, 47.

7. Alba M. Edwards, *Comparative Occupation Statistics for the United States, 1870–1940*, pp. 93, 100–101; *Historical Statistics*, pp. 63–64; Paul H. Landis, *Population Problems*.

8. *Historical Statistics*, p. 15.

9. W. H. Shaw, *Value of Commodity Output.* Shaw's output data in current prices for total commodity output, consumer durable output, consumer semidurable output, and consumer perishable output were deflated by his price indices for each category to yield the series graphed in Figure 3: pp. 34–35, 39–40, 51–52, 61–62, 290–295. Total commodity output excluding food (more meaningful for purposes of growth than including food) was derived by subtracting out manufactured and nonmanufactured food products, using the above-mentioned techniques of deflation; pp. 30–31, 290. For Figure 4, the building material purchases (1913 prices) was taken from the table on pp. 76–77. Frickey's Durable and Nondurable production indices are taken from his work, *Production in the United States, 1860–1914,* pp. 54, 64, 117.

10. Construction materials are subject to cyclical as well as longer-term forces affecting the degree of fluctuation. According to Long, "building as a whole fluctuates in long cycles lasting about a generation." Cf. C. D. Long, *Building Cycles and the Theory of Investment,* p. 128 and passim. In the nineties, building activity was in a contraction of a "long building cycle" and thus construction materials output declined much more sharply than when a depression occurred while a "building cycle" expansion was on, as in the 1908 depression.

11. Cf. Long, *Building Cycles,* chap. 9.

12. Kuznets, *National Product since 1869,* p. 194.

13. The series on locomotive and railroad-car output is taken from Shaw, *Value of Commodity Output,* pp. 75–76. Annual railroad construction figures are from *Statistical Abstract, 1915* for the years 1869–1882; for subsequent years, *Poor's Manual of Railroads, 1885–1912.* The series on building permit values is from *Historical Statistics,* pp. 172–173. Newman's index of permit values has been set up on a 1913 price base so that price changes are eliminated.

14. *Historical Statistics,* p. 174.

15. The sources for the five price series are: Wholesale Prices of 30 Basic Commodities, *Historical Statistics,* pp. 231–232; Farm Product Prices, ibid.; Metals and Metal Product Prices, ibid.; Cost of Living, ibid., p. 265; Producer Durable and Construction Material Prices, Shaw, *Value of Commodity Output,* p. 294.

16. *Historical Statistics,* pp. 101, 106. See Figure 2 for growth of GNP.

17. The 1869 data are not as reliable for these series as are those in the nineties.

18. *Historical Statistics,* pp. 143, 146, 149. In regard to petroleum development, see Carter Goodrich et al., *Migration and Economic Opportunity,* p. 268.

19. *Historical Statistics,* p. 179.

20. Victor S. Clark, *History of Manufactures in the United States, 1893–1928,* 2:174.

21. U.S. Industrial Commission, *Final Report of the Industrial Com-*

mission 19:595–597 (hereafter cited as *U.S. Industrial Commission Report*). See also I. M. Tarbell, *The Nationalizing of Business 1878–1898*.

22. *U.S. Industrial Commission Report* 20:600–604; Clark, *History of Manufactures 3:7*. By the turn of the century, combinations were mainly found in the rapidly expanding industries. In extractive and related manufacturing activities, combination was widespread. Amalgamated Copper Company's control of copper production was estimated at between 55 and 60 percent; American Smelter and Refining Company (just affiliated with a major competitor, Guggenheim) controlled practically "all the silver-lead smelting interests in the United States." U. S. Steel Corporation, at its inception, controlled about 70 percent of iron and steel production, extending to mines as well as plants. Zinc was also mainly controlled by a few producers, as was anthracite coal, where railroad and financial interests cooperated in control. The Standard Oil Company was characterized as having "practical control of the refining of petroleum in the U.S. and a considerable degree of control over the production of crude oil." See *U.S. Industrial Commission Report*, ibid., pp. 228–236. As we saw in Figure 6 and on p. 29, one consequence of combination in metal production was the more stable price situation. The administered price in steel and related fields is reflected in the metal product price series in Figure 6 after 1899.

23. *Historical Statistics*, pp. 85–96.

24. F. A. Shannon, *The Farmer's Last Stand*, pp. 311–328.

25. See Leo Wolman, *Ebb and Flow in Trade Unionism*, pp. 15–20; John Commens et al. *History of Labour in the United States* 2:396–397, 413–414, and passim.

26. The percentage changes in imports and exports are on a value basis and therefore do not accurately reflect actual changes in quantities. If, however, the figures were adjusted by deflating for price changes from 1869 to 1913, using the wholesale commodity price index, the percentage increases would be greater than the increases based on the value figures tabulated. See *Historical Statistics*, pp. 231–232, for the index.

27. It is assumed, in the absence of good data on other countries, that fluctuations in British economic activity followed generally the same pattern as those in France, Belgium, and Germany. There was a close conformity in the business cycle. Cf. Burns and Mitchell, *Measuring Business Cycles*. The series in Figure 7 are from the following sources: all indices on Great Britain were taken from Walter Hoffmann, "Wachstrum und Wachstumsformen der Englischen Industriewirtschaft von 1700 bis zur Gegenwart" in *Probleme der Weltwirtschaft* (Schriften des Instituts fur Weltwirtschaften der Universitat Kiel), Jena, 1940 53, table opposite p. 284. The index on manufactures in the United States is from Frickey, *Production in the U.S.*, p. 54.

28. The British, French, and German economies were following roughly the same business cycle course, starting in 1890. See Burns and Mitchell, *Measuring Business Cycles*, p. 78.

29. *Historical Statistics*, p. 246.

2

The Economic Annals of the Depression, 1892-1897

Although broad quantitative measures are important and occupy us through most of this work, the single and other interrelated events out of which the aggregates take form must also inform the student of the depression. From the ebb and flow of day-to-day events, one senses the changing moods, attitudes, and tempos which condition decisions determining levels and directions of economic activity. Such knowledge lends the shape and substance of reality to the quantitative dimensions of the economic process.

This chapter's focus—based both on contemporary reports and analyses and later scholarly research—is a summary descriptive analysis of some of the most important economic events from 1892 to 1897. From the last half of 1892 and the economic peak in January, 1893, the narrative takes the measure of the panic and the contraction that reached a trough in June, 1894; then the picture of this severe depression is completed with an account of the recovery to the incomplete December, 1895, peak followed by the second contraction to the June, 1897, low point and the final recovery. Knowledge of the un- even and often opposite movement of economic forces both be- fore and during this twin-bottomed depression should furnish a more complete view of its essential characteristics.

As we have seen from our broad analysis of economic devel- opment in the United States, the depression of the nineties was a contraction of great intensity and long duration. Starting in 1893, economic activity declined to a trough in the summer of 1894, after which recovery set in and expansion continued until a peak was reached at the end of 1895. This peak, however, was "submerged" in that the levels of economic activity at- tained, though about as high as those in 1892, fell far short of the growing capacity of the economy as projected from 1892 peaks. Figures 2 through 6 in Chapter 1 illustrate this. The peak of 1895 was short-lived; it was followed by another significant downturn starting in 1896 and continuing into the first half of 1897. In the summer of 1897, economic activity ceased con- tracting and recovery began once more. By the end of the year, output in many areas again attained 1892 levels. But most eco- nomic activities did not rise to capacity levels measured from the 1892 peak until 1901 or 1907. The recovery after 1897 was a slow process that did not pick up momentum until after 1900.

Europe

While the United States was suffering economic contractions, the major industrial nations of western Europe were also in the throes of deep depression. The downturn in England started after September, 1890, preceding the Baring failure by about a month, and the contraction lasted until February, 1895, after which there was a long expansion until June, 1900. The trough in Germany was also in February, 1895, after a contraction starting in January, 1890; the next peak was in June, 1900. In France, there was a similar cycle; the peak of January, 1891, was followed by a contraction which reached its bottom in January, 1895, with the next peak occurring in March, 1900.[1]

The depression of the nineties in Europe was one of long duration and wide amplitude. The full cycle, from 1890 or 1891 (depending on the country) to early 1900, lasted ten years, about double the average cycle length for the end of the nineteenth century. The period of contraction was also about double the average. In Germany the contraction period was three times the average 1879–1902 length. As for severity—if we use Great Britain as representative—we find that many industrial activities fell to levels below 80 percent of potential capacity at the trough. Compared to previous depressions, the decline was as deep and the duration was longer.[2]

In the United States, there was also a parallel contraction in economic activity in 1890. July, 1890, marks the peak of economic activity. The contraction which followed was short-lived, reaching a trough in May of 1891 after which economic expansion developed until the peak of January, 1893. The next trough was in June, 1894, followed by a peak in December, 1895, and then another trough in June, 1897, with the final peak for the decade in June of 1899. Thus, while the major industrial nations of Europe were coursing through one complete business cycle, the United States experienced three distinct cycles, the middle trough of June, 1894, anticipating the European troughs by some seven or eight months.[3]

As in Great Britain and Germany, in 1890 economic activity in the United States started to contract before the Baring crisis, the peak being reached in July. Though the contraction was widely felt throughout the economy, its intensity and duration were limited. By the summer of 1891, the economy was recovering rapidly and new, higher levels of economic activity were achieved by the end of 1892. In a short period of about ten months—from July, 1890, to May, 1891—the economy completed its contraction. In that short time, some areas of economic activity were not adversely affected by the reaction in trade, but others experienced sharp contractions.[4]

The downturn in the United States economy starting late in 1890 was reversed mainly due to what Noyes characterizes as a "freak of nature." The short supply of wheat in Europe for 1890 and the wheat famine in Europe in 1891 occurred when the United States was producing a fair grain crop in 1890 and the largest grain crop in its history in 1891. The rise in prices on the world market for the two years reflects this fortuitous turn of events. This "concurrence of bad harvests in Europe and abundant harvests in America" stimulated a continuing expansion of American business as the farmers' prosperity generated activity in railroads, trade, mining, and manufacturing. This prosperity kept on an expanding course until the beginning of 1893.[5]

Mid-1892 to Beginning of 1893

The last six months of 1892 foreshadowed, superficially, a continuing and expanding prosperity. High levels of economic activity obtained, but there was evident disappointment among business analysts in the economy's failure to achieve more complete prosperity. Symptoms of impending breakdown were in evidence and in some financial circles the ambivalence mirrored confidence in business activity but lack of confidence in government. The *Commercial and Financial Chronicle* reported: "There is unbounded confidence in the business vitality and resources of the country, but only a feeble confidence that Congress will do what it ought to do to put our finances on a sound basis."[6]

Generally, business leaders did not consider the last half of the year as favorable as the first. High among controlling influences was the agitation over silver policy which, certain financial circles claimed, unsettled business. The slackening in economic activity was traced to the agricultural sector where poor market conditions adversely affected railroad earnings, exports, commerce, and industry.

But, despite some business leaders' disappointment in not reaching expected high levels, most financial and business analysts felt restrained optimism about general economic conditions. This business optimism stemmed from the persistence of certain strong expansionary forces and was underscored repeatedly in the business journals by reference to these significant indicators. During the last half of 1892, bank clearings surpassed the previous year's totals. With prices generally lower or stable, this represented real economic expansion. A companion indicator, business failures, also supported business confidence. Failures were lower both in number and dollar value of liabilities than for the previous year and half-year periods. Since business enterprises had grown in size and number, this represented a significant relative decline. Trade statistics also supported optimistic views. *Bradstreet's* estimated that trade in 1892 was greater than in 1891 by about 10 percent. Businessmen took further heart from reports that the South, which had been having economic difficulties earlier in the year, was slowly recovering in most sectors.[7]

The picture reflected by railway dividends was more shadowy. Earnings expectations had been very bright early in 1892; thus the results of the year, though far from discouraging, fell short of anticipations. Most railways reported the same or higher rates of yield on investment. In the South, however, where generally depressed conditions prevailed, railroad dividends either were the same as during the previous year or lower. The trunk lines, the anthracite railways, and the New England railways, on the other hand, declared dividend payments that were the same or even higher.[8]

Some business and financial leaders hoped that the International Monetary Conference which opened in Brussels late in November would advance some solution to the currency problem. Called for the purpose of "increasing the use of silver," the Conference was expected by many silverites to establish universal bimetallism. Such was the anticipation of the American party led by Senator Allison. Once the meetings were under way, however, it became clear that the ambitious aims of silverite and inflationist Americans were doomed to failure. Attempts to increase the monetary use of silver were wholly unsuccessful; yet many bankers and businessmen still feared that there would be continued attempts in the United States to extend the use and purchase of silver.[9]

Meanwhile, the results of the recent presidential election were being assessed. Since the election of Cleveland was not viewed with alarm by business leaders, many of whom supported him despite their usual Republican allegiance, the failure of the stock market to react favorably was wholly unexpected. There was some trepidation that low tariff and silver groups in Congress would complicate the tariff and currency problems, but most business leaders felt major problems could be avoided under Cleveland's conservative leadership.[10]

Although these indications of prosperity and confidence in the future were widespread, hindsight analysis of several series reveals that the economy was headed for difficulties. Most production totals for 1892 were higher than those for 1891. But there were some notable exceptions: in agriculture, the quantity of grain and flour sold at the Produce Exchange declined. Exports were about 4 percent less in dollar value, while imports rose about 6 percent. This narrowed the export surplus considerably from about $140 million to about $60 million. Railroad construction was down about 10 percent. Cotton output dropped sharply. Petroleum production was also off, declining almost 10 percent. Immigration also fell off, though not very sharply.[11]

The continued easing in wheat and other agricultural prices had significant implications for the entire economy. It explained partially the reduction in the favorable balance of trade and the continuing export of gold. This growing drain of gold was symptomatic of the difficulties which had developed in the economy and was a major factor in the near panic of the stock market on December 19. One journal weighed the adverse factors affecting the economy and took the popular business position linking economic distress with monetary factors:

> This large outflow of gold, at a season of the year too when we are accustomed to look for an import, should obviously lead to . . . correct a situation that includes it. Neither business nor enterprise can thrive while so abnormal a movement is in progress . . . if it were a mere temporary affair induced by any ordinary cause it would be of little consequence. But it . . . has been gathering force for a number of years now, especially for the last five years.
> . . . gold not only leaves us, but leaves us in spite even of [a favorable trade balance]. . . . It is . . . the lack of confidence which our [monetary] policy is causing Europe to feel in our financial stability. No more foreign capital comes to the United States [sic], and as fast as Europeans can dislodge their holdings in America they take the money away.[12]

During 1892, the stock market reflected the contradictory forces at work. The very bright prospects expected at the year's opening were never realized. The market was narrow and irregular throughout the year, and even large foreign sales of American securities during the summer were not unsettling. But the persistent outflow of gold over the year finally took its toll. When this gold drain continued contraseasonally in the last quarter, many dealers reacted strongly and the sharp December break in the market resulted. Call-loan rates soared, temporarily, to 40 percent. Some people labeled the market break a panic, but the early recovery belied this and by the close of the year stock prices were not at sharply lower levels. The market's quick retreat indicated, nevertheless, the sensitivity of traders to adverse forces and foreshadowed the storm ahead: the panic was months off, but the conditions determining it were already taking shape cumulatively.[13]

The year 1893 started without proclamations of great hope or predictions of dire events. Businessmen expected currency reform and emphasized that continued expansion was contingent on solving the vexatious silver problem. The business outlook and its apparent dependence on the currency question left many businessmen with mixed expectations.[14]

First Signs of Trouble: February to April, 1893

The first dramatic, though not completely unexpected, sign of trouble came on February 20 when the Philadelphia and Reading Railway Company went into bankruptcy. This failure can be explained satisfactorily by the internal corporate situation rather than general economic conditions. Nevertheless, the combination's support by powerful Wall Street financial houses and the questions raised by the failure of so large and significant a firm precipitated suspicion and led to a greater awareness of unstable conditions. The bankruptcy of the Reading combination caused many businessmen to question the soundness of other railways and the financial houses behind them.[15]

Once reaction to the Reading failure had subsided somewhat, there followed a short interlude during which many people took heart at the absence of any other spectacular failure or disturbing event. President Cleveland's inaugural address "gave general satisfaction, especially that part which emphasized the importance of sound and stable currency." His accession to office was viewed with confidence by most businessmen. He was expected to "maintain our nation's credit [and] avert financial disaster" and among his desirable qualities the one of "sober and dignified patriotism" was viewed as a key to his future actions.[16]

Despite this faith in Cleveland, economic affairs definitely did not improve. Little more than a month and a half after his new administration took office, an event more clearly symptomatic of the state of the economy than the Reading failure occurred— the decline of the Treasury gold reserve below the $100 million minimum. On April 22, 1893, this minimum was violated for the first time since the resumption of specie payments in 1879 —the result of a process of long duration, reflecting cumulative changes in economic relationships with Europe and adumbrating growing difficulties in the domestic economy.[17]

These two events early in 1893 were not the only distress signals. There were more pervasive forces bringing about a steady economic contraction. Late in January, prices declined in staples such as wheat and iron, foreshadowing a general cyclical economic contraction. General business activity suffered a severe check that was recognized at once in the business journals. The stock market gave ominous signs of falling prices before any sharp drop took place; and money flowed contraseasonally to the interior. A dwindling favorable trade balance evoked further pressure on gold holdings and consequent contraction in bank reserves.[18]

Whatever the complex of interrelationships engendering the economic contraction, its reality became more apparent as the months slipped by. Depressed trade conditions, developing in the early months of 1893, continued and business failures swelled in number and value. Credit was steadily contracted, especially by the New York banks, while loans declined almost 10 percent from February to the beginning of May. Nevertheless, banks were in a solid reserve position, their surplus reserves increasing slightly in the first four months of the year. Credit contraction, early in the year, was attributed to widespread fears about the maintenance of the gold standard and, thus, the early business failures were viewed as the next chain in the causal link of economic decline.[19]

While the forces of depression were gathering, evidence of expansion still persisted as various economic activities continued their momentum from the high levels of 1892. Even after the stock-market panic in May, some economic aggregates were above levels of the corresponding 1892 periods—for example, bank clearings for the first five months of 1893 were above the totals for the same 1892 period. Railroad gross earnings also continued to grow in the first part of 1893. Except for February, 1893, when gross earnings were about 3 percent lower than in February, 1892, gross earnings for each month were higher than in the previous year and for the first half of 1893 were about 3 percent higher than in 1892. The economic retreat starting at the beginning of 1893 was thus a gradual one.[20]

The Reading failure of February ushered in a period of uneasiness which subsequent events failed to allay and mounting business failures suggested that a pervasive economic downturn was occurring. The seriousness of the situation was more dramatically demonstrated with each succeeding failure of well-known firms. The Reading collapse was followed by the failure of numerous financial and industrial firms. A few Wall Street firms failed in the subsequent weeks. In April, the stock-market decline was attributed to uneasiness arising out of these failures and the difficulties confronting the Whiskey Trust. Later that month the Pennsylvania Steel Company went into receivership. Although not a firm of great size, with capital amounting to only

$5 million, its failure signaled weakness in still another industrial sector. By the beginning of May the atmosphere was a tensely expectant one. The news of the failure of the 150-branch Bank of Australia was considered by some as a gloomy omen of the dire conditions inevitably expected in the United States.[21]

May to July: The Panic Begins and Spreads

May 3 marked the commencement of a series of disturbing events called the "Panic of 1893"—among the worst in this country's annals. On that date, the stock market took its sharpest drop since 1884 with industrial shares off most—some losing as many as 15 points. Next day the National Cordage Company, whose stock had dropped 15 points, was in the hands of receivers and three Wall Street brokerage houses failed.[22] The beginning of a series of failures and suspensions was abruptly at hand.

The "panic" consisted, first, of precipitate declines in the stock market with attendant financial stringency and, second, of many bank failures and suspensions leading to widespread financial and commercial dislocation. These conditions prevailed from May to August, 1893, after which the financial mechanism operated more normally. Bank failures, issuance of clearinghouse loan certificates, suspension of payments, a currency premium, the spread of hoarding, gold exports, and then gold imports were all part of the panic syndrome. After the panic started, depression forces developed more rapidly as employment fell off and price declines became more marked and more widespread. The panic, like the 1929 stock-market crash, complicated and intensified the contraction already under way.[23]

Bank failures and suspensions for 1893 were the greatest on record. Most occurred in the South and West with few in the

East. Of 158 national bank failures for 1893, 153 were in the South and the West. The total of other bank failures was much greater: 172 state banks, 177 private banks, 47 savings banks, 13 loan and trust companies, and 16 mortgage companies. These failures outside large cities had disruptive repercussions beyond their localities. Interior banks with liquidity problems withdrew money deposited in New York, affecting the stock market and the money market banks' reserves.[24]

Gold-standard advocates blamed these failures on currency redundancy and inveighed loudly against past silver legislation, yet basic structural and cyclical factors more adequately explain the failures. One incisive evaluation reveals a weakness of the gold partisans' argument:

> In the eastern money centers bank failures and suspensions were attributed almost entirely to the silver influence. But . . . they occurred principally in the West and Southwest, where there is no evidence that people were distrustful of silver money. Had the monetary influences been potent, we should expect to find numerous failures in the Eastern States and also some discrimination on the part of depositors between different kinds of money in circulation. Distrust of the solvency of the banks rather than dissatisfaction with the circulating medium . . . brought about runs upon banks and the numerous failures and suspensions.[25]

These bank failures raised problems for the New York City banks and contributed, along with other factors, to sharp declines in their reserves which had been more than adequate before the crisis. Thus, while surplus reserves in New York City banks in the middle of June were over $8.5 million, they dropped sharply below legal requirements in July and the continued or renewed pressure of gold exports threatened them further. In these circumstances and in the confused atmosphere of bank failures throughout the country, many people questioned the solvency of the New York banks. So despite the fact that no New York bank was in difficulty, on June 17 these banks, at an earlier phase of a crisis than ever before, set up a mechanism for using clearinghouse loan certificates. Issued by the clearinghouse with high-grade assets as collateral, these certificates economized on the use of cash, being substituted for it to clear differences in bank claims. Their use implied a shortage of cash funds, though the action was actually taken as a precautionary move to forestall suspension of cash payments and reduce pressures leading to further bank failures. As money became scarcer at the close of the fiscal year, loan certificates were relied on more heavily. Bank reserves dwindled and the July 8 statement showed a reserve deficiency exceeding $5 million. The situation was alleviated momentarily by an inflow of currency from the interior after the banks tried to ease the reserve deficiency through loan contraction.[26]

The respite provided by the flow of funds to New York early in July was short-lived and during the third week in July withdrawal of funds was resumed. As bank failures in the West and South grew in number, cash withdrawals increased. The Erie Railroad went into receivership July 26 and the stock market took another sharp drop. One journal noted somberly, "Our markets have been more disturbed and excited this week than at any time this year. . . . Neither banks nor trust companies are making loans on time."[27] President Cleveland's June 20 proclamation convening a special session of Congress to repeal the Sherman Silver Act did not noticeably boost the morale of the business community to whose pressure he had yielded.[28] New York banks continued to lose reserves. More prominent institutions were now involved in bank failures. During the last two weeks of July, over thirty national banks suspended operations. In New York, the savings banks announced their intention, July 28, of enforcing the 60-day rule on withdrawals. Two days earlier, for the first time, Chicago banks approved the issuance of clearinghouse loan certificates. These events foreshadowed the inevitable suspension of cash payments by banks.[29]

Early in August, the New York banks were forced to suspend cash payments partially and they were followed by banks throughout the country. Just before such suspensions, these banks had a reserve deficiency of over $14 million and were in a very much more precarious position than they had been in June, when with a reserve surplus of about $24 million they were faced with large withdrawals by interior banks. Such withdrawals in July forced suspensions. Confidence in the New York banks was still maintained by the community so that there was no immediate danger yet of a general run. The larger banks were subject to the major impact of the withdrawals and suspension was not complete: cash payment was refused on drafts remitted in ordinary business dealings; currency was still being sent to interior banks drawing on balances.[30]

The use of clearinghouse loan certificates for the vast majority of interbank settlements, reaching 95 percent in August, made suspension inevitable. With all banks using this means of settlement, those banks with many correspondent relationships were subject to severe pressure. Some banks had adequate reserves while others did not. Unequal reserve positions led to suspensions while the interior drain, which ended before the beginning of September, continued. These suspensions intensified panic conditions and gave impetus to further financial and commercial dislocation.[31]

During practically the entire month of August and the first two days of September, currency was at a premium in New York City and in other parts of the country. To attract cash to the banks to replenish the deficient reserves, rates were raised to a high of about 4 percent. The currency premium resulted from partial suspension which led to a more complete suspension that was further extended by the currency premium, with many depositors withholding money so as to meet payrolls. Other depositors withdrew money by guile and then profited by the sale of such money to banks at a premium. In these circumstances, partial suspension could not long be maintained. During the early period of currency premium, the interior banks were large purchasers of cash. Later, when the panic was abating, the premium dwindled as demand eased and less money flowed to the interior. After the middle of August, the reserve position of the New York banks steadily improved and by the middle of September reserves were once again above the legal requirement. By then, currency premiums had ended throughout the country.[32]

There was not very much hoarding before the currency premium occurred and most hoarding that did take place was confined to the parts of the South and West where bank failures and suspensions were widespread. Once currency was at a premium and banks had suspended, many people reduced their cash deposits. What happened was that "various substitutes for money served in a measure to take the place of money which would have moved into and out of the banks in ordinary course had they not resorted to suspension."[33]

The gradual increase in the reserves of the New York City banks was not the result of dishoarding or of the inflow of money from the interior, as money conditions eased somewhat. The restoration of reserves was achieved mainly through gold imports. In the four weeks of currency premium gold imports to New York exceeded $40 million; even interior banks, especially those in Chicago, imported gold.

A casual survey of imports would seem to explain the gold inflow fully by the currency premium. But the contradictory facts were that foreign exchange rates were near or at the export point and the differential in money rates between London and

New York during August was hardly sufficient to attract money to the New York money market. Yet gold imports persisted. Undoubtedly the currency premium played a role, but other factors were much more significant. Some gold had been contracted for before the currency premium arose. (Even after the premium was in effect, the risks involved for gold importers discouraged importing for that purpose.) The main factor in the gold inflow, undoubtedly, was the change in the balance of payments. During the months of July and August, the merchandise export surplus rose absolutely and relatively compared to earlier months and the previous year. Furthermore, there were significant purchases of securities by Europeans taking advantage of bargain prices in the United States during July and August.[34]

The degree to which bank suspension of cash payments aggravated the contraction of industrial and commercial activity is not susceptible of precise measurement. But it is quite clear that suspension intensified economic decline. Business was undergoing serious contraction before banking difficulties reached their climax in August. By July many business sectors, such as railroads—which had withstood the effects of contraction through the first part of the year—were at last giving evidence of declining activity. In this developing depression situation, suspension complicated the many difficulties which already confronted industry and commerce.[35]

While the banking and financial panic was under way, other sectors of the economy were going through the painful catharsis of liquidation and contraction. Many of those business sectors which had resisted contraction early in the year were now fast succumbing. Price declines continued throughout the summer; failures spread in all sectors of the economy. Stock-market prices continued to drop, reacting sharply to each report of bad news. Near the end of July, for example, when the Erie Railroad went into receivership, stocks sank lower. On occasions the market would effect a short recovery, as happened when London buyers entered the market July 20 to take advantage of bargains, forcing some prices upward. By the late summer, however, it was clear that depression was the pervasive economic force at work.[36]

Summer 1893 to Summer 1894

During the summer of 1893, all the elements of industrial, commercial, and financial depression were in evidence as a sharper downturn followed the panic. The economy retreated steadily into a deepening contraction of major proportions.

The increase in business failure was underscored by the great number of receiverships in the strategic railway industry. The failure of the Philadelphia and Reading Railroad was the first significant railway failure early in 1893, before the panic's onset, and it heralded increasing difficulties in a major industry. Still, many railways continued to prosper early in 1893. The failure, however, of the Erie Railway, announced on July 26, marked clearly the advent of severe depression for the railroads. Once receiverships began to grow, they assumed record proportions. As one historian records, "All records in this regard . . . were broken by the panic of 1893, when the control of an unprecedented mileage was handed over to the officers of the state and federal courts." For the year ending June 30, 1894, over 125 railroad companies went into receivership. At that time, 192 companies—involving about one-fourth of all railroad mileage and capitalization—were in the hands of receivers. For the same period, over 63 percent of railway stock paid no dividends. Many railroads had been on the verge of financial difficulties when the depression took hold; as the depression spread, it was impossible for them to avert bankruptcy. Railroad reorganization on such a grand scale was one dimension of the intensity of the depression.[37]

In the summer of 1893, while the panic continued and the depression developed further, the nation's attention was dramatically focused on the silver question. So many people had mechanically related depressed economic conditions to the Sherman Silver Act that, less than a week after Congress convened in special session in August, one business journal remarked with deep disappointment that "the long desired meeting of Congress had not brought the improvement anticipated." Yet this sort of anticipation persisted throughout the congressional debates as well as after the Sherman Act's repeal at the end of October. When recovery failed to come speedily, the bugbear was still silver: "Panics come in a day; but they wholly disappear only after years. This is the penalty the country is paying, and still must pay, for its costly experiment in silver legislation."[38]

As was noted above, the Treasury gold reserve declined below the $100 million minimum to $96 million in April. This event had been foreshadowed by the long-term gold drain starting in 1889. As the government fiscal deficit grew and was met by using Treasury gold, the Treasury gold reserve necessarily declined sharply. Many business and financial leaders expressed lack of confidence in the Treasury and voiced fears that the gold standard would be repudiated. The continuing decline in Treasury gold led the conservative gold-standard group to press strongly for repeal of the Sherman Act; the decline in the price of silver, resulting partially from the demonetization of silver by India in June, aroused the silver groups to resist repeal efforts and to press for legislation enacting full bimetallism.[39]

In these trying circumstances Congress, convened by President Cleveland, met in August to act on repeal. The debate was sharp in both houses and most of the press clamored unsuccessfully for swift action to end the depression through repeal. The House passed the Wilson repeal bill with dispatch on August 28 by 239 to 108. In the Senate, where delay was more easily achieved, a strong minority pressed the debate for months. When, on October 11, cloture was imposed, further delay was accomplished by a forced adjournment. But finally the repeal bill passed, 43 to 32, following the President's suggestion, except for a paragraph in favor of bimetallism.[40]

Many businessmen contended that despite the repeal of the Sherman Act the stage would be set for recovery only when the requirement of upward tariff revision was met. So legislative action on the tariff was begun. The administration had been elected on a tariff-reform plank, but the depression and the government deficit were more compelling reasons given why such action was urgently pressed. High-tariff advocates blamed the depressed conditions on industry's fear of a lower tariff; confidence would be restored only by a "good" (higher) tariff act. The administration, faced with a mounting deficit, explained it by pointing to the effects of the McKinley Tariff of 1890, which raised rates protectively and thus reduced revenue. One historian, however, argues convincingly that the main factor in the federal deficit was the depression, which induced a decline in imports and consequently lower revenue. Moreover, he maintains that "No one change in the McKinley Act had done so much to upset the federal budget as the removal of the duty on sugar, and no one change was so certain to bring an additional revenue as the reimposition of this tax."[41]

The tariff bill was bitterly contested. After a tortuous path through the Senate, the bill was passed after considerable delay in the House; it was allowed to become law without the President's signature in August, 1894, after the depression's trough had been reached. The Wilson Tariff was a jumble, the result of compromise and conflicting motives with little attention given to the government's fiscal situation. The majority in the House "was planning a law to remit taxation; those who held the balance of power in the Senate were secretly contriving to retain as much protection as they dared. Between the two, the urgent question of a deficit had little hearing."[42]

The tariff's enactment was marked by bitter clashes and theatrical disclosures of attempted bribery of some Senators and the sugar interests of certain Senators. The tariff which finally emerged mainly reflected the Senate version—sugar duties favorable to the refining companies and duties on coal and iron, struck off by the House. Raw wool was put on the free list. The Wilson Tariff in its final form also included a tax of 2 percent on income over $4,000, but within a year and a half the Supreme Court declared this income tax unconstitutional.[43]

The Wilson Tariff failed to produce adequate income for the federal government. Revenue continued to decline during 1894 and 1895 as depressed economic conditions persisted and the income tax was invalidated. Despite the efforts of free traders, the principle of protection was not seriously undermined even though freer trade in raw-material imports was enacted.[44]

While headlines chronicled the battle over silver and the tariff, industrial production declined all along the line in the closing months of 1893 and the first half of 1894. By the end of 1893, the production of heavy woolens had fallen off about 60 percent and springwear orders were about 30 percent of normal. The production of woolen hosiery declined 50 percent, while cotton hosiery output decreased 10 percent. Fine yarn cottons were off 25 percent and print cloths 10 percent. Export cottons declined about 20 percent since the start of the year. New England shoe shipments declined 24 percent from July and shoe factories, which had had their worst decline in August, produced at a level 15 to 20 percent lower than in 1892. The iron industry's output fell to a low in October, and its modest recovery by December still left about 40 percent of the industry's work force idle.[45]

A broad list of consumer and producer goods shows production declines of about 20 percent for the year from June, 1893. Most resistance to the downward trend appeared in certain essential consumer goods. One journal reported aggregate grocery sales for the last half of 1893 higher by 1 percent than for the preceding year.[46]

Prices declined in varying degrees: cotton and wool prices were down 20 percent, pork at wholesale 10 percent, steam lard 21 percent, sugar 36 percent, while coffee prices rose 6 percent for the year. In the steel industry, pig-iron prices declined almost one third, steel billets over a third, and steel rails about 17 percent. Such dim developments led one journal to declare dolefully: "The business year 1893 promises to go into history with heavier net losses in financial, commercial and industrial circles throughout the United States than in the more severe among other panic periods in the past eighty years."[47]

Most contemporary journals ignored unemployment until the numbers defied this disregard at the end of the year; other sources clearly reported that the labor market was quite slack. By July and August, unemployment was substantial. Factory employment began to fall off in June, increasing its rate of decline in July and August. Wage reductions also commenced in the second quarter of the year and continued thereafter. One source put the decline in wages from April, 1893, to the year's end at over 9 percent. Another reported wage rates, hours worked, and total wages declining much more sharply over the period November, 1892, to November 1893. The drop in workers' earnings was softened somewhat as the cost of living also declined, the decrease for the entire year 1893 approximating 3 percent.[48]

From the summer of 1893 until that of 1894, when the depression reached its low point, millions of families experienced extreme hardship. Unemployment grew and gave rise to violent strikes, varied but limited efforts were made to bring relief to hundreds of thousands of families, and unique forms of protest such as the industrial armies were organized.[49]

For many industrial workers, conditions were not to improve

greatly for many months and for some not for years. During the winter, there was frequent reference to the hardships the unemployed had to endure. Emergency relief action was taken during the winter to mitigate some effects of unemployment. Such assistance was handled locally and its extent and efficiency varied with local conditions and attitudes. Late in the fall of 1893, a conference of representatives of leading relief societies was held in New York to define needs and to ask for substantial, ordered contributions rather than indiscriminate alms. Extra workers and more volunteers were put to work. For example, the local New York society increased its working force and expenditures by about 50 percent.[50]

It is doubtful that these relief measures were adequate. In New York, for instance, all sums available for relief, during the winter of 1893–1894, totaled just under $2.5 million. Assuming 50,000 in need, unquestionably a gross understatement, the money amounted to $48.30 per needy family head or individual. The winter of 1893–1894 was extremely cold and natural and economic conditions visited untold hardship on hundreds of thousands of families scattered across the nation.[51]

Such mass misery gave rise to various forms of expression. One type of unusual expression was the industrial army, the most famous of which was Coxey's "Commonwealth of Christ." Conservative opinion belittled such a group which, they claimed, "attracted a degree of attention to which it has not been entitled." Nevertheless, while such armies attracted old hangers-on and hoboes, they did represent an extensive, spontaneous, genuine protest movement of workers concerned with the pressing problem of unemployment. The armies, which included besides Coxey's those under the leadership of Fry and Kelly on the West Coast, had coherent goals and policies which they pressed dramatically to alleviate the depressed conditions in which millions of workers found themselves.[52]

Violence, conflict with local authorities, and the seizing of trains were striking events in the industrial armies' vicissitudes that received wide publicity and gave rise to many fears of the possibilities of disturbance and disorders. Yet, at no time did the combined armies reach more than 10,000, and they probably numbered a lot fewer. Organized in the first two months of 1894, they began the trek to Washington in late March and early April. Coxey's group left Massillon, Ohio, on March 25, some nine days after Fry's army left the Los Angeles area. Kelly's army, the largest, left San Francisco on April 14. Their peregrinations across the continent were marked with violence on the part of local police and the marchers' seizure of railroad trains in the West. Kelly's group picked up Jack London as a recruit in Iowa. In the long march to Washington, the groups were decimated by arrests and defections. The armies arrived in Washington at different times between May and July, but at no time were there more than 1,000 in the capital. There the movement died of its own inadequacy; the arrest of its leaders for walking on the Capitol grass was an incongruous anticlimax.[53]

Less theatrical, but representing more economic force, were the numerous strikes which gave deep expression to the discontent of many hundreds of thousands of workers. The hard winter, marked by severe blizzards and cold reminiscent of the '88 blizzard, was scarcely over before a series of strikes occurred. In April, 1894, more than 40,000 workers were reported involved in over thirty strikes. In some regions, such as the Pennsylvania coke area, violence led to deaths. On April 18 deputy sheriffs killed two Polish rioters and many workers and deputies were injured in Grosse Point township near Detroit in a dispute over the payment system on a city waterworks extension project. Four days later, 130,000 coal miners of the United Mine Workers, led by President McBride, went on strike for a wage increase of twenty to twenty-five cents a ton. Seven weeks later, the strikers were forced to return to work empty-handed.[54]

The greatest of all the strikes, the Pullman strike, started in

May among a group of Pullman workers who insisted that the company restore the wage scale of 1893. This demand mushroomed within little more than a month into a historic labor dispute manacling the main railroads of the country. The railroad workers of the American Railway Union rallied to support their Pullman co-workers. In desperation, the workers tied up twenty-two railroads totaling 50,000 miles in their boycott starting on July 26. Intervention of the federal government with troops and through the courts succeeded in ending the strike.

Obscured somewhat by the Pullman strike was another violent labor dispute—the Cripple Creek, Colorado miners' strike. Starting in February, it ran a violent course "beyond the stage of ordinary industrial disturbances." An attempt of the mine owners to reopen the mines led to violence, which motivated the owners and their allies to denounce the "reign of terror . . . instituted by the strikers" and to call for police protection, denouncing the governor for his failure to take "proper" action.[55]

The declining Treasury gold reserve, which had received such attention in 1893, continued to chronicle the disequilibrium in the economy's relations with Europe. From June, 1893, when the banking panic was on, until a year later, the reserve declined from about $95 million to $65 million, though there were some increases above the $100-million mark when the Treasury received some gold through ordinary inflows and more gold from a 5 percent, ten-year bond issue in January, 1894. This issue, taken reluctantly by the New York banks to avert its failure, yielded over $58 million. The golden cushion furnished by the loan did not last long in the face of Treasury deficits and the gold outflow abroad so that by June, 1894, its gold reserve dwindled again to about $65 million.[56]

The process generating Treasury gold depletion was a complicated one. A direct influence was the government deficit, which persisted through fiscal year 1897. After the panic, the federal government had a deficit each month through May, 1894, ranging from just under a million dollars to just under $10 million and averaging throughout about $6.5 million a month. This deficit was due mainly to diminishing revenue as imports declined. To meet these shortages, the Treasury used its gold reserve since it had no other form of legal money with which to make payments. Thus, it was the deficit rather than redemption of legal tenders which mainly effected the shrinkage in gold reserve.[57]

While the gold reserve declined and the government deficit persisted, there were important changes in the international flow of gold. During the banking crisis in the summer of 1893, gold flowed into the United States. This inflow halted in December, after which there was a constant outflow of gold until the late summer of 1894. The period from June, 1893, to June, 1894, was one in which there was a continuous export surplus in United States trade averaging about $18 million a month. The outward gold movement was due, therefore, to changes in the invisible and capital accounts.

One government statistician estimated that from June, 1892 to June, 1893 at least $200 million in payments had to be made abroad and a sum half that amount had to be paid by foreigners for purchases of United States securities. The net outflow of payments was thus over $100 million. For 1893, movements in and out were often determined by panic conditions. There were foreign purchases of American securities during the summer of 1893 and the spring of 1894 when bargains were obtained. Throughout the period foreign purchases in smaller amounts are also recorded. When the market recovered, foreign sales of American securities stimulated gold outflows.[58]

Summer 1894 Through 1895

The industrial and commercial stagnation that reached its

nadir about June, 1894, was not followed by rapid recovery. But there were perceptible signs in the summer of improvement in trade. Certain strong forces which had begun as early as 1893, such as the expansion of exports, developed further and stimulated the economy, slowly but with growing influence.

Among the more favorable developments were: general trade improvement reflected in shipments, sales, and so on; cessation of price declines; strong export expansion, as manufacturing industry extended its markets abroad; rise in bank clearings; continued decline in business failures. Although these developments were pushing the economy forward, there still were many retarding forces. The Treasury was beset with the drain on its gold reserve as the deficit continued, and gold exports continued to disrupt the economy. Earnings in many important industries, such as railways, remained low. There was no upsurge in foreign investment in the United States, a condition for which poor management by the railroads was a facile but inadequate explanation offered by many observers. The money market had ample funds—some claimed there was a glut of money—but they were not being absorbed to stimulate recovery. The passage of the Wilson Tariff in August failed to work the miracles some of its proponents had predicted.[59]

The recovery from the trough of June, 1894, to the December, 1895, peak was marked by general though restrained economic expansion. The 1895 peak was not a complete recovery to full employment. Seasonally adjusted outside bank clearings showed an increase of almost 15 percent from a $57.6 million daily average in June, 1894, to $65.9 million in December, 1895. For 1895, however, outside clearings were only 10 percent over those for 1894. After June, 1894, clearings did not increase at first, but in the fall they increased gradually until the end of 1895. The high $68.8 million daily average in October, 1895, was the highest achieved since early 1893. The restricted nature of the recovery in clearings is illustrated by the fact that the 1895 peak was more than 20 percent depressed below capacity as projected from the 1892 peak. Business failures had already fallen off sharply in 1894, both in number and in dollar values. For the two years, 1894 and 1895, the total liabilities of business failures were almost the same: $150 million and $159 million. In number of failures, 1895 exceeded 1894 by 292. Here, too, the signs were not those of great buoyancy.[60]

Retail trade increased during the early months of 1895, though the upward movement was not uniform or sharp. In cities such as Chicago, Denver, and Omaha, increases in retail sales in March, 1895, were at last 5 percent over the trough of 1894. This level of sales, however, was still about 15 percent short of the March, 1893, level. As 1895 proceeded, retail sales continued to improve, though in many cases the levels of the peak preceding the contraction of 1893–1894 were not reached.[61]

Unlike most economic indicators, pig-iron production increased rapidly after June, 1894; average daily production in July was over 35 percent above that of June. By the end of 1894, production was more than double the June rate. The high of over 30,000 gross tons daily production, reached in November of 1895, was almost 35 percent above the rate in January, 1895. The annual figures illustrate further the rapid recovery in pig-iron production: in 1894, roughly 6.7 million gross tons were produced; in 1895, about 9.4 million gross tons were produced.[62]

Building construction, according to the index of building permit values, exhibited some increase in the recovery, though the high levels of early 1893 were not reached even by the end of 1895. From July, 1894, to November, 1894, the index rose about 35 percent. Throughout 1895, the level was high, though there were downward fluctuations: the lowest level in November, 1895, was almost 80 percent above the July, 1894, level which was a very low bottom point.[63]

Fluctuations in employment during the period reflected the general recovery pattern. The low for the depression, according to Jerome's index of factory employment, was reached during August of 1894, a level almost 15 percent below that of January, 1893. In the autumn months of 1894, factory employment rose rapidly to a point about 10 percent over August. Throughout 1895, employment was at least 13 percent greater than in August, 1894, and attained, at the peak in November, 1895, a level about 18 percent above August, 1894. This peak was still short of that early in 1893 since which time the labor force in manufacturing had grown considerably.[64]

In manufacturing and transportation, unemployment declined from 1894 to 1895, but not very greatly. An estimate of unemployment in these two sectors for 1894 was over 900,000, but for 1895 the decline was only about 300,000. For 1894, this represented almost 17 percent of the labor force in these industries, while the 1895 total was just under 12 percent. The expansion starting June, 1894, did not absorb all of the unemployed before recession set in again. Douglas' estimates show unemployment throughout the period June, 1893–1898 fluctuating about 10 percent.[65]

In 1894 and throughout 1895, restrained recovery characterized other areas too. Production of anthracite coal increased by about 12 percent in 1895, while Bessemer steel-rail production rose 30 percent. Producer durable goods production increased by over 13 percent, paralleled by consumer durables. Output of all finished commodities increased, but not by as much, the increase averaging only about 8 percent.[66]

The recovery movement was also seen in the improvement of the stock market. Through most of 1895, the trend of the market was upward. For the first time in some years, railroad securities played an important bullish role in the market. In general, save for short periods, industrial securities reached better levels than had been attained since the depression started. The steady upward movement began in March, 1895, and reached its culmination in September, anticipating the economic peak by three months.[67]

Agriculture showed only slight signs of recovering from the deep depression. Income gains for farmers were very limited, amounting generally in 1895 to 5 percent over 1894 levels. The wheat crop was about the same for 1894 and 1895. Prices did not change greatly, and wheat farmers' income rose only slightly. The corn crop for 1895 was about 75 percent greater than in 1894 and prices fell over 40 percent from 45.7¢ a bushel in 1894 to 26.4¢ in 1895. Actually, in both years, income for corn farmers was about the same. Cotton farmers produced only about 75 percent as much as in 1894; thus their prices rose sharply from 4.6¢ a pound in 1894 to 7.6¢ and their income increased slightly.[68]

While the economy was emerging from the 1893–1894 depression, there were many forces impeding a full recovery. Railroads did not contribute much to the general revival of the economy. Railroad construction in 1894 totaled only about 2,100 miles compared with the 4,700 of 1892. In 1895, after recovery was well on its way, construction fell off further to 1,800 miles, a low for the decade.[69]

Confidence in railroads was shaken, both at home and abroad, after the spurt of failures in which mismanagement and criminality often became indistinguishable. The falling off in earnings reflected heavy burdens of reorganization as well as decline in traffic. Both gross revenue and net earnings dropped in the middle nineties. Gross operating revenue reached a low of about $1,073 million in the fiscal year 1894, which was only $2 million less than the gross of fiscal year 1895, while the net income low of $69 million obtained for both years. During most of the economy's expansion, gross and net income remained about the same as in the July, 1893–June, 1894 period.[70]

The balance of payments reflected changes which made full expansion impossible. During 1894, the foreign trade of the United States reached a low for the decade. The sharp decline in imports eased somewhat the gold outflow, which nevertheless persisted throughout most of 1894. In that year, the export surplus of $310 million was not adequate to prevent a gold outflow, which reached a high of over $80 million. During 1895, exports maintained the same level as in 1894, about $808 million, but with recovery imports rose sharply and almost equaled exports for the year, totaling $802 million. During this period, net gold exports were less than in 1894 by about $10 million despite the virtual balance of trade.[71]

The continued gold outflow implied either that the invisibles account was a larger debit than in the past; that more capital was flowing abroad; that foreign investors in the United States were disinvesting; or that there was a decline in foreign investment in the United States; or a combination of these. The annals indicate that disinvestment was occurring in significant amounts. While some of the evidence shows foreign capital flowing to the United States in response to bargain conditions, the general consensus was that European disinvestment assumed great proportions. The contemporary business journals provide some evidence of the disinvestment. Less apparent but certainly very significant was the decline of foreign investment in the United States.[72]

As 1894 drew to an end, the export surplus was accompanied by a decline in the Treasury gold reserve to a low point of about $60 million in November. The gold outflow to Europe ceased temporarily as importers abroad sought dollar exchange to meet their obligations here, but this situation was short-lived; in December, 1894, and in January, 1895, about $35 million in gold flowed abroad, apparently in response to foreign disinvestment. The gold loan that the Treasury placed in November, 1894, yielded over $100 million when a New York banking syndicate was hurriedly formed to prevent the loan's failure. Much of the gold obtained for the loan, however, was secured through redemption of legal tenders. In December, the Treasury's gold reserve totaled about $111 million. But this amount rapidly dwindled as gold flowed abroad, legal tenders were redeemed, and the government deficit persisted. In February, 1895, the gold reserve reached a low of $41 million. To replenish it, the Treasury again resorted to a gold loan. Merchants and banks were rather dubious of the Treasury's ability to remedy the situation and drastic action was feared.[73]

The government turned to the Morgan-Belmont investment banking group to handle the loan and to insure that the gold of the loan would not come from the Treasury gold reserve through the redemption of legal tenders. The syndicate was pledged to "protect the Treasury against the withdrawal of gold," which really meant obtaining credit and gold in Europe to avert the export of gold. A gold outflow of the proportions of 1894 could not be handled by short-term credit arrangements and would upset the project. Here both the syndicate and the government took a bold chance, which succeeded for much of 1895. To maximize the possibility of success, the syndicate joined all banks and banking houses in New York and the Morgan-Belmont connections in Europe. The loan yielded over $65 million and boosted the Teasury gold over $100 million. During the spring and summer of 1895, the Morgan-Belmont syndicate carried out its agreement and kept a close watch over the foreign exchange market which it in effect had cornered.[74]

Increased European demand for United States securities supported by American bullishness pushed prices up on the security markets. At the same time, favorable economic conditions increased imports while exports remained the same in value but declined slightly in volume as prices rose. The force of foreign investment was stronger than that of increased imports as gold flowed into the United States.

But, as the market approached its peak in September, Europeans began to realize on some of their holdings. The temporary relief from gold outflow and loss of Treasury gold was short-lived. This was foreshadowed during the summer when foreign exchange rates were being held at $4.90 by the Morgan-Belmont syndicate. This rate was above the gold export point but was maintained by the syndicate's cornering of the market. The syndicate's high price for sterling was a hedge against the failure of their loan agreement, the possibility of which was growing daily while the syndicate had large debts in London.[75]

This situation increased the incentive to compete in foreign exchange since the spread between the syndicate's $4.90 and the gold export point was 1½ cents. In July, a New York coffee-importing house with connections in Europe began trading in foreign exchange, selling at $4.88 ½ and getting gold from the Treasury by presenting legal tenders. Others followed suit, ending the corner. After that, gold flowed out and the old problem was intensified as European investors liquidated more holdings to realize profits and for other reasons. The Morgan-Belmont group's efforts failed under such strains, though technically the syndicate fulfilled its obligations by October at which time the gold outflow continued. In December, the Treasury's gold reserve was down again to about $60 million after having reached $107 in June and July. Once again, the monetary system was severely strained as disequilibrium with Europe and the rest of the world worsened.[76]

As these balance-of-payments forces were interacting, there were other influences in the domestic economy militating against full recovery. Agriculture, while it experienced a slight expansion, was not enjoying the full measure of prosperity. Throughout the economy, the level of unemployment was quite high, much higher than customary in expansion periods. Although the business and general press ignored unemployment, it remained at a level of at least 10 percent. In general, the 1895 "peak" was submerged.[77]

Thus the regenerative process, starting in the middle of 1894, progressed throughout 1895 and raised economic activity to a new peak level before contracting factors again reversed the economic course. This level, however, was at least 10 percent below output capacity. Prices had risen in many sectors; iron and steel production was at new high levels; bank clearings had recovered somewhat by the end of 1895; business failures were at a stable level; coal production had surpassed former highs; employment was higher, though not at former peak levels; construction had recovered somewhat in the expansion—in short, the economy had recovered less than completely from the sharp contraction of 1893–1894 and then proceeded into another downturn. One appraisal of the year implied this incomplete recovery: "While 1895 . . . was not a year of . . . full prosperity, it was a very much better year than its predecessor, and . . . improving conditions continued to make steady headway almost through the whole of the twelve months."[78]

The Contraction: 1896 to Summer 1897

The downturn of a business cycle often occurs quite unobtrusively and its advent is not usually discovered until well after the fact. In some instances, however, a dramatic event coincides with the downturn. In 1895, this happened when President Cleveland's message on the Venezuelan boundary dispute precipitated stock-market declines of panic proportions. The market panic culminated on December 21, only four days after the presidential message was released. By coincidence, this sharp market decline marked the beginning of another contraction period, lasting through 1896 and much of 1897.

The short market panic in December aroused fears that another bank panic might follow. Prompt action was taken by the New York banks which immediately caused the clearing house to issue loan certificates to reduce the use of cash in interbank payments. The money market quieted after the first sharp increase in call money rates during the market decline to a high of 80 percent. Commercial loan rates rose to 6 percent as banks extended money cautiously. Bank failures grew in number after the market panic in December but nothing approaching a bank panic developed; the economy was in a much stronger position than in 1893. Though total failures in 1896 were almost 50 percent greater than in 1895 and liabilities were two and a half times as great, this only represented about one-third of both the number and total liabilities during 1893. The proportion of national banks failing doubled, reaching forty-two for 1896. Many of these failures were in larger urban centers. Bank failures occurred in the later months of 1896; more than half the yearly total in number and liabilities was recorded after July.[79]

Fortunately the pressures on the Treasury gold reserve and on bank gold holdings were not as great as when the economy started its downward movement again. At the end of 1895, Treasury gold reserves declined after the Morgan-Belmont syndicate consummated its contract agreement. From August to December, the reserve fell from $100 million to about $63 million and by February, 1896, before another gold loan was transacted, a low of about $45 million was reached. The Treasury gold loan of $100 million at 4 percent announced early in January was the most successful of all the gold loans; it was offered in open competition with over 4,600 individual bids for the over $560 million being entered. Greater public confidence in the

Treasury had developed and economic conditions were more favorable. While legal tenders were presented for gold redemption by potential subscribers, the number of these outstanding had previously been appreciably reduced.[80]

Thus by "converting its floating debt into a funded loan" and going into a competitive market, the government was able to replenish its gold reserve in more favorable circumstances than before. The loan elicited gold imports at a premium with salutary effects on the monetary gold stock. The Treasury gold reserve still suffered somewhat from the continuation of a budgetary deficit, which persisted through most of 1896 and much of 1897. There were, however, forces developing to raise the reserve again above the $129 million level attained in March. Although the reserve fell slightly below the $100 million mark once more in July, after that it grew steadily and was no longer a cause for concern, becoming instead a measure of rapidly expanding industrial output.[81]

This favorable turn of events was due mainly to changes in the balance of trade. November, 1895, was the last month until April, 1897, in which merchandise imports exceeded exports. The seasonal pattern of foreign trade was changing. The growth of industrial exports, as the economy became more industrialized, made the active trade balance continually larger. This steady export surplus helped dampen the downward fluctuation of the economy in 1896. The outflow of gold was reversed and at year's end about $45 million in gold was imported as against gold exports of over $70 million in 1895. No longer was there a constant strain on the Treasury and the banks for gold. Credit expansion was made easier.[82]

In this complex of circumstances, the downward movement of the economy was not accelerated by monetary convulsions. The economic contraction in the United States coincided with expansion in Europe, which aided the growth of exports. European recovery also reversed the heavy repatriation of foreign capital and the slackening of foreign investment in the United States, which were of great moment in the 1893–1894 contraction. During 1896, Wall Street transactions revealed no steady and heavy withdrawal of foreign capital; only speculative transactions served, occasionally, to give Europeans claims on dollars for their securities. In fact, foreign investment of some moment occurred in the middle months of the year.[83]

Other developments of a favorable nature were not difficult to discover despite the contracting movement of the whole economy. The momentum of these forces continued into 1896; some of them were merely slowed in their forward movement. Steel production did not decline sharply below the 1895 highs; pig-iron production fell off less than 10 percent during 1896. United States iron and steel products were encroaching more on British markets in Europe and even in India. Even at the trough of the depression, iron and steel production was at 1895 levels. Iron and steel prices had risen sharply throughout 1895, declining somewhat at the end of the year as trade fell off. During 1896, prices for these products remained high, though never rising to the highs of 1895 or, for that matter, falling to the lows of that year.[84]

In 1896, many prices reached their low points in the long decline from the sixties and seventies, so that with these prices now on the upturn many business firms' profit expectations brightened. The rise in the prices of farm products, fuel, chemicals and drugs, producer durables along with scattered other commodities reflected, in some measure, the fact that European economies were in an expansion period and thus one important market was exercising an upward pressure.[85]

The intensity of the contraction was somewhat mitigated by the strength of the expansionary forces. Railroad earnings, increasing slowly since the spring months of 1895, continued at higher levels with the exception of the early part of 1897. Mexican railroads, an area of United States investment, reported increased earnings. Insurance companies enjoyed steady growth with no important company defaulting in investment value. New issues of stocks and bonds listed by the New York Stock Exchange in 1896 declined in value only by 15 percent.[86]

The contraction of the economy, however, was clear-cut. Seasonally adjusted outside bank clearings remained high for the first half of 1896 but then fell sharply in the months of August and September to levels almost as low as those of the summer of 1893. Deflated clearings suggest the economy was 25 percent depressed—worse than in 1894. Marked and continuous improvement in outside clearings did not develop until June, 1897, clearings in the period from January to June, 1897, being some $950 million less than for the first half of 1896, when totals were about $37 billion.[87]

Another clear sign of business stringency was the data on business failures. More individual firms and corporations failed in 1896—some 15,122—than in 1895 by some 16 percent. Total liabilities involved were almost $250 million, an amount about 55 percent greater than in 1895 and the highest total for failures during the decade except for 1893, the panic year. A more meaningful measure of failures relates them to the total number of businesses. Here, too, 1896 was second only to 1893. In the latter year, the failure rate was 1.5 percent, whereas in 1896 it was 1.4 percent. (In the prosperity year 1892, the rate was 1.0 percent.)[88]

The year 1896 was one in which businessmen felt ambivalent about the future. It was a year of "dire decision," in which the fate of the nation supposedly hung in the balance. The "anxiety and demoralization" arising out of the political situation gave rise to opposing security market tendencies: prices and orders fluctuated in response to the psychology of the moment. The stock market mirrored reactions to the political vicissitudes of a climactic presidential year. The issue was joined between "free silver" and "sound money" and most business and financial leaders, most of whom were unequivocally for the gold standard, predicted economic events by political events. For many a Democratic victory meant chaos; on the other hand, a Republican victory would save society and thrust the economy to untold heights of wealth. The Republican victory gave psychological relief, but the predicted economic advances that were so mechanically associated with political victory did not appear for some time. Actually this victory was an anticlimax since the gold standard was firmly secured by the buttressing of the Treasury gold reserve early in 1896. Not until 1897 was well under way did the economy as a whole expand again.[89]

The stock market was an excellent barometer of changes in the political atmosphere and oscillated anxiously. The market decline at the beginning of the year, traced to the Venezuelan affair, continued as the Treasury gold reserve dropped to a low in February. After the Treasury loan was successfully floated, a short recovery ensued. This erratic movement continued beyond the political conventions. The Republican Convention at St. Louis in June stimulated confidence by its gold plank and prices rose; the Democratic Convention in Chicago in July terrified the market into a decline with widespread liquidation. The liquidation subsided but prices did not rise except for technical situations of short sellers covering. In the week after the election, there was a sharp rise to the year's best level. Profit realization led to declines and then dullness followed at the end of the year.[90]

As 1897 started and political events became less significant, the market began more to reflect economic conditions and developments. In the early months of the year, the market did not vary widely, being an area mainly for professional activity. Business stagnation was reflected in the lack of market buoyancy. There was some foreign selling, but this did not unsettle the market. Contemporary observers related the market's dullness to political problems such as the Cuban question and the tariff and blamed foreign disinvestment on uncertainty about financial and political questions in the United States. Nevertheless, as crop prospects grew more promising, the market responded favorably; in the middle of April, a recovery began. Despite continued foreign sales and gold exports, in the spring the widening market kept rising and no reaction occurred until September. By November, however, the setback was reversed and prices recovered again. The tone of economic recovery was echoed in the market's lift.[91]

One of the major factors in the recoiling of the economy was agriculture. In the nineties, agricultural conditions still determined, in very important degree, the shape of the economy's expansion or contraction. In 1896, agriculture fared no better than in 1895: more of some commodities were sold at lower prices; others sold less at higher prices. In 1896, farm income and prices reached the decade low point. Since the economy was already in a depression as 1896 started, this slightly worse agricultural situation intensified the contraction.

In 1897, however, the economy was given a lift by agriculture. Wheat and cotton led the way with sharp increases in output; the corn and oats markets enjoyed modest improvement. Price advances were strategic in this agricultural recovery as world markets absorbed more American farm products. The smaller harvests of Russia, Germany, France, and Hungary gave rise to greater agricultural exports from the United States to all of Europe at better prices than had prevailed since the bumper year of 1891. In the first nine months of 1897, wheat exports were valued about 75 percent above 1896; corn exports were over a third greater in value; other grains and agricultural exports also rose sharply in value. Total agricultural exports reached the highest level in value for the entire period 1890–1897. This contrast between 1896 and most of 1897 emphasizes the strong check which agriculture exerted on the economy in 1896 and early 1897.[92]

The dragging effects of agriculture in 1896 were paralleled by other retarding forces. Unemployment rose markedly. According to Douglas, it increased during 1896 to 22 percent above 1895, at which time unemployment in manufacturing and transportation was estimated at over 15 percent of the working force. In bituminous-coal mining, idleness grew insignificantly but in anthracite mining the increase was about 20 percent. During 1897, unemployment in these areas persisted, though for the entire year it declined about 5 percent to roughly 15 percent of the working force. Even after business expansion was under way in 1897, unemployment continued at relatively high levels into 1898; apparently it was a deep-rooted phenomenon of the decade.[93]

Many businessmen offered tariff revision as a device which, properly manipulated, would stimulate recovery. Most advocates of higher protective tariffs loudly and somewhat inconsistently proclaimed that a "good" tariff would end the government's deficits and give the economy a lift out of the depression. The passage of the Dingley Tariff in July, 1897, was reported by one journal to have "been welcomed by people generally throughout the country" who were "anxious for the removal of all influences making for the maintenance of . . . economic disturbance and against the return of that tranquillity and confidence which are so necessary for the development of business."[94]

The Dingley Tariff extended the principles of protection beyond some previous levels. The duty on wool was reimposed and rates on carpet wools were raised, as were those on hides which had been on the free list since 1872. Rates of the 1890 tariff were restored on many woolens, some reaching 55 percent. Duties on cotton goods were generally lowered below the 1890 levels while those on silks and linens were raised: some linens were dutiable at 80 percent. Chinaware rates were raised to 1890 levels. Most metal schedules were left at 1894 levels. (Improved cost conditions in certain metal industries diminished the need for high protective rates.) The duty on raw sugar was practically doubled to get more revenue. Refined sugar duties were raised, giving the United States refiner a protection of one-eighth of a cent a pound.[95]

The optimistic predictions of protectionists that deficits would end were not correct, though their prognostications on recovery were borne out by the upturn in business which fortuitously followed the passage of the Dingley Tariff. The Treasury deficit did not end until 1899, due both to the lingering effects of the depression and to increased expenditures for the Spanish-American War. The continuing deficit probably had some inflationary impact on the recovery.

Construction industries did not contribute to rapid recovery. Railway building, for example, showed some slight signs of greater activity. In 1895, railway mileage constructed reached a decade low of about 1,800 miles; in 1896, the total was greater by less than two hundred miles. Although railway construction never again attained the level of earlier years, by the end of the nineties the annual rate was about double the 1895 rate. Throughout the depression, the railway industry was a major weak sector in the economy; its construction and investment statistics as well as earnings and receiverships demonstrate this.[96]

While railway construction did rise in 1896 and somewhat more in 1897, building construction was sluggish throughout the country. From 1892 to 1899, building construction in the United States was in the contraction phase of a long "building cycle." There were increases as well as declines in the period. The decline in construction from the peak in 1892 to the trough in 1894 was almost 40 percent while the rise from the trough to December, 1895, was just under 25 percent. From that point, during the contraction of 1896 and part of 1897, construction declined less than 5 percent, though the maximum drop from June, 1895, to December, 1897, was about 19 percent. Generally, from the end of 1895 to the trough of the depression in 1897, there was a low declining level of construction. Throughout the period, the 1892 peak level was never approximated.[97]

Expansion: From Summer 1897 Onward

By the end of 1897, the economy was moving ahead at a much faster pace and its growing importance and impact were being felt in much of the world. There was more money in circulation than ever before; bank clearings were 10 percent short of the 1892 all-time high. Business failures were declining to rates of the predepression period; railway earnings were at higher rates than in any year of the decade. Agricultural output and exports were high and prices were up. Iron and steel production was at an all-time high with the United States producing more than any other country. Production of pig iron was almost 30 percent of the world total. The stock market was at its highest level in years. Throughout 1897, the economy generated "a larger aggregate of business . . . than for any year since 1892."[98]

The Treasury gold reserve was about $160 million, the highest level since the end of 1890; gold imports were again becoming the usual pattern. Exports had passed the billion-dollar mark, while imports also rose but at a rate that insured a very active trade balance and made possible large exports of capital to Canada, South America, and other parts of the world. Prices were still not very high, but they had reversed their earlier downward movement and their relatively low but rising level was an incentive to industrial expansion, as was the large number of unemployed who were not fully absorbed into industry until after 1898. The total output of all finished consumer and producer commodities was at the highest level in history.[99]

And yet, despite these clear-cut evidences that the economy was recovering from the deep trough of 1894 and 1896–1897, economic activity in 1897 and the years immediately following did not approximate capacity. In the period from 1892, the economy had aged five years and was thus capable of much higher output, assuming modest annual capacity growth. From 1897 to 1901–1902 or 1906–1907 (depending upon which series are analyzed), the economy increased production but its level of output remained close to 90 percent of capacity. Thus the downturn starting in 1893 was such a severe one that complete recovery was retarded until after the turn of the century. The depression of the nineties was a major disorder in the rapid growth of an economy transforming itself into an industrial-manufacturing order.

NOTES

1. A. F. Burns and W. C. Mitchell, *Measuring Business Cycles*, p. 78. Cf. also W. C. Mitchell, *Business Cycles*, p. 48; W. W. Rostow, *Brittish Economy of the Nineteenth Century*.

2. Burns and Mitchell, *Measuring Business Cycles*, pp. 78–79, 401. See Figure 7 in Chapter 1 for a graphic view of British fluctuations from 1869 to 1913.

3. Burns and Mitchell, *Measuring Business Cycles*, pp. 78–79, 401. Australia went through a crisis in 1895 too.

4. Ibid.

5. A. D. Noyes, *Forty Years of American Finance*, pp. 157–170; *Financial Review*, 1893, p. 5.

6. *Commercial and Financial Chronicle*, December 31, 1892, p. 1102 (hereafter cited as *Chronicle*). See also *Bradstreet's*, December 31, 1892, pp. 835–836, where the comments are similar. Disappointment was expressed at the failure of the economy to attain the ends anticipated early in the year.

7. *Chronicle,* January 7, 1893, pp. 11–20, *Bradstreet's,* December 3, 1892, p. 779; ibid., January 7, 1893, pp. 2–3; ibid., December 31, 1892, p. 834; ibid., October 15, 1892, p. 667; ibid., November 5, 1892, p. 706.

8. *Chronicle,* December 31, 1892, pp. 1098–1100.

9. *Chronicle,* November 26, 1892, p. 874; *Bradstreet's,* November 26, 1892, p. 753; ibid., December 3, 1892, p. 769; *New York Times,* November 21, 1892, p. 1; ibid., November 23, 1892, p. 1.

10. *Chronicle,* January 7, 1893, pp. 15–20. While *Bradstreet's* was noncommittal on Cleveland's election, the *Chronicle* on November 12, 1892, expressed "a hope of something better to come through the [election]" by the way of "relief to our currency embarrassment." They were certain that "the new President's influence . . . will be used" to provide such relief. (Pp. 784–1785) The *Banker's Magazine* pointed out (December, 1892, pp. 405 ff.) that the election did not unsettle business because "the great mass of business men . . . are confident that their interests are safe in the hands of either [party]. . . . This confidence existed before election, and has not been shaken since."

11. These declines were for the entire year; near the end of the year, the rates of decline were sharper. *Chronicle,* January 7, 1893, pp. 11–15; *Financial Review, 1893,* pp. 5, 56; *Bradstreet's,* January 14, 1893, pp. 19–20.

12. *Chronicle,* December 17, 1892, p. 1102.

13. *Bradstreet's,* December 24, 1892, p. 819; ibid., December 31, 1892, pp. 835–836; *Chronicle,* August 6, 1892, pp. 196–198; ibid., January 7, 1893, pp. 4–5; *New York Times,* December 20, 1892, p. 1. *Chronicle* characterized the year cautiously as "not . . . a conspicuously prosperous year" though "no one would hesitate to say that 1892 has proved far more prosperous than either 1891 or 1890."

14. *The American Banker,* February 11, 1893, p. 8.

15. The Reading Combination, formed in February, 1892, had a capital of about $40 million and debts of over $125 million.

16. *Chronicle,* March 11, 1893, p. 392; *Bradstreet's,* March 11, 1893, p. 145; *The American Banker,* April 5, 1893, p. 8.

17. See D. R. Dewey, *Financial History of the United States,* pp. 440–445, for a thorough analysis of the gold situation. It is interesting to note an article in the London *Statist,* July 23, 1892, which in effect predicted a gold run and bank panic in the U.S. The prediction was in response to the wave of selling of U.S. securities by Englishmen, which was explained by lack of confidence in the U.S. due to the monetary situation. The predicted disaster was to start with a run on banks, then a run on the Treasury, after which gold hoarding was to occur and lead to a premium on gold and finally a panic and disaster. While the sequence of events in the 1893 panic did not follow exactly the pattern predicted, all of the events alluded to occurred in the spring and summer of 1893.

18. *Bradstreet's,* January-April, 1893, U.S. National Monetary Commission, *Statistics for the United States, 1867–1909,* p. 101.

19. See O. M. W. Sprague, *History of Crises under the National Banking System,* pp. 162–167; U.S. National Monetary Commission,

Statistics for the U.S., p. 101; *Bradstreet's and Chronicle*, January-May, 1893.

20. See *Bradstreet's*, April 8, 1893, p. 211, and June 3, 1893, p. 342, and *Chronicle*, February 25, 1894, p. 328, for evidence of continuing high levels of economic activity.

21. *New York Times*, April 14, 1893, p. 1; ibid., February 21, 1893, p. 1; ibid., April 22, p. 1; ibid., May 1, 1893, p. 1. See also *Bradstreet's* for the same period. The Australian banking crisis was considered the result of national conditions. Details are to be found in *Bankers Magazine and Statistical Register* 47 (June, 1893):900–902.

22. *New York Times*, May 4, 1893, p. 1; ibid., 1893, May 5, p. 1; ibid., June 25, 1893, p. 4. The *Times* termed these events a "near-panic."

23. Wholesale prices started declining from April to June. By the end of the year most prices had declined between 5 and 10 percent from January levels. See U.S., Bureau of Labor Statistics, *Retail Prices, 1890 to 1928*, p. 2. For a view of a parallel situation in 1929, see J. K. Galbraith, *The Great Crash*.

24. *Annual Report of the Comptroller of the Currency, 1893*, pp. 10, 80; *Bradstreet's*, February 17, 1894, p. 102.

25. Sprague, *History of Crises*, p. 169.

26. Sprague, *History of Crises*, pp. 168–174; Noyes, *American Finance*, pp. 191–193; *New York Times*, June 15, 16, 1893.

27. *Chronicle*, June 29, 1893, p. 162; see also *New York Times*, July 27, 1893.

28. President Cleveland delayed calling a special session after his inauguration despite pressures brought to bear by such influential businessmen as Henry Villard, August Belmont, and J. P. Morgan. After the panic in May, Cleveland was pressed further to call a special session and he finally issued the proclamation on June 20, asserting that the crisis resulted from "a financial policy which the Executive Branch of the government finds embodied in unwise laws which must be executed until repealed by Congress." See Allan Nevins, *Grover Cleveland*, pp. 523 ff.

29. Sprague, *History of Crises*, pp. 175–180; Noyes, *American Finance*, pp. 193–194; *New York Times*, July 21, 27, 29, 1893.

30. Sprague, *History of Crises*, pp. 181–182.

31. Ibid., pp. 181–186; Noyes, *American Finance*, pp. 193–195.

32. Sprague, *History of Crises*, pp. 186–191.

33. Ibid., pp. 195–199; Noyes, *American Finance*, pp. 195–196.

34. Noyes, *American Finance*, pp. 190–195; ibid., pp. 195–196; U.S., National Monetary Commission, *Statistics for the United States*, p. 192.

35. Sprague, *History of Crises*, pp. 199–203. Sprague described the situation thus: "It increased the general feeling of distrust which, as always in a crisis, does so much to bring about greater inactivity than the actual condition of affairs warrants. A more definite consequence was the difficulty in securing money for pay rolls, which led to the temporary shutting down of many factories. Finally, it deranged the exchanges between different parts of the country, causing a slackening in the movement of commodities and needless delays in collections which were al-

ready slow on account of the general situation . . . . In August . . . the most frequently assigned cause of the shutting down of the factories was inability to procure money for pay rolls." (pp. 200, 202)

36. *Bradstreet's,* May-August, 1893; *Chronicle,* May-August, 1893; *New York Times,* May 12, June 4, 12, July 1, 27, August 6, 1893.

37. Receivership for the Erie had been "a customary feature of our commercial crises for half a century" (in 1857, 1873, 1884, 1893, and almost again in 1908). See W. Z. Ripley, *Railroads: Finance and Organization* (New York; Longmans Green & Co., 1927), II, 374 ff.; Noyes, *American Finance,* pp. 276–277; E. G. Campbell, *The Reorganization of the American Railroad System, 1893–1900,* pp. 9–61, 303–318; *Annual Report of the U.S. Interstate Commerce Commission, 1894,* pp. 68–69; S. Daggett, *Railroad Reorganization,* and *Bradstreet's* August 19, 1893, p. 519; ibid., October 14, p. 656; ibid., December 23, p. 807; ibid., December 30, p. 823.

By the end of 1893, the Erie, Northern Pacific, Union Pacific, Santa Fe, and the Philadelphia and Reading comprised nearly three quarters of the total mileage of seventy-six roads in receivership. On the other hand, as the depression continued the minor roads did almost as well as they had done in the decade preceding 1893. The great systems suffered the most. Most of the failures were either the result of overexpansion, past management mistakes, or poor or criminal management. Northern Pacific provides a good example of overexpansion—its capitalization was almost $50,000 per mile with fixed charges of about $1,800 per mile per year. Union Pacific was an example of a road failing due to past management mistakes, while Philadelphia and Reading was one of those whose demise was the result of criminal or poor management.

38. *Dun's Review* 1 (August 12, 1893): 1; *Banker's Magazine* 48 (December, 1893): 405–407.

39. Early in 1893, government expenditures rose slightly, due to increases in pension payments and slight increases in Army, Navy, and Indian Affairs disbursements. Receipts also increased. The deficit arose from this greater increase in expenditures. In March and June, there were slight surpluses. Thereafter the deficits rose as receipts fell off with customs revenue showing the main decline. See U.S., Bureau of Foreign and Domestic Commerce, *Monthly Summary of Imports and Exports of the United States, 1893–94.*

40. D. R. Dewey, *Financial History of the U.S.,* pp. 445–46.

41. F. W. Taussig, *Tariff History of the United States,* pp. 305, 324; Noyes, *American Finance,* pp. 222–223; *New York Times,* August 29, 1893 and October 31, 1893; Nevins, *Grover Cleveland,* pp. 540–562; and Gerald T. White, *"The U.S. and the Problem of Recovery after 1893"* pp. 11–35.

42. Noyes, *American Finance,* p. 225.

43. Taussig, *Tariff History of the U.S.,* pp. 284–320.

44. Noyes, *American Finance,* pp. 224–230; *New York Times,* February 2, March 7, May 17, August 14, 24, 26, 1894; Taussig, *Tariff History of the U.S.,* pp. 299–314.

45. *Bradstreet's,* July 8, 1893, pp. 408, 428; ibid., December 30, 1893, p. 825; ibid., December 16, 1893, p. 791.

46. Ibid., December 30, 1893, p. 825; ibid., December 16, 1893, p. 791.

47. *Dun's Review,* December 30, 1893, p. 1; ibid., January 6, 1894, p. 2.

48. *Bradstreet's,* May-August, 1894; *Chronicle,* May-August, 1894; and *New York Times,* May 12, June 4, 12, July 1, 21, 27, August 6, 1893.

49. H. Jerome, *Migration and Business Cycles,* pp. 97, 248; *Dun's Review,* December 29, 1894, p. 2; *Historical Statistics,* p. 236; Michigan, *Annual Report of the Bureau of Labor and Industrial Statistics,* pp. 423-434; *Bradstreet's,* May-August, 1893.

50. H. Leibowitz, "Unemployment Relief during the Depression of 1893-1894", pp. 2-6; F. D. Watson, *The Charity Organization Movement in the United States,* pp. 249-263; Leah H. Feder, *Unemployment Relief in Periods of Depression,* pp. 98-125; and S. Rezneck, "Unemployment, Unrest, and Relief in the United States during the Depression of 1893-97," *Journal of Political Economy,* pp. 327-328, 330-331. One student of relief during the depression described three lines of relief in New York City: (1) permanent societies and churches increased their activities; (2) temporary private organizations were formed to dispense relief; and (3) private and public emergency funds were created and administered by the creators. The city did not increase appropriations to the Board of Charities and Correction except for a trifling amount for coal. The state legislature authorized $1 million for park commissioners to use in relief public improvements. Cf. "Report of NYC," *Journal of Social Science,* November, 1894, pp. 28-32.

51. See "Report of NYC," *Journal of Social Science,* pp. 28-32.

52. *Bradstreet's,* April 28, 1894, p. 257; *New York Times,* April 23, 1894; and D. L. McMurry, *Coxey's Army,* pp. 3-20. The industrial armies received some support and sympathy from populist groups. Their orientation was mainly reformist and democratic and their demands that the government provide work opportunities and secure decent levels of living were in line with the notion "That the right to work is the right to life, that to deny the one is to destroy the other. That when the private employer cannot or will not give work the municipality, state or nation must" —which the AFL resolved at its December, 1893, convention. The ridicule and contempt with which these armies were treated reflected the contemporary rejection of collective action and responsibility. See McMurry, *Coxey's Army,* pp. 260-285.

53. McMurry, *Coxey's Army,* pp. 127-196; *New York Times,* May 2, 3, 9, 22, 1894.

54. *Bradstreet's,* April 7, 1894, p. 209; *New York Times,* April 19, 22, June 12, 1894.

55. *New York Times,* June 28, July 1, 3, 11, 1894; *Bradstreet's,* June 2, 1894, p. 337; July 7, 1894, pp. 418-419.

56. The net gold yield to the Treasury was actually less since many of the bond purchasers redeemed legal tenders for gold and then bought the bonds. See D. R. Dewey, *Financial History of the U.S.*, pp. 447–450; *New York Times*, January 8, June 23, 1894; Noyes, *American Finance*, pp. 182–218.

57. Noyes, *American Finance*, pp. 204–206; and U.S., Bureau of Statistics, *Monthly Summary of Imports and Exports of the United States, 1893–1900*. Since silver was not held by banks and businessmen, the Treasury had to build up its cash balances to be able to hold silver. This meant that receipts of borrowing had to cover this contingency.

58. U.S., Bureau of Statistics, *The Foreign Commerce and Navigation of the United States for the Year Ending June 30, 1893*, pp. xxiii–iv. Worthington C. Ford, Chief of the Bureau, lamented the absence in the United States of series measuring these accounts. See also Noyes, *American Finance*, p. 201; *Bradstreet's* March 31, 1894, p. 203, and April 7, 1894, p. 219; *New York Times*, July 21, 1893.

59. *New York Times*, August 31 and September 1, 1894; *Bradstreet's*, August-December, 1894. See also Bureau of Labor Statistics, *Retail Prices*, p. 2.

60. *Historical Statistics*, p. 337. See also *Bradstreet's*, July 7, 1894, p. 419; ibid., November 2, 1895, p. 690; ibid., December 28, 1895, p. 818; ibid., January 4, 1896, p. 5; ibid., December 3, 1898, p. 770; ibid., December 31, 1898, p. 839.

61. *Dun's Review*, April 13, 1895, p. 2; *Bradstreet's*, December 14, 1895, p. 788. Since retail food prices (the only retail series available) declined almost 2 percent from 1894 to 1895, actual increases in quantities sold were probably greater than the value figures indicate.

62. *Historical Statistics*, p. 333; *Financial Review*, 1894–1897.

63. *Historical Statistics*, p. 342.

64. Jerome, *Migration and Business Cycles*, p. 248. In Pennsylvania, employment increased by 16.5 percent in 1895, while in Massachusetts, the average number of days in operation for all industries increased by almost 6 percent. Pennsylvania, *Annual Report of the Secretary of International Affairs, 1899*, Part III, p. 258; C. D. Wright, "The Relation of Production to Productive Capacity," *Forum*, November, 1897, pp. 290–302.

65. Paul H. Douglas and Aaron Director, *The Problem of Unemployment*, pp. 26–28; Jerome, *Migration and Business Cycles*. It would be very interesting to be able to break down unemployment by industry to see whether there was large-scale technological unemployment as U.S. industry expanded and consolidated into larger units. This had particularly important implications in terms of the process whereby industrialization was taking place and the way in which the burden of such technological change was being borne. Was the high rate of unemployment a symptom of the metamorphosis under way?

66. *Financial Review*, 1895 and 1896; and *Historical Statistics*, p. 231.

See also *Bradstreet's*, September 7, 1895, p. 562. Being out of phase with the European business cycle complicated our economy's recovery.

67. *Bradstreet's*, January 11, 1896, pp. 20–21.

68. F. Strauss and L. Bean, U.S., Bureau of Agricultural Economics, *Gross Farm Income and Indices of Farm Production and Prices in the United States, 1869–1937*, pp. 24, 36, 39, 64. (hereafter cited as Strauss and Bean, *Gross Farm Income*).

69. *Financial Review*, 1896.

70. *Historical Statistics*, p. 205; *Bradstreet's*, January 12, 1895, p. 18; January 15, 1898, p. 35.

71. U.S., Bureau of Statistics, *Monthly Summary of Imports and Exports*, 1894–1896; *Bradstreet's*, 1895, various issues; *Chronicle*, April 13, 1895, pp. 630–633; ibid., March 30, 1895, pp. 542–544; ibid., May 4, 1895, pp. 769–772; and Noyes, *American Finance*, pp. 230–233. Europe, particularly England, was in a depression and capital outflow had contracted. In the period 1890 through 1893, English capital issues shrunk by almost two-thirds. After 1893, capital issues expanded but by the end of 1895 they were not yet 75 percent of the 1890 level. At this time, there was also some outflow of U.S. capital into South America. *Economist* (London), Supplement, "Commercial History and Review of 1895," February 22, 1896, pp. 5–6.

72. See *Bradstreet's*, January 11, 1896; *Financial Review*, 1895.

73. Noyes, *American Finance*, pp. 230–233.

74. Ibid., pp. 234–235; *New York Times*, February 19, 1895. See also *New York Times*, June 26, August 21, September 5, 22, 1895, for accounts of the syndicate's operations.

75. Noyes, *American Finance*, pp. 242–247.

76. Ibid., pp. 247–250; *Bradstreet's*, May–December, 1895.

77. U.S. Bureau of Labor, *Statistics of Unemployment*, Bulletin 109, 1912, p. 28; Douglas, *Problem of Unemployment*, p. 26.

78. *Chronicle*, January 4, 1896, p. 5. The recovery proceeding throughout 1895 coincided with the start of recovery of the major European economies which were at their low point at the beginning of 1895.

79. *New York Times*, December 18, 21, 23, 30, 1895; *Bradstreet's*, December 28, 1895, p. 819. The declines of 1896 were not as steep as those of 1893.

80. Noyes, *American Finance*, pp. 248–251; *Bradstreet's*, December 28, 1895, p. 819; ibid., November 7, 1896, p. 710; ibid., January 8, 1898, p. 20; *Historical Statistics*, p. 346; U.S., National Monetary Commission, *Statistics for the United States, 1867–1909* 21:124.

81. Noyes, *American Finance*, pp. 252–253; U.S., Bureau of Statistics, *Monthly Summary of Imports and Exports*, January, 1898, p. 1066. The renewed confidence in the Treasury meant that silver and paper money could be used once again for payments by the government.

82. Ibid.

83. Ibid.; and *Bradstreet's*, June 13, 1896, p. 373; ibid., June 20, 1896, p. 387; ibid., July 18, 1896, p. 453.

84. *Bradstreet's,* January 11, 1896, p. 22; ibid., January 9, 1987, p. 24; F. C. James, *Cyclical Fluctuations in the Shipping and Building Industry,* p. 78.

85. U.S. Bureau of Labor Statistics, *Retail Prices,* p. 2.

86. British insurance companies did important business in New York and increased their holdings during this period. It is not known to what extent this increased the amounts of money flowing to England. See *Dun's Review,* March 14, 1896, p. 203; also New York State, *Insurance Reports,* 1892–1898.

87. *Bradstreet's,* January 11, 1896, p. 22; ibid., January 9, 1987, p. 24; ibid., November 13, 1897, p. 734; ibid., January 13, 1898, p. 35; ibid., February 19, 1898, p. 114; ibid., March 2, 1898, p. 184; ibid., December 3, 1898, p. 770; U.S., Bureau of Statistics, *Monthly Summary of the Commerce and Finance of the United States,* January, 1900, p. 1946; *Financial Review,* 1893 and 1899, p. 14 and p. 16, respectively; Jerome, *Migration and Business Cycles,* p. 248; C. D. Wright, "The Relation of Production to Productive Capacity," pp. 290–302.

88. *Historical Statistics,* p. 337.

89. *Bradstreet's,* January 1, 1898, pp. 4–5; ibid., December 31, 1898, p. 839. Increased failures in 1896 in the face of price upturns in important areas suggest that the depressive forces were powerful since it is usually easier to maintain solvency when prices are rising.

90. *Bradstreet's,* January 2, 1897, pp. 3–4; *Dun's Review,* November 7, 1896, p. 1.

91. *Bradstreet's,* January 2, 1897, pp. 3–4; ibid., January 1, 1898, pp. 6–7.

92. *Bradstreet's,* March 27, 1897, p. 197; ibid., July 10, 1897, pp. 434–435; ibid., December 11, 1897, p. 792; *Financial Review,* 1899, pp. 25–26; Strauss and Bean, *Gross Farm Income,* p. 24; F. Strauss, "The Composition of Gross Farm Income Since the Civil War," Bulletin 78, National Bureau of Economic Research, pp. 14–15.

93. Douglas, *Problem of Unemployment,* pp. 26–28; *Bradstreet's,* January 15, 1898, p. 36. The business annals contain practically no reference to unemployment, though such references are to be found in labor journals and other sources. Feder, *Unemployment Relief,* alludes to the expenditure during 1896–1897 of over $28,000 by a New York City typographical union for unemployment relief. Cf. also U.S., Bureau of Labor, *Statistics of Unemployment,* Bulletin 109, 1912, p. 28.

94. *Bradstreet's,* July 31, 1897, pp. 483–484; Taussig, *Tariff History of the U.S.,* pp. 321–360.

95. Taussig, *Tariff History of the U.S.,* pp. 321–360.

96. *Financial Review,* 1894, 1899.

97. Long, *Building Cycles,* p. 216.

98. *Bradstreet's,* January 1, 1898, p. 2.

99. *Financial Review,* 1899; William H. Shaw, *Value of Commodity Output Since 1896;* Theodore E. Burton, *Financial Crises and Periods of Industrial and Commercial Depression.*

Appendix to Chapter 2
Note on Unemployment Estimates During the Depression

Verification or rejection of unemployment estimates for the bottom of the depression of the nineties is made very difficult by the paucity of reliable data. Most newspapers and journals only mentioned unemployment in the winter of 1893–1894. Some calculations of unemployment figured during the winter of 1893–1894 ranged from about half a million to as high as 4.5 million.[1]

Table 12
Unemployment Estimates, 1893

Source	Number	Period
Closson	523,000	Mid-November
Bradstreet's	800,000+	Mid-December
C. D. Wright	2,000,000+	September-October
Colorado Bureau of Labor Statistics	2,500,000	January, 1894
Knights of Labor	3,000,000	beginning October
A.F.L.	3,000,000+	December

Closson's estimate of 523,000 was based on data from 300 replies to a questionnaire sent to public officials and others in all cities over 20,000 and answered mainly for the second and third weeks in November, 1893. These figures were higher than most local police estimates but far below others. Closson compared his results with those of *Bradstreet's,* whose totals reached over 800,000 for the early part of December, 1893.[2]

Doubts are raised about the reliability of these two figures. For those cities where both made estimates, at about the same time, wide differences are established. In many instances, Closson's estimates exceeded *Bradstreet's;* in others, the situation was reversed. For some, there was no appreciable disparity. The conflict in estimates, as well as the limited coverage, leads one to question them seriously. Only one set of numbers lower than those of Closson's was circulated—those of the local police. In some instances, their estimates were one-seventh of what Closson termed a "conservative" estimate: in Boston, the police figure was just under 5,100, while the "conservative" estimate was 35,000.[3]

When one examines the sources and how they were used by Closson, initial doubts are reinforced. The major sources of information were the various state labor departments. Two factors cause one to be skeptical of some of the information gathered by *some* of these departments: their limited resources and the crude manner in which unemployment estimates were often arrived at.[4]

The inadequate facilities and personnel with which some of the twenty-seven labor bureaus in the forty-four states operated usually arose from their minuscule appropriations. In the mid-nineties, Maryland's bureau received $5,000 annually, almost all of which went for salaries. Iowa's annual fund was $500, while Minnesota's bureau enjoyed over $10,000 each year. In most states, appropriations were low; in others, appropriations reached $25,000, but these were unusual. Collections of accurate and comprehensive data on ad hoc problems were often not possible, though on longer range, routinized projects better results obtained, even with limited funds. Most bureaus were thus not in good condition to gather reliable unemployment data effectively.[5]

A further manifestation of the unreliability of some of the data and estimates of some of the bureaus emerges from analyzing their reports. While there was reference to unemployment and depressed conditions in many reports, practically no concrete information was furnished. In most cases, the entire report was devoted to routine accounts of strikes, activity of industries, labor chronology, trade reports, child labor, and the like.[6] In some states, where agriculture was the main economic activity, the reports consisted mainly of agricultural statistics.

The fact-finding function of most of these bureaus did not extend to unemployment statistics in either prosperity or depression. Data gathering was usually confined to matters of concern to the more important economic interests in the state, which expected the limited funds and staff to be devoted only to such activities. Unemployment was an individual problem to be solved by the individual and too much government solicitude with it implied socialism.[7]

In some instances, however, reports gave reliable evidence of the degree of unemployment. Here the data were sometimes incomplete but in the main they proved useful. In New York, for example, direct efforts were made to get information on unemployment and the effects of the depression. Manufacturing establishments were circularized by letter in December, 1893, and the results were compiled and tabulated without analysis or interpretation. The replies came from 2,011 manufacturing concerns in sixty-four general industries and dealt with effects of the depression on operations, the percentage of employees kept at work, the length of time the factories were closed, wage reductions, and the like. It was the bureaus in states such as New York and Massachusetts that were able to provide the most reliable and meaningful data.[8]

Closson's complete reliance, therefore, on state bureaus' estimates without any critical evaluation of their data and methods rests his estimates on shaky grounds.[9] Even when attempts were made to get broad unemployment estimates, the results were also open to question; some of the methods used hardly instilled confidence. For example, take the Maryland bureau's estimate of 10,000 unemployed (or 11 percent of the working force) in Baltimore. This was a rough guess; the police estimate was 7,000 to 8,000. Later, in its *Third Annual Report,* however, the bureau questioned the accuracy of its own figures by citing a later, more comprehensive study it made which revealed that unemployment in selected trades amounted to 38 percent. Its "refined" estimate, *which Closson never received,* amounted to a total of just under 34,000!

Bradstreet's estimate of over 800,000 was scarcely more reliable than Closson's. The calculation was derived from telegrams sent by correspondents from 119 cities during the middle of December, 1893. Incredibly, some reports (for example, from both Augusta, Maine, and Georgia) stated that there was *no* unemployment. The level of industry and commercial activity in such cities makes it extremely improbable that there was *no* unemployment at all.

The *Bradstreet* estimate for Baltimore was 20,000—more than half the Maryland bureau's revised estimate. *Bradstreet's* estimate of unemployment in New England was 66,200 while that of the Massachusetts bureau for that state alone was over 71,000.[10] This latter figure represented over 22 percent of the work force. Connecticut's Bureau of Labor Statistics reported that even in those industries least affected by the depression only 90 percent of the 1892 labor force was employed while in industries most affected by the decline in business activity only about 60 percent were employed.[11] These figures cast doubt on those of *Bradstreet's;* a review of similar percentage estimates of other state bureaus (where data seem reliable) fortifies that doubt.[12]

Another unemployment estimate reveals the statistical methods used by the Colorado Bureau of Labor Statistics. Data were gathered by circulating forms in post offices throughout the state. (Since only $300 a year was appropriated for expenses, a most economical method of gathering data was mandated.) On this basis it was estimated that in March, 1893, about 8,000 were unemployed in the state. After the repeal of the Sherman Silver Act, another circularization was undertaken and on the basis of 60 percent of the blanks having been returned, an estimate of 45,000 additional unemployed was arrived at. It was also estimated that for lack of work over 22,000 left the vicinity where they had been employed.[13]

The head of the Colorado bureau also made an estimate for the entire nation for January 1, 1894. His method was simple, direct, and reasonable, if crude. He utilized reported unemployment statistics where available from the various large towns in different states, getting the percentage of unemployed to population. He then applied these percentages to all towns in the state. He indicated this would be too low a figure since only towns with population over 8,000 were included. The total he inferred for unemployment in towns over 8,000 exceeded 1,850,000. To reach a more comprehensive total, he analyzed unemployment trends in towns under 8,000 and came to a 2 percent figure; this yielded an additional 700,000 unemployed. The total for the nation, therefore, came to over 2.5 million.[14]

C. D. Wright, United States Commissioner of Labor, also gauged unemployment. He estimated over 2 million out of work in the late autumn of 1893 before unemployment reached its peak during the winter of 1893–1894. Since the method he used is not available, no evaluation is possible. Nevertheless, Wright's reputation and competence requires that we consider his estimate a serious one. While Wright's estimate was discussed in the *Journal of the Knights of Labor,* it was not accepted; instead the Knights held that unemployment was "not less than 3,000,000, and this number is increasing daily." [15]

The AFL convention in Chicago during December, 1893, met at a time when unemployment was growing and was receiving wide public notice. With ominous words, Samuel Gompers welcomed the delegates to the convention, apprising them of the dismal situation: "Since August . . . we have been in the greatest industrial depression this country has experienced. It is no exaggeration to say that more than three million of our fellow toilers . . . are without employment." [16] This estimate approximated that announced in the rival labor movement's journal. At the Denver convention in 1894, Gompers still complained of the workers' suffering "from the paralysis of industry resulting from the incompetency of our modern captains of industry." The fact that Gompers did not give an unemployment figure at that time and that he anticipated revival and prosperity suggest that unemployment had subsided somewhat. [17]

Other estimates were current, some going even higher than those already mentioned. But these had no substantial statistical backing. In attempting to arrive at a more acceptable figure, we must evaluate the above estimates within a framework of occupation statistics and corroborated unemployment data. We shall set up the limits of unemployment on the basis of occupation statistics and different assumptions as to the percentage of unemployment. This should eliminate those estimates which are completely out of focus.

Analysis of census figures on occupations provides a set of limits. By interpolating between the 1890 and 1900 census figures on occupation distribution by various categories, a first approximation of 1894 occupation estimates results: the total of all gainful workers by occupation was 26,195 million. From this figure we subtract those in three of the ten occupation categories: agriculture, public service, and professional service. While there must have been some unemployment among those groups, it is very likely that the percentages were very much lower for them than for others. The resultant total—the primary base for an unemployment estimate—was 14.5 million. This figure represents the total number of gainful workers in the remaining categories.[18] It is reasonable to expect that in these categories the variations in the proportion of unemployed were slight compared to those in the three categories listed.[19]

Starting from this base of 14.5 million gainful workers, various results based on different assumptions are possible. On the basis of a 10 percent unemployment ratio, a total of just under 1.5 million unemployed would obtain; assuming 15 percent would yield 2.175 million; a third assumption of 20 percent would establish a total of 2.9 million. Any unemployment in the three omitted categories would be at a much lower ratio than for the rest of the economy, certainly not more than 5 percent and probably less. The 11.695 million in the three omitted groups were divided: agriculture, 10.425 million; professional service, 1.028 million; and public service, 242,000. In agriculture, more than half of the gainful workers were owners or tenants; no more than 4.8 million were agricultural workers. Among professionals about 65 percent were either teachers, dentists, physicians, lawyers, or judges. Thus only about 375,000—if that many—could be considered vulnerable to unemployment. In the public service group, most unemployment would be fractional and random since most of the security and service forces remained intact during the depression; government expenditures did not fall off.[20]

It seems unlikely that of the total 11.695 million gainful

workers in the three groups more than 5.3 million would be liable to unemployment. A 5 percent unemployment figure for this group would be very high and would yield a total of a little over 250,000. This can be viewed as an upper limit to any unemployment arising in these groups. If unemployment in this sector were between 1 and 5 percent, the limits in absolute numbers would be between 50,000 and 250,000.

Thus far only analysis of occupational groups has been used upon which to base an unemployment estimate. In terms of our earlier evaluation of unemployment calculations, we may place the unemployment ratio somewhere between 10 and 20 percent, though there is scattered evidence of much higher rates in different industries and geographic areas over a period of many months. In its survey of 1893, *Dun's Review* estimated that 40 percent of the labor force in the iron industry was unemployed despite a marked recovery in iron output by December 1. In woolen manufactures, over half of the industry was said to be idle.[21] Another source gauged that from June, 1893, to September, 1894, in Connecticut industries the range of time worked as a ratio of full time was from 47 percent in musical instruments and parts to 80 percent in printing and bookbinding.[22] In Massachusetts, average unemployment in all industries was estimated at 22.3 percent in September, 1893, and 14.8 percent in December. In carpeting, unemployment was estimated at 62 percent in September; in woolen goods, 30.9 percent; in paper and paper goods, 14 percent; in metals and metallic goods, 16 percent. The average for the year, which included lows of the early months, was estimated at 8.5 percent.[23] In Michigan, among 2,066 factories inspected starting September, 1893, 377 were idle, 1,689 were operating wholly or otherwise (of these 1,117 were working full time). An unemployment estimate of 48,752 (considered "conservative") and the estimate of plant operation led to an estimate of plants inspected operating at about 58 percent of full employment capacity.[24]

In New Jersey, unemployment was also quite high. On the basis of some 252 responses to a schedule of questions circulated by the Bureau of Statistics, a fair notion of unemployment was obtained. The decline in employment from June, 1892, to June, 1893, was negligible—1 percent. After June, 1893, however, the decline became more marked. From June to July, 1893, the drop was 9 percent. Following is the percentage decline in employment by month from June, 1893: [25]

Month	Percentage Decline
July	9
August	18
September	21
October	21
November	23
December	24
January, 1894	27
February	27
March	25

In Pennsylvania, on the basis of returns from 424 establishments in iron, steel, textiles, glass, and miscellaneous industrial activities, one impact of the depression was calculated. It was found that the average number of employed declined from 155,299 in 1892 to 135,165 in 1893, a decline of almost 13 percent. Aggregate wages paid declined over 16 percent and the value of product over 18 percent. Decreases for major groups were: [26]

Commodity	Employment	Wages
Cotton goods	9.0%	26.5%
Woolen goods	15.3	25.8
Carpets	11.8	23.9
Glassware	9.8	29.7
Iron and steel	13.0	16.7

Data on employment in New York followed the same pattern. On the basis of information gathered from 66 identical establishments in the state employing over 20,000 on May 31, 1893, the decline in employment by May 31, 1894, was estimated at 25.4 percent.[27]

Study of other state labor departments' statistics bears out the general pattern thus far detailed. Unemployment varied in different activities and areas. In some instances, high proportions of the total labor force were out of work, while in others the unemployment ratio was about 10 percent and in some cases even below. According to available estimates from eight of the ten leading manufacturing states, unemployment was quite high in the winter of 1893–1894. Table 13 gives a summary of the highest unemployment percentages (at a specific period or on an average basis) in these states.[28]

Table 13
Unemployment Percentages in Eight States, 1893–1894

State	Percentage Unemployed	Date
New York	35	December, 1893
Pennsylvania	25	1893–1894
Massachusetts	22.3	September, 1893
Ohio	11	1894 average
New Jersey	15	June, 1894
Missouri	20	November, 1893
Michigan	43.6	September 1, 1893
Connecticut	20+	January, 1894

The only figures below 20 percent are those in Ohio and New Jersey. In the former situation, the figure is an average for 1894 so it is reasonable to expect that in the winter of 1893–1894 the percentage was at least 20 percent. The New Jersey percentage for the 1893–1894 winter also was probably about the same. This summary suggests that where manufacturing was concentrated, unemployment was appreciably over 20 percent in the worst spell of the depression. In states where manufacturing was not as significant, unemployment was probably somewhat lower. But the average for all manufacturing and allied activities must have been pulled up by the high incidence of unemployment in major manufacturing areas. On the basis of these scattered reports, it seems sensible to place the overall ratio somewhere between 16 and 20 percent and most probably closer to the upper limit.

Douglas' employment studies, undoubtedly based on some of the above data, show large proportions of unemployed in manufacturing and transportation for the period 1893–1899: [29]

Year	Percentage Unemployed
1890	5.1
1891	5.6
1892	3.7
1893	9.6
1894	16.7
1895	11.9
1896	15.3
1897	14.5
1898	13.9
1899	7.7

His estimate for 1897, including mining and building trades, is 18 percent. Undoubtedly, the addition of mining and building trades data for the earlier period would raise the general percentage too. Moreover, since the percentages are averages for the year, the percentage at the peak of unemployment was most probably above the yearly average. Scattered qualitative data seem to substantiate this.[30] Frickey also constructed an employment series covering the nineties and he asserts that "Professor Douglas' totals for manufacturing employment—setting aside certain minor divergencies—show close correspondence of short-run fluctuation with . . . our own employment index."[31]

Harry Jerome computed an index of employment which also helps in our estimate of unemployment. His index of factory employment by months, 1889–1923, is based on various state indices and other available data. For the period under survey, the main sources were estimates of factory employment in Massachusetts and New Jersey. Measuring the change in the index from its peak in April, 1893, to its trough in August, 1894, yields a percentage decline of just under 19 percent.[32]

Assuming then that the proportion of unemployment at its greatest intensity during the winter of 1893–1894 falls within the range 15 to 20 percent, we can put together an approximate absolute estimate. We indicated above that the primary base of gainfully employed was 14.5 million. This base needs refinement since some gainfully employed were owners and managers. To arrive at a base upon which a ratio of unemployment can be applied, we must first exclude owners and managers. From census data, we see that about 1.4 million should be omitted, giving as a base 13.1 million.[33] On the basis of our census data, the absolute range of unemployment corresponding to the ratios from 10 to 20 percent follows:

Percentage Unemployed	Number Unemployed
10	1.310 million
15	1.965
16	2.096
17	2.227
18	2.358
19	2.489
20	2.620

These estimates, however, do not involve employment among the three occupational groups which were omitted from the 14.5 million base figure and among owner and manager groups. The total in the three groups was 11,695 million; the total of owners and managers was about 1.4 million. We saw above, however, that unemployment for the three occupational groups was not likely to be over 250,000 and the lower limit was placed at 50,000. It is difficult to say whether there is a high correlation between the ratio of unemployment in the major occupational groups and the three under consideration for the period. To straddle the issue, an absolute estimate of 150,000 will be made. Among owners and managers, unemployment must have been more marked than among the three occupational groups since business failures were exceedingly high at this time. Arbitrarily we will assume an unemployment ratio of 5 percent, yielding an unemployment figure of about 75,000. Thus, assuming an unemployment ratio of 16–20 percent for workers and assuming the conditions above, we estimate that total unemployment is between 2.190 and 2.845 million.

It seems safe to say that a 17–19 percent unemployment ratio is a reasonable one. The absolute estimate on this basis is between 2.452 million and 2.714 million for the winter of 1893–1894. The margin of error is likely to be wide. About one in every six gainfully occupied in industry and commerce was out of work at the height of unemployment during the depressed period 1893–1897. Unemployment began to assume significant proportions in July, 1893, and increased rapidly as the year ended, reaching a trough for a period going into the early part of 1894. The rapid and heavy increase in unemployment was one measure of the depression's severity.

The sharp rise in unemployment in the autumn of 1893 reached a level sustained through most of 1894. In the incomplete recovery of 1895, unemployment fell off slightly after which, in 1896, the increase in the jobless grew as the economy contracted again. The trough level of unemployment in 1896–1897 was not as low as in 1894 but hovered around 15 percent. With the recovery that started in 1897, unemployment declined slowly, but even as late as 1899 almost 8 percent of the labor force was still without work. This slow recovery in employment accords with the notions suggested above that capacity levels were not reached until 1901–1902 or 1906–1907. The depression of the nineties was a deep contraction, making the rebound to capacity a task of many years.

NOTES

1. Leah H. Feder, *Unemployment Relief in Periods of Depression,* p. 79.
2. Carlos C. Closson, Jr., "Unemployed in American Cities," *Quarterly Journal of Economics* 8 (January and July, 1894): 168–217, 257–280, 453–477, 499–502; *Bradstreet's,* December 23, 1895, p. 806. *Bradstreet's* figures were based on telegraphic reports from correspondents in 119 cities.
3. Closson, "Unemployed in American Cities," pp. 499–502.
4. Since Closson wrote his article right after the sharp rise in unemployment, he was not in a position to see the shortcomings in the estimates of some state bureaus, as we are from our vantage point of time.
5. U.S. Commissioner of Labor, *Third Special Report of the Commissioner of Labor,* pp. 5–6. See the state annual report: Maryland, *Annual Report of the Bureau of Labor Statistics,* p. 196 and passim; Iowa, *Biennial Report of the Bureau of Labor Statistics, 1892–93;* Minnesota, *Biennial Report of the Bureau of Labor, 1895–96,* passim. In Iowa, for example, only general statements about unemployment were made: "Reports from correspondents of this bureau residing in the larger cities of the state, covering the first six months of the present year (1893), show hundreds of laboring people out of employment, affecting largely the building trades and factory employes." Iowa, *Biennial Report, 1892–1893,* p. 286.
6. In addition to the states listed above, see the following for the years 1890–1897: Massachusetts, *Annual Report of the Bureau of Statistics and Inspection;* Missouri, *Annual Report of the Bureau of Labor Statistics and Inspection;* New Jersey, *Annual Report of the Bureau of Statistics of Labor and Industries;* Ohio, *Annual Report of the Bureau*

of Labor Statistics; and Pennsylvania, *Annual Report of the Secretary of Internal Affairs. Part III: Industrial Statistics.*

7. Cf. H. Leibowitz, "Unemployment Relief during the Depression of 1893–1894," pp. 25–34, for evidence of such attitudes. In order to cleanse the relief agencies of the taint of socialism, some social workers made a point of proclaiming their support of the status quo.

8. See, for example, New York, *Annual Report of the Bureau of Labor Statistics, 1893.*

9. Had his estimate been made after the bureaus had checked their data more carefully, he might have weighed the evidence more attentively, and probably would have made a more correct estimate.

10. Massachusetts, *Annual Report, 1894,* p. 128.

11. Connecticut, *Annual Report of the Bureau of Labor Statistics, 1894,* p. 185.

12. *Bradstreet's* found it necessary to defend its unemployment estimate from the charge of its being too high. On p. 81 of its February 10, 1894 issue, *Bradstreet's* reported that the police census of unemployment yielded a total unemployment for New York City of 67,280—16 percent less than its own estimate. In its haste to defend itself, the journal did not raise any questions regarding the validity of the police estimate. Samuel Gompers criticized the police census in the March, 1894, *American Federationist* (p. 11), pointing out that the *New York Sun* had also questioned the police figures. It was asserted that the police failed to go into many areas. *Bradstreet's* reconciled its estimate with those of the police by pointing out that its estimate "was made in December . . . when the industrial situation was much darker than it is today . . . the fact that the difference between the police census and the estimate of this journal is no greater than it is may be fairly regarded as evidence confirmatory of the soundness of our earlier estimate." It is very difficult to accept this line of reasoning, let alone the estimate of either the journal or the police.

13. Colorado, *Fourth Biennial Report of the Bureau of Labor Statistics,* pp. 23 ff. Usually repeal of the Sherman Silver Act was hailed as a great boon to economic activity and it was predicted that once this dreaded impediment was eliminated prosperity would return at once. It is evident, however, that one of the direct effects of the Act's repeal was to throw thousands of miners out of work, adding to the growing army of unemployed. See Allan S. Everest, *Morgenthau, the New Deal and Silver,* p. 4. The sharp rise of unemployment in Colorado gives substance to this view.

14. Ibid., pp. 361–364. While this method may appear questionable, it represents a more reasonable approach than most others. The significant question is whether the sample upon which the percentages were based was representative. The estimate, perhaps quite accidentally, was probably close to the actual figure.

15. *Journal of the Knights of Labor,* October 12, 1893, p. 1.

16. American Federation of Labor, *Report of Proceedings of the Annual Convention,* p. 11.

17. Ibid., p. 10.

18. Such categories included Forest, Fisheries, Trade, and Transportation and Communication.

19. See Alba E. Edwards, *Comparative Occupation Statistics for the United States, 1870–1940,* p. 100. In the interpolation, it was assumed that the 1894 data would be midway between the figures for 1889 and 1899.

20. Ibid., p. 104 ff.

21. *Dun's Review,* December 30, 1893, p. 1.

22. Connecticut, *Annual Report, 1894,* p. 185.

23. Massachusetts, *Annual Report, 1894,* pp. 124–125.

24. Michigan, *Annual Report of the Bureau of Labor and Industrial Statistics, 1894,* pp. 423–434. It was estimated that in the period between September 1, 1893, and February 1, 1894, a total of 1,763,080 labor/days were lost in the 2,066 factories inspected. Of this total, 706,676 labor/days were lost due to hours worked less than the usual ten hours and 1,056,294 were lost due to layoffs. The greatest sufferers in Michigan were the miners in the upper peninsula iron-ore mining area.

25. New Jersey, *Annual Report, 1894,* pp. 24–77. Of the 252 "complete" returns from industrial establishments (70 from general industry), over half were from metals, metallic goods, and textiles. The percentages are based on establishments employing over 42,000 in June, 1892.

26. Pennsylvania, *Annual Report of Secretary of Internal Affairs, 1893, Part III,* sec. G, p. 87. In gathering data, the bureau found that some plant officials declined to give information. Bureau representatives did not, however, visit every plant.

27. Cited in Theodore E. Burton, *Financial Crises and Periods of Industrial and Commercial Depression,* p. 330.

28. The percentages are derived from the following state labor bureau reports: New York, *1893 Report,* pp. 3,212, 3,240; Pa., *1894 Report,* p. E4; Mass., *1893 Report,* p. 1,268; Ohio, *1894 Report,* pp. 342–343; New Jersey, *1894 Report,* pp. 24–25; Mo., *1894 Report,* pp. 64, 137; Mich., *1894 Report;* Conn., *1894 Report,* pp. 167 ff., 184, 186.

29. Douglas, *Problem of Unemployment,* chap. 2 and p. 26; Paul Douglas, *Real Wages in the United States 1890–1926,* especially pp. 440, 460.

30. Cf. Colorado, *Biennial Report, 1893–94,* pp. 23 ff.

31. Edwin Frickey, *Economic Fluctuations in the United States,* p. 220.

32. Harry Jerome, *Migration and Business Cycles,* pp. 66–72, 248.

33. Edwards, *Comparative Occupation Statistics,* pp. 104–112.

3
Investment During the Depression

Now that the broad structural changes in the economy and the events of the depression have been outlined, some of the major quantitative changes during the depression can be more meaningfully analyzed to view investment as a strategic factor in economic activity. In a business economy, investment activity is of signal importance in shaping the general course and nature of all economic fluctuations, which in turn interact affecting the nature of investment activity. Investment is a volatile economic force that exercises strategic influence on overall economic activity. Especially during rapid industrialization, an understanding of investment activity is essential for the comprehension of the nature of economic oscillations. We analyze fluctuations in different areas of investment, therefore, to see more clearly the nature of the depression. Evidence on investment in plant and equipment but not on inventory changes makes possible only an incomplete view of total investment.[1]

That there was a marked decline in investment during the depression is implicit in the decline of gross and net national product. For 1892, these measures of output were at historic peaks.

By the 1894 trough, gross and net product had declined almost 10 percent in real terms; this marked the maximum decline during the depression. It is reasonable to assume that the decline in real investment was greater than that in GNP. Once the depression was over, recovery proceeded at a rapid rate so that by the end of the decade GNP had increased about 50 percent in real terms. The fact that most of this increase came after 1896 suggests that the depression significantly retarded economic growth in general and investment growth in particular.

Stock and Bond Issues

One general indicator of investment activity for the entire economy is to be found in the listings of new stock and bond issues on the New York Stock Exchange. Unfortunately, the available data on such listings are in aggregate form and can only be used to give a general sense of what was happening to overall investment. The data cover only a portion of total financial investment. Nevertheless, such data do provide a rough measure of the direction and timing of overall investment.

Table 14 illustrates that new financial investment in the middle nineties was at greatly lower levels than at either end of the decade. Recoveries from the troughs of investment activity did not reach earlier highs. Throughout the period 1893–1897, there was a general slack in new investment activity. The decline varied for stocks and bonds: stock issues receded by greater amounts and also showed sharper recoveries than bond issues. The downward trend, starting at the beginning of the decade, led to the generally depressed economic conditions marking the severe depression of the middle nineties. A more comprehensive understanding of varying influences of the different areas of investment must await analysis of the more specific data on major economic sectors dealt with below.

Table 14
Listings of New Issues of Stocks and Bonds
on the New York Stock Exchange, 1890–1898
(*millions of dollars*)

	Stocks		Bonds	
Year	New Issues	Percent Change	New Issues	Percent Change
1890	$164.5	—	$198.2	—
1891	96.5	− 41	191.4	− 03
1892	99.9	04	175.1	− 09
1893	93.7	− 06	139.3	− 20
1894	36.6	− 61	184.8	33
1895	77.1	110	166.5	− 10
1896	76.6	− 01	147.3	− 12
1897	33.3	− 30	87.7	− 40
1898	69.8	31	246.2	180

Source: *Financial Review*, 1893, p. 14; ibid., 1899, p. 16.

Major Investment Areas

In the nineties, there were certain sectors of the economy in which most of the capital investment took place. It is mainly in these areas that available evidences of changes exist and make possible a partial reconstruction of the course of capital investment. The following listing records the increase in value of real estate improvements and equipment for major sectors of the economy in billions of 1929 dollars and in percentages from 1890 to 1900:[2]

Electric light and power	$ .663 billion	470%
Street railways	2.466	330
Telephone and telegraph	.772	173

Mining	.792	95
Manufacturing	5.838	65
Shipping and canals	.390	45
Steam railroads	4.929	34
Agriculture	2.489	33
Other industrial	2.332	24

These sectors of the economy accounted for most of the increase in national wealth during the decade and they represented the areas where the most significant changes occurred, with repercussions affecting the whole economy. While the expansion of railroads—an expansion resulting from and stimulating wider markets—slowed up somewhat, a new transportation development of great moment was spreading rapidly: the electric street railway. This transportation development was a concomitant of the accelerated urbanization process in the nineties. Agriculture—quantitatively still an important segment of the economy—recorded an increase in wealth of one-third and in this total the rise in the value of equipment was only 20 percent. This rise in equipment investment amounted to only $500 million, a relatively small sum for the vast agricultural segment. Apparently mechanization of agriculture was advancing at a modest pace while other areas of the economy showed more widespread introduction of equipment. (For example, railroads, utilities, and other industries amenable to mechanization used much more equipment in line with the industrialization process sketched in Chapter 1.)

These are the industries, then, that should yield the key to investment changes during the decade, for they were the areas into which most of the increasing savings of the economy were channeled for further improvement and development. Significant changes in these investment areas have to be noted and analyzed in order to understand the general character and dynamics of the depression.

PRODUCER DURABLE OUTPUT

Some notion of what happened to investment in manufacturing and allied industries during the depression may be obtained from data on producer durable output. Table 15 below summarizes fluctuations in producer durable output during the nineties in 1913 dollars—reflecting variations in real terms. From it we see in which areas of manufacturing and allied industries investment in equipment fell off most and when these declines occurred.

Total producer durable output destined for domestic consumption, set forth in Table 15, illustrates equipment investment fluctuations during the depression after the high levels of 1892 were reversed.[3] The rate of increase in such investment early in the decade was very modest and neither foreshadowed the sharp decline of the depression nor the very great rise after the depression. Over the decade, output of producer durables increased by about 55 percent; the increase from 1897 to 1900 alone amounted to about 53 percent, indicating the strong retarding effect of the depression. From 1893 to 1897, there were violent fluctuations in output, reflecting the volatility of this sector of the economy.

From 1892 to the trough in 1894, producer durable output fell by almost 25 percent. Significantly, while this was occurring, exports of durables were either increasing or maintaining their previous levels. By 1895, the level of output of 1892 was not quite reached, but in 1896—a year of general economic contraction—a new peak of output was attained to be followed by another sharp decline, almost reaching a decade low, as the depression worsened. The decline in 1897 amounted to 17 percent. Recovery after 1897 was at first slow and then sharp as industry hit a new stride. Output of producer durables led business in its 1893 decline but lagged behind in the 1896 contraction; in both contraction periods, the decline in this sector was extreme. Industry's investment in equipment declined sharply and this was a major force in the depression. The drop in producer durable output was roughly twice that in GNP.[4]

Several categories of producer durable output showed early and sharp declines. Electrical equipment for industrial and commercial uses fell by almost 37 percent from 1892 to 1894, as Table 15 shows. Output of ships and boats also started declining in 1892; by 1894, the decline totaled 30 percent. The output of farm equipment commenced its decline earliest of all, reflecting the depressed economic conditions in agriculture. The decline from 1890, arrested temporarily in 1892, amounted to about 27 percent. These three categories, amounting to about 20 percent of all producer durable output, were leaders in the industrial decline starting at the beginning of 1893. In the contraction of 1896–1897, decreases in these categories were more moderate and closer to the overall drop in total producer durable output.[5]

With the exception of miscellaneous subsidiary durables and locomotives and railroad cars, the remaining categories declined starting in 1893 and in amounts clustering around the fall in total output. Output of office and store furniture and fixtures fell off least of the group—by only about 18 percent—while that of industrial machinery and equipment fell off most—by almost 25 percent. In the 1896–1897 contraction, the pattern changed with industrial machinery and equipment and office and store machinery and equipment outputs declining by amounts approaching 40 percent, while total output declined only by about 17 percent.

The remaining output categories—locomotives and railroad cars and miscellaneous subsidiary durable equipment—declined after the 1893 contraction started. The decrease in the latter category was very moderate, amounting to only about 15 percent. The tardiness and moderation of this decline probably derive from the residual nature of the category. The decline in output of locomotives and railroad cars was the sharpest of all producer durables, exceeding 50 percent. The lateness of this sharp decline is probably due to the length of time necessary to build railroad cars. Indications are that orders fell off as early as 1892 so that the actual decline in output reflects earlier decisions. In the 1896–1897 contraction, output of railroad cars and miscellaneous subsidiary equipment declined by about 11 percent, an amount moderately less than that for total output.

These fluctuations in output of producer durables conformed generally to the usual pattern of business-cycle variations. They all displayed sizable declines in output in the depression years, though different categories started receding at different times. The lead decline of farm equipment output reflected the widespread agricultural depression. All the other categories exhibited parallel sharp increases in the expansion of 1895, some outputs continuing to increase in 1896. These fluctuations in the different categories of producer durable equipment output suggest concretely why the depression was so severe and what business factors determined its shape in a major way.

BUILDING CONSTRUCTION

Building construction is an activity cutting across all industrial sectors and as such is a good general index of investment. There is an important relationship between the level of overall investment and the level of construction, though particular circumstances may modify that relationship. One student of the building cycle outlines the usual relationship between building construction and general business conditions:

> In the absence of war, major movements in building and in general business appear to be associated. On the one hand, when either building or business is depressed, the other does not seem to remain long at an active tempo; on the other hand, when either building or business is active, the other does not

Table 15

Annual Percentage Changes in Producer Durable Output Destined for Domestic Consumption, 1890–1900, 1913 Prices

Year	Total Output	Industrial Machinery & Equipment	Electrical Equipment, Industrial Commercial	Farm Equipment	Office & Store Machinery & Equipment	Office & Store Furniture & Fixtures	Locomotives & Railroad Cars	Ships Boats	Carpenters' & Mechanics' Tools	Miscellaneous Subsidiary Durable Equipment
1890	—	—	—	—	—	—	—	—	—	—
1891	9	10	19	−12	13	4	9	12	7.5	21
1892	5	7	− 3	1.5	10	13	5	− 6	—	10
1893	− 2	− 6	−27	− 4	− 3	− 6.5	17	− 2	− 8	3
1894	−23	−20	−10	−15	−15	−17	−53	−24	−25	− 7
1895	23	49	53	4	51	22	17	31	18	− 9

Table 15 (Continued)

Annual Percentage Changes in Producer Durable Output Destined for Domestic Consumption, 1890–1900, 1913 Prices

Year	Total Output	Industrial Machinery & Equipment	Electrical Equipment, Industrial Commercial	Farm Equipment	Office & Store Machinery & Equipment	Office & Store Furniture & Fixtures	Locomotives & Railroad Cars	Ships Boats	Carpenters' & Mechanics' Tools	Miscellaneous Subsidiary Durable Equipment
1896	15	22	16	−19	22	6	41	− 8	− 2	12
1897	−17	−37	−13	30	−39	− 3	−11	− 1	−10	5
1898	7	− 1	31	52	2	−11	−16	−12	19	−11
1899	24	30	53	13	26	12	33	41	16	7
1900	16	32	23	− 2.5	40	—	12	28	3	2

Source: W. H. Shaw, *Value of Commodity Output Since 1869*, pp. 75–77.

seem to remain long inactive. This agreement of the major movements is . . . due to economic interdependence. Building activity is naturally a derivative of national income and depends upon the prosperity of business in general . . . [and] inversely . . . business prosperity is intimately dependent upon building activity.[6]

We have seen in Chapter 1 that after 1892 the nineties was a period of relative stagnation in overall construction. This condition must have had an important bearing on general economic activity and must be examined more closely to determine the general nature of the relationship. Figure 8 depicts the detailed fluctuations in building activity from 1891 to 1905.[7]

Figure 8 helps to assess the impact of building activity on the economy and especially its role in the sharp declines and long duration of the depression. In 1893, the sharp drop in building activity from May to June was in line with such declines in other sectors of the economy. This precipitate counterseasonal decline of 29 percent in one month—followed by a continuous drop to October, totaling 57 percent from May—must have had a very significant effect on general economic activity. It helps to put the panic and start of the depression in a more meaningful perspective.

The recovery in building activity in 1894 was quite limited. Not until the fall did any marked improvement occur and then, with the exception of December, the expansion was steady in 1895, a peak being reached in May, 1895. This recovery from 1894 to 1895 was somewhat retarded. Despite the fact that the level attained in 1895 was in line with the highs of 1891 and 1892, it was still below potential capacity by at least 15 to 20 percent, assuming an annual growth of about 2 percent. Nevertheless, the relatively strong recovery in 1894–1895 must be reckoned a significant force in the general economic recovery of that period. If the new peak attained was submerged for building activity, so was it for the entire economy.

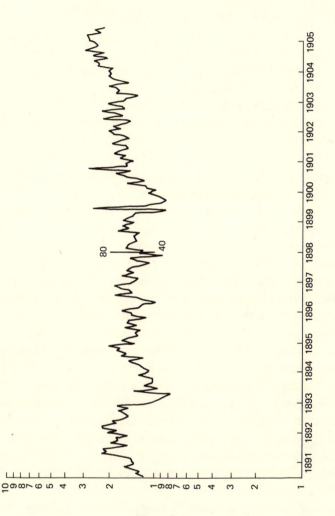

Figure 8
Monthly Index of Building Permit Values, in 1913 Prices

The decline in building activity in 1896 was, like that in 1893, sudden and sharp, coming in both cases in the second half of the year. Building activity dropped by 41 percent from July to October, following by a few months the general downturn in the economy. Although the level of activity at the 1896 trough was greater than that at the 1893 trough, in view of annual increases in capacity, the 1896 level was about the same amount below capacity as that of 1893. Recovery from the 1896 trough was also sharp but short-lived with activity fluctuating greatly in 1897. The 1896 year-end drops in building activity carrying over into 1897 were in line with the generally submerged level of construction during the depression.

While the economy as a whole was beginning to recover in 1897, building construction declined sharply at the end of the year and then in 1898 the lowest point since 1893 was reached. Both 1898 and 1899 were thus relatively depressed for building as economic activity as a whole expanded, though at a retarded rate. By the beginning of 1900, building activity was lower than in 1892, if growth is taken into account. After that trough, there was a general recovery leading to capacity levels by 1906.

As we saw in Figure 5 of Chapter 1, the nineties were a period of greatly submerged building activity—a contraction phase in the long "building cycle." The data in Figure 8 give us the details of this stagnation during the depression. In the recovery of 1895, the buoyancy of building was a factor in the economy's upsurge, but apparently building orders were not sustained and this softness in building construction must be considered a factor of some moment in the subsequent contraction period. After the 1895 recovery, the protracted retardation in building activity must also be recognized as a major factor in the slow movement of the economy to levels of full capacity.

Long's Monthly Index measures overall building activity; for further clues on the impact of building activity on different facets of the economy, a breakdown of building activity into categories such as nonresidential, residential, public, and so on is helpful. Use of annual data obscures crucial turning points of the respective series; nevertheless, in the absence of monthly data, annual data must be employed if any refinements of the above generalization are to be possible.

The annual figures, quite naturally, display less amplitude of fluctuation than the monthly data, as Table 16 bears out. Multifamily dwelling, private nonresidential, and public building construction show less contraction than the others and some significant increases. The totals for residential, nonresidential, and new building show sharper declines than those above, but not as sharp as Long's Monthly Index. Alterations and detached dwelling construction show similar declines. These differences in annual data suggest that certain areas sustained their building activity—those related to industrialization, urbanization, and government building.[8] The sharp declines for the economy reflected in Long's Monthly Index must be qualified with these notions in mind.

AGRICULTURAL INVESTMENT

Of all the economic sectors, agriculture was the most significant in total wealth and increase in wealth during the period. If the changes in agricultural capital investment could be detailed, valuable insight into the processes of the depression would result. The available data, however, do not allow of the sort of tracing of agricultural investment accomplished in building activity. Scattered data and impressions must be relied upon to piece together the jigsaw of agricultural capital development during the depression period. We have seen above that output of farm equipment—one element in agricultural investment—fell off before and during the depression and not until 1897 and 1898 did it increase greatly. Its annual fluctuations are one clue

Table 16
Building Activity Indices, 1892–1898

(1892 = 100)

Year	Total Residential	Total Non-Residential	Total New Building	Detached Dwellings	Multi-family Dwellings	Public Building	Private Non-Residential	Alterations
1893	77	75	74.5	87.5	75	209	87.5	95
1894	71	81.5	68.5	76.5	92	82	81.5	73.5
1895	86	81.5	77	96	192	91	125	95
1896	75.5	81.5	71.5	81	125	82	137.5	95
1897	85	69	68.5	81	175	218	112.5	105
1898	47	62.5	57	32	167	73	62.5	79

Source: C. D. Long, *Building Cycles and the Theory of Investment,* pp. 224, 228.
Notes: The first three indices are of number and the remaining of value. The first three are based on thirteen to twenty cities during the period covered, whereas the remainder are based on only three. Long's index numbers were converted to an 1892 base.

to the question of how agricultural investment fared.

Investment in farm equipment in the nineties was only about one-fifth of total farm investment in land, improvements, and equipment. We have no series on these other elements of agricultural investment so that we must speculate on what probably happened. Our analysis of economic growth in Chapter 1 indicated that the rate of growth in land and improvement investment in agriculture for the nineties was lower than for the eighties, whereas investment in equipment during the nineties was at a higher rate than in the eighties. The series on output of farm equipment demonstrated that contraction in output was significant and came before the general downturn by two years. It seems reasonable to infer that investment in improvements and land declined approximately the same or even possibly to a greater degree than the decline in investment in equipment, especially since farm prices and income were severely depressed in this period.[9]

RAILROAD INVESTMENT

Among the major sectors of the economy, railroad transportation occupied a prominent place: in absolute accretion of wealth during the nineties it stood second to agriculture. The strategic importance of railroads in the economy cannot be gauged alone by such quantitative measures of capital growth. Their linking together of the evergrowing plants, mines, and farms of the nation was paralleled by the tremendous impact of their expenditures on rails, locomotives, passenger and freight cars, as well as on construction and maintenance of the railroad network. Moreover, the railroads were integrated into a complex of financial interrelationships, tying the many lines to the offices of financiers in New York and Boston and thence to the investors of the Old World. Almost 40 percent of the railroad mileage of the world was in the United States.[10] Difficulties which the railroads had during the nineties—mismanagement, bankruptcies, reorganizations—foreshadowed contraction in investment with its adverse repercussions on the economy.

A major aspect of railroad investment was construction. Railroad mileage had mounted continuously over the years: in 1865, total mileage was less than 35,000 miles, whereas at the onset of the depression in the nineties the total was over 175,000 miles. Although total mileage constructed in the early nineties was less than the high levels of the eighties, in 1892 the total was still at a high level—over 4,500 miles. During the depression, however, railroad construction fell to new low levels. One source puts the low at 1,800 miles in 1895, while another estimates a low of about 1,600 miles in 1897. Not until the turn of the century was the 1892 level regained.[11] Whichever trough figures are used, it is clear that during the depression years there was a very sharp decline in construction from which a clear-cut recovery did not set in until after 1896, and this early recovery was an extremely modest one:

Table 17
Gross Railroad Mileage Constructed,
1891–1898

Year	Mileage	Percentage Change
1891	4,620	—
1892	4,584	− 1
1893	2,789	−39
1894	2,264	−19
1895	1,938	−14
1896	2,068	7
1897	2,161	5
1898	3,199	48

Source: *Poor's Manual of the Railroads of the United States*, 1894–1899.

Table 17 shows gross railroad construction figures during the nineties and the percentage changes each year. The decade of the nineties contrasted with the great construction activity of the eighties; in five of its ten years, total construction was less than 2,800 miles—a figure much below the low point for the eighties. No recovery occurred in construction during the upturn of 1894–1895 and the later improvements were of limited impact until after 1897 when the depression was over.

Railroad purchases of rolling stock—locomotives, freight and passenger cars—were a significant portion of railroad investment and they contributed substantial support to the growing machinery and iron and steel industries. During the depression, railroad purchase of rolling stock fell off sharply and recovery was limited both as to quantity and duration. From 1894 to 1898, there was a decrease in the number of freight cars per 100 miles of road and from 1892 to 1897 there was a shortage of at least 250,000 freight cars. In the two-year period, 1898–1899, about 290,000 freight cars were built—an amount greater by 33,000 than the total for all the years from 1893 through 1897. From 1894 to 1899, total cars operated by the railroads increased by less than 13 percent. The depression period was one in which the railroads consumed much of their capital in the form of rolling stock.[12]

The decline in purchases of locomotives was a very sharp one and was sustained throughout the depression.[13] This decline in railroad locomotive purchase orders preceded the business downturn. The peak late in 1892 was about 205 locomotive orders per quarter; the decline reached its bottom early in 1894 when quarterly orders were less than 20 locomotives. After that there was a gradual increase in orders to a peak just under 80 per quarter in the latter part of 1895. Another decline was reversed temporarily in the spring of 1896, followed by a decline to a trough in the spring of 1897, whence a sharp recovery set in. In the 1891–1894 cycle, locomotive orders led the reference cycle (the economy's overall fluctuations) by a few months, whereas in the 1894–1897 cycle they lagged behind very slightly.[14]

Orders for freight cars followed the same general path of decline as locomotives, but there was a marked recovery in the 1894–1895 expansion period to levels barely surpassing the peak plateau of 1891–1892—over 6,750 cars quarterly. The downturn in freight-car orders commenced in the middle of 1892 and was almost completely continuous to a trough of 1,400 car orders in the summer and autumn of 1894. This instance of the trough following that of the reference cycle gives a slight difference to the contour of freight-car order fluctuations compared to that of locomotives. From the trough, however, freight-car orders increased steadily, unlike the locomotive series, and attained its peak coincident with the reference peak at the end of 1895—a quarterly rate of about 7,500 cars. The subsequent decline, which conformed to the reference cycle, did not reach a trough as low as that of 1894. Nevertheless, the trough quarterly figures of about 2,250 freight cars in the early part of 1897 were less than one-third the level of the peak. From 1892 on, the decline was more gradual and over a longer period. The contraction from the beginning of 1896 was somewhat sharper and the recovery from the trough anticipated that of the reference cycle upturn in the summer of 1897.[15]

Passenger-car order fluctuations were the sharpest of all rolling stock from 1892 to the trough in the summer of 1894. Thereafter, while such orders recovered somewhat, the new level was relatively very low and fluctuations were not very great, absolutely. From 1892 to 1897, this series conformed closely to the reference cycle, lagging behind only by a few months in the 1896 downturn and leading the 1893 downturn by a few months. The first peak of over 230 cars ordered per quarter occurred in the latter part of 1892, a few months before the general peak. The precipitate decline after that settled at its trough of 11 cars per quarter at the reference trough—June, 1894. From that point, recovery was not sharp, absolutely. The next peak, in the early months of 1896, was about 56 passenger cars per quarter, a rise of 26 from the previous period and of 45 from the trough. After the beginning of 1893, passenger-car orders did not attain a "prosperity" level until after 1897.[16]

Purchases of rolling stock, for the most part, led economic activity by some months in revivals and declines. This conformed to the usual pattern. Historically, locomotive orders have fluctuated most, freight-car orders have varied almost as much, and those of passenger cars least. Although the decline in passenger-car orders was greatest in the downturn starting in 1892, the other two series followed the historical pattern more closely, locomotive orders declining more than those of freight cars. During the depression, the contraction in freight revenues was greater, both absolutely and relatively, than that in passenger revenues. Since total railroad profits and revenues depend mainly upon freight with passenger traffic secondary, during this severe depression passenger facilities suffered enforced economies and postponements of replacement to a greater degree than freight facilities.[17] From the summer of 1894 to that of 1897, a complete reference cycle, passenger-car orders fluctuated least, freight-car orders most, and locomotive orders in between. Locomotive orders should have fluctuated most, according to the historical pattern. Their failure to follow the historical pattern may have resulted from two important factors: (1) capacity and efficiency of locomotives were growing rapidly in this period; and (2) the sustained expansion of iron and steel and related industries as well as export trade may have called for a greater number of freight cars, of which there was a serious shortage, in order even to maintain freight traffic at moderate levels.[18]

Changes in rail orders historically have preceded similar changes in other railway equipment and have fluctuated least of all railway purchases being considered.[19] Yet, despite this usual pattern, during the period 1892–1897 there were very sharp fluctuations in rail orders. From the peak of 77,000 long tons per quarter, at the end of 1892, to the trough of just under 20,000 long tons, in the summer of 1894, the decline—conforming to the reference cycle pattern—amounted to 74 percent. This decline had been somewhat anticipated since an earlier peak of about 63,000 long tons, at the end of 1891, was followed by a low plateau, averaging about 25,000 long tons for almost all of 1892. The sharp rise to 77,000 long tons, at the end of 1892, was followed by the precipitate drop described above.[20]

In the next cycle, starting from the trough in the summer of 1894, there was, at first, little increase in rail orders until, in the last months of 1895, paralleling the 1892 short-lived rise, orders for rails rose sharply from about 29,000 to 60,000 long tons. There was then an immediate relapse to roughly 30,000 long tons. This level was maintained until, in the first six months of 1897 (which included the trough of the reference cycle), there was a phenomenal rise in orders to over 155,000 long tons, followed by just as sudden, but not as sharp, a drop to 55,000 long tons at the reference trough in June, 1897. This phenomenal rise in orders must be associated with the prices of steel rails at the time. Prices reached their lowest points in the period, June, 1891–June, 1897, ranging between $17.99 and $21.16 a long ton. Apparently the railroads were taking advantage of the price situation to purchase large amounts of rails which together with other equipment had been put off while depression conditions prevailed.[21]

Thus, fluctuations in railroad investment were very great and undoubtedly played a major role in the depression, both in timing and amplitude effects. Many of these fluctuations had a depressive effect before the depression actually was under way and particularly affected in significant degree the output of the strategic machinery and iron and steel industries.

MINING INVESTMENT

We have seen that the wealth of mining industries increased during the nineties by almost 60 percent, rising from $1.2 billion to $1.9 billion. This relative increase was surpassed only by that in street railways, among major economic activities; in absolute terms, mining's growth ranked fifth. Advances in mining techniques and the opening up of new areas provided many industrial activities with the necessary quantities of good-quality raw materials at favorable prices. Changes in industrial techniques also affected mining operations. The interactive relationships between mining and industrial and technological changes furnish an interesting example of the rapidly changing nature of the economy during the nineties.

Data on the quantity and timing of investment in mining activities are not available as they were for producer durables output or for railroad investment, so that the direct impact of changes in mining investment, as they affected economic fluctuations from 1893 to 1897, is not clear. Gauging the impact of mining investment, therefore, must proceed by the use of indirect evidence such as development of new areas, implementation of new techniques, and fluctuation in output.

The development of the Mesabi iron-ore range in the nineties reflected a complex of reactions to changing market conditions. The area was opened by railroads in 1892 and developed rapidly in response to the growing need for high-quality ores as iron and steel techniques advanced. Throughout the depression years, extraction of Mesabi iron ore escalated: in 1893, about 600,000 tons were shipped, while in 1894 the amount was close to 2 million tons. In 1895, it was the most productive iron-ore area. Almost half of its ores were of Bessemer quality. By 1900, the area produced almost one-third of the nation's iron-ore output—greater than the total output of the United States in 1890.[22]

Changes in industrial techniques facilitated the opening of new mining areas. Petroleum, natural gas, bituminous coal, and producer gas were being used more and more economically in metallurgical and industrial fields. Anthracite coal steadily declined in importance. The advance of industry also provided new, more efficient equipment for mining. For example, in bituminous-coal mining the use of coal-cutting machinery increased significantly during the nineties. In addition, there was a spread of mechanized technique in the hauling and handling of coal as well as in the drainage of the pits. In metal mining, the utilization of steam drills and electrical equpiment expanded.[23]

Rapid growth of the industry from 1889 to 1902 is reflected in data on growth of horsepower. In different areas of mining, horsepower increased:[24]

Mineral	1889	1902
Coal, anthracite	160,983	434,220
Coal, bituminous	54,795	521,165
Copper ore	34,390	198,507
Gold and silver	78,343	195,805
Gypsum	2,045	7,319
Iron ore	57,976	119,558
Lead and zinc ore	1,133	41,901
Limestones-dolomites	22,362	64,500
Siliceous crystalline rocks	15,199	46,986

Value and production data also give some indication of which mining areas most probably had the bulk of capital investment in the period. The following figures on the value of mineral products during the nineties and percentage changes show mineral output in years of depression, prosperity, and transition:[25]

Year	Value of Output	Percentage Change
1890	$619.5 million	12.5
1891	623.0	.6
1892	648.7	2.5
1893	574.3	−11.9
1894	526.6	− 8.3
1895	621.3	18.0
1896	622.5	.2
1897	630.9	1.2
1898	697.8	10.6
1899	972.6	39.4
1900	1,070.1	10.0

With prices of fuel products declining about 10 percent and those of metals over 40 per cent from 1890 to the trough of the depression, it is quite probable that the contraction in value of mineral output to the trough of the depression by about 19 percent represented mainly a price decline rather than any real decline in output.[26]

The figures in Table 18 clearly demonstrate that mining output did not contract as much, proportionately, as most economic activities during the depression. Most of the products listed show production declines of 5 percent or less. Demand for mineral output did not slacken as it did for most other commodities.[27]

Table 18
Production of Ores and Related Products, 1890–1900

Year	Copper [a]	Refined Lead [b]	Spelter Zinc [b]	Pig Iron [c]	Steel [c]	Anthracite [c]	Bituminous [c]	Petroleum [d]
1890	116	144	64	9.2	4.3	42	99	46
1891	127	179	81	8.3	3.8	45	105	54
1892	154	173	87	8.2	4.9	47	113	51
1893	147	163	89	7.1	4.0	48	115	48
1894	158	163	75	6.7	4.4	46	106	49
1895	170	170	90	9.4	6.1	52	121	53
1896	205	188	82	8.6	5.7	48	123	61
1897	221	212	100	9.7	7.3	47	132	61
1898	235	222	115	11.8	9.1	48	149	55
1899	254	210	129	13.6	10.8	54	173	57
1900	271	271	124	13.8	10.2	51	190	63

Source: U.S., Industrial Commission, *Final Report of the Industrial Commission* 19:208, 210, 212, 214, 217, 219.
(a) Thousand gross tons.
(b) Thousand net tons.
(c) Million gross tons.
(d) Million barrels (42 gallons per barrel).

Investment in mining during the depression probably did not decline sharply, as it did in the sectors of the economy already surveyed. Overall investment in mining during the decade was high, as mining grew relatively greatly. Expansion in some mining areas occurred even during the depression. Mining output declined in the worst depression years by slight amounts. The introduction of new techniques apparently continued throughout the decade. In these circumstances, it seems clear that the fluctuation in mining investment did not contribute to the stream of contractive forces in the depression; the continued level of mining investment probably was a countercyclical force acting to keep economic activity at a high level.

STREET RAILWAYS

Among the major sectors of the economy, street transportation showed the greatest relative growth during the nineties, and during the depression that growth continued unabated in some sections of the country. In 1890, the total capitalization for street railways approximated $400 million; by 1900, that amount had risen to $1.6 billion—quadrupling in ten years. Even discounting for price increases, this was a significant increase. During that period, equipment capitalization grew to a level five times the 1890 level. The absolute increase in capitalization was surpassed only by agriculture, manufacturing, and steam railroads.[28]

The early years of the nineties saw the increasing development of street railways both of the electric variety and the older types. Expansion of electrical machinery output fed such growth. By 1892, it was clear that this area was a most promising one for investment. One journal pointed out that the securities of street railways were becoming increasingly attractive to European investors as well as those at home. This type of investment was considered, on grounds of safety and return, as falling between industrial and railway stocks and bonds. In the face of growing distrust of South American and other overseas securities investments, underwriting street railway expansion was viewed optimistically.[29]

By 1892, the growth of surface transportation in urban areas had advanced significantly; a boom was under way.[30] With the development of the peripheral areas surrounding the older sections of cities—a type of growth spanning several years and not easily stopped once started—street railways also expanded. In Chicago, for example, from 1894–1898—a period including almost all of the depression—there was a continuous extension of new surface transportation lines. In every year of the depression, some surface transportation development was carried on.[31]

Since street railway development did not occur on a large scale until 1892, and since most of the development did not occur from 1898 to 1900, it follows that from 1892–1898 there was a high level of street railway expansion. We saw that growth in this sector during the nineties was relatively and absolutely very great—amounting to an increase of capitalization of about $1.2 billion. And our measures of capital growth in the nineties indicate that investment in electric light and power increased over 450 percent. This corroborates expansion in electric railway development.[32]

Summary

During the depression, investment fell off sharply, in some cases preceding the contraction in economic activity, in others following it. The most significant declines occurred in producer durables output, building construction, agriculture, and railroad investment. The decline in mining investment was most probably of minor impact, while investment in street railways unquestionably increased during most of the depression period. (As we shall see below, there probably were increases in the amounts being invested abroad by Americans as manufacturing industry expanded.) In terms of timing, there is evidence indicating that investment in railroad construction, rolling stock, and steel rails, as well as in building construction and agriculture, preceded the downturn of business. Investment in industrial and commercial electrical equipment and ships and boats likewise began declining prior to the general contraction. The continued heavy investment in street railways and certain types of building construction related to urban development indicates that despite the all-but-pervasive process of economic contraction, perhaps because of it, urbanization was pushed during the depression.

NOTES

1. There are useful monthly and quarterly data on railroad construction, railroad rolling stock purchase orders, building construction (residential and non-residential), and steel-rail purchases by railways. In addition, annual data reflecting some components of investment are available in some detail in Shaw's value of output series. Indirect indications of what was happening to investment are to be seen in production figures of output going into investment areas such as steel production, pig-iron production, shipbuilding, and so on. Some of these will be reviewed in our analysis later in this chapter.

2. Simon Kuznets, *National Product Since 1869*, p. 231.

3. Total producer durable output was about 5 percent of GNP in the mid 1890s. In that period, capital depreciation was stable in absolute terms but showed a relative increase as gross and net national product declined. Cf. Kuznets, *National Product Since 1869*.

4. William H. Shaw, *Value of Commodity Output Since 1869*, pp. 75–77.

5. Ibid. This is the source for analysis of producer durable output data.

6. Clarence D. Long, *Building Cycles and the Theory of Investment*, pp. 154–155. See also Alvin H. Hansen, *Business Cycles and National Income*, chap. 3, on the nature of building and its relationship to the business cycle.

7. The data in Figure 8 are derived from Long's monthly index of building permit values which the NBER has adjusted seasonally. See *Historical Statistics*, p. 342. These data were then deflated using the BLS wholesale price index on building materials to yield an index in 1913 prices. See BLS *Index Numbers of Wholesale Prices on Pre-War Base, 1890–1927*, pp. 2–6. The data were then converted to a 1913 base

so that the series charted gives a clearer view of fluctuations in real construction related to 1913 construction.

8. In Chicago, for example, despite declines in real estate values and general building activity during the depression, certain types of buildings thrived. Skyscrapers, a vogue coming into effect just before the World's Fair, were still being built during the depression. In 1893, four were built; in 1894, two. The north and northwest sides of Chicago replaced the South Side as centers of residential real estate speculation as a building boom progressed and the depression was "scarcely felt." Thus despite generally depressed building conditions in Chicago there were areas in which activity did not slacken and in some instances building expanded. See Homer Hoyt, *One Hundred Years of Land Values in Chicago*, pp. 152, 179, 181–184.

9. *Historical Statistics*, p. 9; *U.S. Industrial Commission Report* 11: 110–112. See also F. Strauss and L. Bean, U. S. Bureau of Agricultural Economics, *Gross Farm Income*, p. 24.

10. *Historical Statistics*, p. 202.

11. *Financial Review*, 1894, 1899; E. G. Campbell, *The Reorganization of the American Railroad System 1893–1900*, pp. 26–29.

12. *U.S. Industrial Commission Report* 19: 262, 292-293, 299-300, 517.

13. Locomotives, averaging about 150,000 pounds and costing, on the average, about $12,000 during the depression, were taking on their modern technological characteristics and were significantly advancing the efficiency of railroad transportation.

14. *U.S. Industrial Commission Report* 19: 262, 292–293, 299–300, 517; and J. E. Partington, *Railroad Purchasing and the Business Cycle*, p. 222. The data on rolling stock and rail orders are taken from the NBER nine-stage analysis. The failure of locomotive orders to rise in the 1894–1895 expansion to anything approximating the 1892 level may have been due partially to the increased load-carrying capacity of the new locomotives. See also T. Hultgren, *American Transportation in Prosperity and Depression*, pp. 148–157.

15. Partington, *Railroad Purchasing*, and NBER files on his series.

16. Ibid.

17. Partington, *Railroad Purchasing*, pp. 3–7; *Historical Statistics*, pp. 202–203; Hultgren, *American Transportation*.

18. Partington, *Railroad Purchasing*; Hultgren, *American Transportation*; NBER.

19. At the beginning of the decade, only about 80 percent of these rails were steel but by the turn of the century, over 90 percent were steel and iron rails were only being manufactured for repairs. Technological improvements in steel-making reached the roads.

20. Partington, *Railroad Purchasing*; Hultgren, *American Transportation*; *U.S. Industrial Commission Report*.

21. Partington, *Railroad Purchasing*; Hultgren, *American Transportation*; *U.S. Industrial Commission Report*.

22. F. W. Taussig, *Some Aspects of the Tariff Question*, pp. 123–124; *U.S. Industrial Commission Report*, 19: 201, 225–226, 238; *Historical Statistics*, p. 9.

23. Ibid.

24. Bureau of Census, *Special Reports, Mines and Quarries, 1902* (Washington, D.C.: Government Printing Office, 1905), p. 117.

25. *U.S. Industrial Commission Report*, 19: 202.

26. *Historical Statistics*, p. 231.

27. With inventories probably being depleted, the actual demand may have declined even less. Anthracite coal was being replaced by bituminous and other fuels in industry, yet it managed to maintain its level of output; this probably resulted from overall increases in demand for fuels as industry mechanized. Lead and zinc mining grew greatly during the decade, though in the worst depression years production contracted slightly. In the Kansas zinc areas, Galena and Empire City, even the depression failed to halt mining growth. Output rose by 50 percent from 1895 to 1896—a period of economic contraction. Cf. Kansas, *Annual Report of the Bureau of Labor and Industry 1896*, pp. 45–48. Sharp increases in mineral output occurred while the labor force either declined or increased only slightly. This increase was due to the extension of mechanization. Cf. Bureau of Census, *Special Reports, Mines and Quarries* p. 59.

28. *Historical Statistics*, p. 9. In the period 1890 to 1902, electric railways expanded tremendously. The number of employees doubled, while the number of passenger cars used almost doubled. Mileage increased by over two and a half times as did the amount of revenue car-miles. Operating revenues also increased by over two and a half times and net operating revenues were up almost four times. These indices of growth during the nineties compared favorably with the growth in the decade from 1902 to 1912. For documentation, see U.S. Federal Electric Railways Commission, *Proceedings together with Final Report to the President* 3:2221–2223, 2228.

29. Cf. *Street Railway Journal*, January, 1892, p. 29.

30. The National Association of Street Railway Employees was formed in 1892 to represent the growing number of employees manning the spreading intraurban networks. An AFL affiliate, the Association grew during the decade to a membership of about 15,000 scattered in 40 cities throughout the country.

31. On the north and west sides of the city, both elevated railroads and electric surface lines were extended. Elsewhere, new transit facilities were installed and old horse-drawn lines were converted. Even during the depression, these projects were pushed, many new ones even being conceived and started.

Other business activities were also affected: Yerkes formed syndicates in 1895 to purchase land along the routes of new lines. Businessmen in the Loop area started many new stores as these lines integrated the greater Chicago community. See *U.S. Industrial Commission Report*,

8:200–203; Hoyt, *100 Years of Land Values,* pp. 181–184; *A.F.L. Proceedings, 1893,* p. 7.

32. Issues of stocks and bonds on the New York Stock Exchange for street railways reached a high of over $50 million in 1897. Such data are not very useful in gauging totals for the economy; they only help to identify such investment for a small sector of the economy. For example, in 1897 about one fourth of the total (NYSE) issues was for the Metropolitan Street Railway in New York City. For the entire nation, investment in street railways for the year might reasonably have been ten or twenty times that of this one railway. Cf. *Financial Review,* 1894–1899.

4
Consumption During the Depression

We have seen that during the depression investment in major sectors of the economy declined sharply, following the usual business-cycle pattern with variations reflecting the distinguishing characteristics of the 1893–1897 depression. To continue our analysis of major structural parts of the economy, we will now review what occurred to consumption levels over the period. This will give us some notion of the depression's impact on the consumer and of how the contraction in consumption in turn affected general economic activity.

Although consumption is mainly determined by the level of total income, when total income rises or falls consumption also moves in the same direction but by proportionately less than the change in total income. This varies, of course, according to the general income level of the individual or family. Lower-income groups are more likely to spend all of any increment in income on consumer goods, just as upper-income groups will maintain consumption by reducing savings when income contracts. When total income declines greatly in a recession or depression, all groups resist lowering their consumption level by reducing current savings, drawing upon past savings, borrowing, and so on. Only when these alternatives have been exhausted will consumption be curtailed. Such curtailment of consumption will ordinarily start with postponable items (usually durable goods) and reach necessities only under the greatest pressure. Thus, one measure of the severity of an economic contraction is the extent to which consumption is diminished. In many contractions, consumption does not decline absolutely but rather its growth rate slackens. In the severest economic contractions, not only does total consumption decrease but all or most categories of consumer goods, including perishables (sometimes even food), contract.

Ideally our analysis would be more complete and meaningful if we had series on savings, family expenditures, and aggregate consumption expenditures broken down into meaningful categories and according to different income groupings. Such series are available today, but for the nineties we must count ourselves fortunate in having available some aggregative annual consumption series compiled by W. H. Shaw.[1] On the basis of these series, some important generalizations about consumption changes, both in aggregative and per capita terms, are possible.

Shaw's data are divided into three major categories: perishable, semidurable, and durable consumer goods.[2] In all cases, the figures on consumption refer to the value of output of commodities destined for domestic consumption, in constant (1913) prices, imports and exports having been taken into account. Shaw's series measure the flow of finished goods from factories, corrected for foreign trade, so that at the beginning of the depression inventory changes may have been significant. To equate, then, his series with consumption, at that time, involves the possibility of some error. For most periods, however, the fluctuations in the series probably reflected actual changes in consumption. This is assumed throughout the following analysis.

In calculating changes in real per-capita consumption, a 2 percent yearly increase in population is employed.[3] Admittedly, per-capita figures leave much to be desired in analyzing cyclical changes. More ideally, a frequency distribution of family consumption expenditures would lead to more meaningful generalizations concerning changes in consumption. In the absence of such data, however, real per-capita figures serve a useful purpose in reflecting the aggregate changes in consumption and, by the nature of the product, we get some notion of the impact of the depression on the level of living. Combining the information on changes in per-capita consumption for various commodities with various other data on changes in consumption, we gain a clearer impression of how the consumer fared during the depression than contempoary qualitative statements yield.

Consumption of Perishables

Analysis of fluctuations in the value of output of consumer perishables in Table 19 indicates that during the depression of the nineties such consumption fell off significantly. In the first part of the depression, the decline amounted to about 5.6 percent. From 1889 to 1939, there were only three times when there was a greater decline—1908, 1921, and the early thirties.[4] In these instances, the general economic contractions were extremely sharp though their duration varied. In addition, there is some evidence that suggests consumption did not decline as greatly in the early phases of the 1929–1933 depression as in the 1893–1894 downturn.[5]

During the contraction which began after Cleveland's message on the Venezuelan dispute in December, 1895, consumption of perishables dropped again, though not by as much as in

1893. The decline for 1896 amounted to 3 percent compared to 5 percent during 1893. However, the trough levels of 1893 and 1896 represented much lower per-capita consumption levels than in previous years since population increased by 2 percent each year while total consumption was down by these two years by the indicated proportions. In the trough years of 1893 and 1894, per-capita consumption was considerably lower than in 1891 and 1892 and about the same as in 1890.[6]

Scanning Table 19, we see that all categories of consumer perishables fell off in real terms by significant amounts in the early stages of the depression. Sharp declines, exceeding 10 percent, were recorded for such perishables as tobacco products, toilet articles, and printed matter. A more moderate decline occurred for nonmanufactured fuel and lighting products, reaching levels about 5 percent below those of the predepression period. Manufactured fuel and lighting products output did not decline in this stage of contraction, its earlier decline occurring outside our cycle framework. In the second contractive phase of the depression, with the exception of fuel and lighting products, which declined appreciably in 1896 and 1897, the remaining perishables experienced only moderate declines—the decline for each category being less than its contraction in 1893. The relatively sharper decline in consumption of fuel products in the second phase of the depression suggests that that contraction was a serious one in which many families were forced to cut down use of fuel products to a greater extent than in 1894. This inference is not clear and is suspect on grounds of no parallel decline in related areas.[7]

The extent of the contraction in perishable consumption can best be visualized if reference to Figure 3 in Chapter 1 is made. Here the degree of per-capita decline from Table 19 takes on fuller meaning in the context of a full-employment or rising-capacity level. We see that the drop in consumption of perishables

Table 19
Annual Percentage Changes in the Value of Finished Perishable Commodities Destined for Domestic Consumption, 1890–1900, 1913 Prices

Year	Total Perish- ables [a]	Cigars, Ciga- rettes, Tobacco	Drugs, Toilet- ries, House- hold Prepa- rations	Maga- zines, News- papers, Etc.	Lighting Products, Manu- factured	Fuel & Lighting Products, Nonman- ufactured
1890	—	—	—	—	—	—
1891	6.0	5.6	9.0	10.0	− .5	9.0
1892	5.0	5.0	14.0	9.5	− 6.0	4.5
1893	− 5.0	− 7.5	− 12.5	− 9.0	5.0	2.0
1894	− .5	− .5	6.0	− 6.5	3.0	− 5.5
1895	5.5	− 6.0	23.5	3.0	9.0	9.5
1896	− 3.0	− 1.0	− 7.5	0.0	.5	− 5.5
1897	0.0	4.0	9.0	3.5	13.5	− 3.0
1898	9.0	7.5	11.0	41.0	− 4.5	2.0
1899	13.6	15.5	12.5	15.0	8.5	12.5
1900	2.0	11.5	− 2.5	− 9.5	5.5	− 2.5

Source: W. H. Shaw, *Value of Commodity Output Since 1869*, p. 70.
Note: Percentages are rounded to nearest .5 percent.
  (a) Excluding food.

in both troughs of the depression stopped at levels 20 percent below the expanding-capacity mark. The second trough of the period was thus more severe, in these terms, than the first trough. In other words, in the dynamic framework of growth, the declines of 1896 and 1897 for some categories, though showing a percentage drop less sharp than those of 1893 and 1894, must be viewed as relatively sharper since the levels reached were further from the potential full-employment mark and population was about 7 percent higher than at the commencement of the economic downturn.

Consumption of Semidurables

Fluctuations in the output of consumer semidurables over many cycles tend to conform in timing to those of the reference cycle more closely than variations in the output of consumer perishables and they also tend to be more marked. As we have just seen, contractions in consumer perishable output during the depression of the nineties were of more than average magnitude. Output of consumer semidurables dropped considerably during the depression, falling much more than that of perishables. The maximum overall decline from 1892 to 1894 exceeded 10 percent for all semidurables, as Table 20 indicates; the overall decline during the contraction of 1896 was quite moderate, totaling only 2.5 percent. Individual series, of course, displayed different rates of contraction.[8]

Real per-capita output of semidurables did not increase markedly during the entire decade of the nineties: it was above the 1890 level after 1897 by about 3 percent. In 1900, real per-capita output of semidurables was probably 8 to 10 percent. For the years 1893–1897, real per-capita consumption of semidurables was below the 1892 and even the 1890 levels, except in 1895. In that year it was above the 1890 but not the 1892 level. The 1894 per-capita consumption level of semidurables was roughly 13 percent below that of 1890 and 15 percent below that of 1892. Clearly consumption of semidurables contracted to a greater extent than that of perishables and was at a level below that of 1890 for a sustained period of at least four years.[9]

Most semidurables listed in Table 20 can be considered necessities of a less urgent nature than most of the perishables already analyzed. Fluctuations in their output conformed fairly closely to the urgency of need of the group of commodities. The outputs of all the categories, except that of house furnishings, declined from 1892 to 1894 by amounts roughly as great or greater than that for all semidurables. Sharpest was the decline in output of dry goods and notions, which dropped over 15 percent. The decline in house furnishings was least of all and amounted to only about 6 percent. In 1896, the second contraction period of the depression, all categories experienced sharper declines than that for all semidurables with the exception of clothing and personal furnishings, which showed an increase in output of almost 4 percent. The sharpest decline (about 15 percent) in this phase of the depression was, as in the first phase, in dry goods and notions output, suggesting that these semidurables were more dispensable than the others.

In real per-capita terms, consumption of each category of semidurables reached decade lows in 1894. With the exception of shoes and other footwear, consumption in 1895 returned above 1890 real per-capita levels. Even dry goods and notions, which showed no real growth during the nineties (probably due to the wider purchase of more finished commodities formerly made at home with dry goods), generated a sharp recovery in 1895. (By 1900, real per-capita output of dry goods and notions was about 15 percent less than in 1890.) With the exception of dry goods and notions, all semidurables surpassed the 1890 real per-capita output level by the end of the decade. That for shoes and other footwear, however, was just barely above the 1890 level in 1900.

Despite the seemingly greater decline in semidurables consumption compared with that of perishables, closer examination of our data (using Figure 3 in Chapter 1 again) makes possible a more discerning set of generalizations. Using full-employment or capacity levels (assumed to grow each year), we see that the decline in consumption of semidurables was greater in the first

Table 20

**Annual Percentage Changes in the Value of Finished
Semidurable Commodities Destined for Domestic
Consumption, 1890–1900, 1913 Prices**

Year	Total Semi-durables	Dry Goods & Notions	Clothing & Personal Furnish-ings	Shoes & Other Footwear	House-furnishings
1890	—	—	—	—	—
1891	2.5	5.0	2.5	− .5	5.5
1892	5.0	− 1.4	6.0	9.0	10.0
1893	− 8.5	−11.5	− 7.0	−10.5	− 5.5
1894	− 3.0	3.0	− 3.0	− 2.0	− 1.0
1895	20.0	29.5	22.5	3.0	16.0
1896	− 2.5	−15.0	3.5	− 3.0	− 5.5
1897	8.5	6.5	7.0	11.5	2.5
1898	.5	− 5.1	− 2.5	8.0	3.5
1899	11.5	1.0	17.0	13.0	11.0
1900	− .5	− 1.0	1.5	3.0	5.0

Source: Shaw, *Value of Commodity Output,* p. 72.
Note: Percentages are rounded to nearest .5 percent.

phase of the depression, stopping at about 20 percent below full employment. The recovery in 1895 was sufficiently sharp [10] so that the modest declines in 1896 did not carry semidurables as far below full employment as they had gone in 1894. This was the reverse of the perishables situation in which the 1896–1897 levels were farther below capacity than those of 1894. Surveying the growth of these areas, we see that in the nineties semidurables were growing faster than the output of perishables. This accounts for the strength of semidurables in 1896 and the weakness of perishables in the second trough.

Consumption of Durables

Fluctuations in the output of consumer durable goods during the depression conformed in timing and amplitude to the usual cycle pattern in the early phase of the depression. Overall durable goods output declined by almost 20 percent from 1892 to 1894, almost double the contraction of semidurable goods output. This more pronounced decline is easily understandable when the different categories are reviewed. Most of the durable goods are easily dispensed with in times of low income. Certainly pleasure craft and musical instruments are consumption items that can readily be eliminated without the level of living being appreciably affected. In many instances, postponement of the purchase of a durable good means delaying replacement of an item which still is capable of providing the consumer service desired. The decline in durable goods output in 1898 was late in coming but did not exceed the relative decline in semidurables output.[11]

Except for miscellaneous housefurnishings and the jewelry category, the outputs of which fell 9 and 14 percent, respectively, during the first phase of the depression, the declines in output of various durables were as great or greater than the overall contraction of 20 percent for all durable goods output. Musical instruments were produced in 1894 at a level almost 40 percent below the 1892 output and pleasure craft production likewise fell sharply from the 1892 performance level, sinking in 1894 to almost 27 percent lower than the predepression year. Output for the two categories, china and house utensils and floor coverings, dropped in 1894 to almost 26 percent below 1892 levels. The 1894 output for household furniture also receded sharply to a level about 22 percent below 1892 production.

The sharp declines of most categories testify to the postponability of these items. Their output contracted most of all con-

Table 21
Annual Percentage Changes in the Value of Finished Durable Commodities Destined for Domestic Consumption, 1890–1900, 1913 Prices

Year	Total Durables	Household Furniture	Floor Coverings	Miscellaneous House furnishings	China & House Utensils	Musical Instruments	Jewelry, Silverware, Clocks, Watches	Pleasure Craft
1890	—	—	—	—	—	—	—	—
1891	3.5	5.5	13.0	3.0	5.5	2.5	− 4.0	11.5
1892	− 8.0	14.5	.5	5.0	5.0	− 4.0	.0	− 7.0
1893	− 9.5	− 6.0	−18.0	− 6.5	−17.5	−31.0	1.5	− 2.5
1894	−10.5	−16.5	− 7.0	− 2.5	− 8.0	− 7.5	−14.0	24.0
1895	24.0	24.5	35.5	19.5	21.5	57.0	19.0	30.5
1896	1.0	7.0	−19.5	− 4.0	13.5	−18.5	−15.5	− 8.0
1897	8.0	− 1.5	7.0	5.0	10.0	6.5	18.5	− 2.0
1898	− 2.5	− 9.5	− 7.5	2.0	2.0	15.5	—	11.5
1899	15.5	12.5	26.5	17.5	13.5	14.0	38.0	40.5
1900	− 5.5	9.0	− 1.5	.0	8.0	14.5	3.0	29.0

Source: Shaw, *Value of Commodity Output*, pp. 73–74.
Note: Percentages are rounded to nearest .5 percent.

sumer goods, and most of these contractions probably affected fewer people's levels of living than the decrease in output of perishable and semidurable goods. Certainly the average level of living was likely to be affected mainly by declines in the consumption of such goods as furniture, housefurnishings, floor coverings, and china, and even here the effect of declines was probably not as disruptive of living as cutbacks in the consumption of foods and other necessities would be.

The declines in output of durables having been the sharpest of all consumer goods, real per-capita output likewise fell off more in durables than in other consumer goods. Recovery of output in the 1895–1897 period was sharp enough so that the per-capita levels for total durables just passed those of 1892 by 1897. In 1894, the real per-capita output of total durables was about 30 percent below that of 1890 and about 25 percent below the 1892 level. Real per-capita output for the various categories of durable goods reached lower depths in most cases than for total durables. In 1894, the real per-capita output of musical instruments, the category that declined the most of all durables, was about 50 percent below that of 1890 and 42 percent below that of 1890 and 42 percent below the 1892 level. These declines represented very significant contractions in consumption—much more than that of either perishables or semidurables.[12]

The relative declines in output of durables versus perishables and semidurables are better seen by referring once again to Figure 3 in Chapter 1. There we see that the rate of capacity growth was about the same in the nineties for durables and semidurables while perishables lagged. The sharpness of durables output contraction vis-à-vis other consumer goods is seen in the decline from 1892 to 1894. The trough of this phase of the depression was about 25 percent below full-employment capacity. The recovery from 1894 on continued through 1897 and, thus, was unlike that of perishables, which sunk farther below capacity, and semidurables, which recouped somewhat to levels closer to capacity. Not until 1898 did consumer durables decline again and by that time recovery had been sufficiently sharp so that the 1898 levels were about 90 percent of capacity. In these circumstances, the increase in output in 1899 pushed durables closer to the capacity mark than either perishables or semidurables.

As consumption fell in both phases of the depression to levels as much as 20 percent below capacity, with instances of levels 25 percent below capacity, we see that the depression was quite severe and affected consumers significantly. While durables and semidurables consumption reached relatively higher levels in the second phase of the depression, the levels attained by perishable consumption were farther from capacity in that phase. Thus it seems that the first phase of the depression was slightly more severe in terms of consumer goods purchased. But the difference in no case is a sharp one. This supports the proposition that the depression was quite severe in its overall impact on consumers. When we follow Figure 3 to 1902 and 1906 and see that consumption levels remained below capacity for most of that period, the severity of the decline in the depths of the depression is underscored. If we see these levels of output in the context of 15 to 20 percent of the labor force being unemployed, the implicit sharp decline in consumption and levels of living for millions of people emerges as a stark characteristic of the depression of the nineties. The pervasive decline in consumption during this depression was another confirmation of its severity.

NOTES

1. William H. Shaw's *Value of Commodity Output Since 1869* provides annual data on the value of output of goods destined for domestic consumption broken down into major classifications within the three categories of consumer goods. This is the statistical basis for this chapter. Although annual data are not adequate for assessing timing and certain causative relationships, the general impact of consumption fluc-

tuations is clear. Scattered data from other sources will be used to fill out the picture. Analysis of such data indicates that although they do not always corroborate Shaw's series, they do not contradict the basic tendencies shown in his data. Although differences in relative degree of decline and details in certain categories of consumer goods do crop up, no serious doubt is cast on Shaw's series by data taken from the annals of the period. Cf. *Dun's Review,* January 6, 1894, p. 2, for an analysis of sales fluctuations in selected activities for the first half of 1892 and 1893, *Dun's Review* and *Bradstreet's* aggregative and per-capita consumption data are also found in government reports: U.S., Department of Labor, *Bulletin No. 17* (July, 1898), on consumption of liquors; U.S., Bureau of Foreign and Domestic Commerce, *Consumption Estimates.* Also U.S., Department of Agriculture, *Yearbook,* in which estimates of per-capita consumption for various staple commodities are given.

2. The three major consumption categories are defined by Shaw: "Perishable commodities include those usually lasting less than six months; semidurable those usually lasting from six months to three years; and durable those usually lasting more than three years. As in any classification, the distinctions cannot always be sharp; but . . . the groups are sufficiently clear cut to facilitate analysis." *Value of Commodity Output,* pp. 6–7.

3. *Historical Statistics,* p. 26.

4. Shaw, *Value of Commodity Output,* pp. 21, 26. Food is excluded from our analysis since crop changes are not cyclically determined. Food consumption did decline in 1894 by just under 3 percent.

5. A. R. Tebbutt, *The Behavior of Consumption in Business Depression,* vol. 20, no. 3.

6. Per-capita figures were derived by using Shaw's deflated series and applying annual population change to them directly.

7. In face of the failure of consumption data for other perishables to decline as much, the question is raised to the reliability of Shaw's data on fuel consumption or of his methods. Another possibility is that fuel utilization became more efficient during the period. Shaw's data show that from 1890 to 1906, a period in which GNP doubled in real terms, output of nonmanufactured fuel products increased by 52 percent while that of manufactured fuel products declined by 1 percent. In this period, bituminous coal, a nonmanufactured fuel product, increased tremendously in importance. During the nineties, production of bituminous coal almost doubled while Pennsylvania anthracite output increased by only 19 percent. See Shaw, *Value of Commodity Output,* p. 70; *Historical Statistics,* p. 142.

8. Shaw, *Value of Commodity Output,* pp. 9–27.

9. Ibid., pp. 70–72.

10. This sharp recovery in 1895 might have been due to increases in inventories as recovery got under way. Without the support of other important sectors of the economy, such as construction or investment in

equipment, such a growth of inventories was unlikely to buoy the economy up in any significant way.

11. The belated decline in output probably relates to the nature of production of durables, which require longer periods than do most consumer goods. With orders and inventories declining in 1897, the effect would show up in the 1898 production figures.

12. Shaw, *Value of Commodity Output,* pp. 73–74.

5
The Balance of Payments During the Depression

During the nineties, the economy responded rapidly to changes in its economic relations with Europe and the rest of the world. A partially reconstructed balance of payments for the period [1] demonstrates that fluctuations in the domestic economy reflected, in some measure, changes in international economic relationships. Within the statistical framework of the balance of payments, some notion of what happened to trade, dividends, investment, short-term loans, immigrant remittances, and freight charges emerges. Assimilating such information and relationships aids in assessing the impact of balance-of-payments changes on its components as well as on the domestic economy. It is therefore important to see to what extent the depression in the United States affected its economic relations with the rest of the world and what impact these changed relations had on the domestic economy.

157

*Foreign Trade and Investment Before and After the
Depression*

In the period before the depression, United States foreign
trade had certain distinct characteristics. From about 1875 on,
the balance of trade was, for the most part, active, with exports
exceeding imports by amounts ranging from $20 million to $250
million each year. In 1892, this pattern was followed: exports
exceeded imports by over $80 million, making possible income
payments on foreign investments, foreign shipping and insurance services, remittances abroad, tourist expenditures abroad,
and so on. The exports and imports for fiscal 1892 represented
highs or near highs for these categories.[2]

EXPORTS

A breakdown of exports and imports before the depression
and after the worst depression years makes clearer the nature of
United States foreign trade. For 1892, exports totaled $923 mil-
lion, while in 1899—a year clear of war influences when economic activity was over 90 percent of capacity—the total was
$1,253 million. Exports were distributed:

Export	1892	1899
Agricultural products	77.0%	62.5%
Manufactures	17.0	30.5
Forest products	3.0	4.0
Mining	2.0	3.0
Fisheries	.6	.4
Miscellaneous	.4	.3

As the export trade before the depression was mainly in agricultural products, changes in its aggregate amount mainly reflected
price fluctuations in agricultural products competing on a world
market. Although the percentage for agricultural exports is
slightly higher for 1892 than for most years, the pattern was for

these products to represent over two-thirds of total exports. Manufactures, although a significant part of total exports, were overshadowed by agriculture. Before the depression, the economy's relations with the rest of the world were thus significantly determined by the vicissitudes of agricultural production and marketing.[3]

In the decade before 1900, the relationship between agricultural products and manufactured products changed significantly. The rapid industrialization taking place in the nineties thrust manufactured products to world markets in ever-increasing quantities. This is emphasized by the fact that agricultural exports did not decline absolutely in this period. By 1899, more agricultural products were exported and at better prices than in 1892. The change in relative figures for agricultural and manufactured products exported was accomplished by exports of manufactures increasing by 150 percent from 1892 to 1899.[4]

IMPORTS

The distribution of imported products was more diversified than that of exports and changed less drastically. In 1892, total imports exceeded $840 million, while for 1899 the total almost reached $800 million. Import ratios follow:

Import	1892	1899
Food and live animals	34.0%	29.0%
Crude articles	25.0	33.5
Manufactures to be used in manufactures	11.0	9.5
Manufactured articles	18.0	15.0
Luxury articles	13.5	13.5

In 1892, the bulk of imports was raw materials and food while partially or wholly manufactured items were also important. Changes in the proportions of imports reflected the growing industrial nature of the economy as raw-material imports rose absolutely and relatively to sustain manufacturing expansion. The growth of domestic agricultural output made less necessary the importation of food and animals in the same amounts: there was an absolute as well as a relative decline in this category. The decline in the relative quantity of partially manufactured articles imported was fairly significant, amounting to an absolute decrease of about 17 percent. Imports of manufactures declined absolutely by about 14 percent. In both instances, there was a subsequent recovery to levels approximating the absolute levels of 1892. The increasingly active trade balance after the depression also made possible expansion of United States investment abroad and other changes in the invisible account.[5]

FOREIGN INVESTMENT BEFORE THE DEPRESSION

While the emphasis in trade relations was changing in tune with the continuing industrialization of the economy, significant changes were occurring in the net indebtedness of the United States. Estimates for this period are very rough. Nevertheless, they provide a basis upon which to draw some reasonable inferences. In the period before the depression began, it is probable that direct and total securities investment in the United States was between $2.6 and $2.8 billion. With short-term credits added, the total for all foreign investment was about $200 million higher, or between $2.8 and $3 billion. For the most part, these foreign investments were in railroads, though some direct investment in mining, oil, breweries, and mortgage companies existed.[6] (This estimate of investment is supported by the following: prior to the depression, annual interest and dividend payments approximated $100 million. If the average return for all foreign investment be set at between 3 and 4 percent, the total amount of indebtedness would be around $2.9 billion.)

UNITED STATES INVESTMENT ABROAD BEFORE THE DEPRESSION

While estimates of the amount of United States investment abroad just before the depression are based on fragmentary data, it is known that the rate of investment abroad quickened after the depression. One source has estimated annual investment abroad during the worst part of the depression between $10 and $15 million. After 1896, more United States loans abroad were made to Mexico, Canada, China, and other countries than before the depression. There is an estimate of total investment abroad in 1898 amounting to about $600 million. If we assume that investment abroad in the period 1892 to 1898 was at an annual rate of $30 to $50 million, except during the worst period of the depression, it seems reasonable to estimate United States investment abroad in 1892 between $350 million and $450 million.[7]

FOREIGN INVESTMENT AFTER THE DEPRESSION

Despite differences in estimates of the investment of foreign capital in the United States after the depression, the order of magnitude of such investment is clear. By 1899, total indebtedness abroad was between $3,330 and $3,600 million.[8] Since foreigners repatriated their capital during the depression at the rate of about $60 million a year and since foreign investment before the depression approximated $30 million, there must have been capital inflow into the United States, if at a reduced rate. The rate of capital inflow easily picked up as economic conditions improved in industrial activities, long the cynosure of foreign investors.[9]

UNITED STATES INVESTMENT ABROAD AFTER THE DEPRESSION

While there is little difference in the estimates of total foreign investment in the United States made by Lewis and Bacon, the estimates on investments abroad are wider apart. Bacon's estimate of $500 million as of January 1, 1898 is about $185 million less than the Lewis estimate for end of 1897. Since most analysts agree that the United States was increasing its foreign investments abroad at the end of the nineties at the rate of at least $50 million a year, this difference represents a sum of some moment—about $235 million.[10] We shall arbitrarily use an estimate of $600 million for the end of 1897. The Lewis estimates are detailed in Tables 22 and 23.

Table 22
United States Direct and Portfolio Investment Abroad,
by Geographic Area, End of 1897
(millions of dollars)

Area	Amount
Europe	$151.0
Canada and Newfoundland	189.7
Cuba and West Indies	49.0
Mexico	200.2
Central America	21.2
South America	37.9
Africa	1.0
Asia	23.0
Oceania	1.5
International, including banking	10.0
Total	$684.5

Source: Cleona Lewis, *America's Stake in International Investments*, p. 606.

Thus from 1893 to 1897 United States investment abroad rose from $350–$450 million to about $600 million at an increasing rate. Foreign investment, while it increased from about $2.9 billion to about $3.3 billion, reflected a retarded rate of

Table 23
United States Investment Abroad, by Type, End of 1897
(*millions of dollars*)

Type of Investment	Amount
Direct Investments:	
Sales Organizations	$ 56.5
Purchasing	5.0
Banking	10.0
Oil Distribution	75.0
Oil Production	10.5
Mining: Precious metals '	88.0
Industrial minerals	46.0
Agricultural enterprises	76.5
Manufacturing	93.5
Railways	143.4
Public Utilities	22.1
Miscellaneous	8.0
Total direct investments	$634.5
Portfolio investments	50.0
All investments abroad	$684.5

Source: Lewis, *America's Stake in Investments,* p. 605.

growth in the five years. The net inflow of capital into the economy during the period was on the average about $50 million a
year, a total sharply reduced from earlier periods. By 1898,
United States net foreign indebtedness approximated $2.75
billion.[11]

The Balance of Trade During the Depression

IMPORTS

While the international indebtedness position of the United

States was changing during the depression years, as already noted, its trade network was also in process of transformation. Many of these changes affected the economy. Reviewing imports, we see in Table 24 that there was relative stability in total imports over the decade with exceptions during the worst years of the depression. For the years 1893, 1894, and 1896, imports fell off appreciably and most of these declines in value represented real declines in quantity. Imports of such commodities as coffee, hides and skins, rubber, rice, nutmeg, tin, leaf tobacco, and wools displayed absolute quantitative declines in some years, reflecting the sharp contraction in production and consumption during the depression. After the depression had run its course and the economy was recovering, imports returned to the predepression level, so that by the end of the century the total value of imports was almost at the 1890 level.[12]

The contraction in imports during the depression may be said to have served a very useful purpose. The sharp declines in imports for 1893, 1894, and 1896 by about $65 million, $100 million, and $120 million, respectively, in the face of the favorable export picture, enhanced the merchandise surplus in the balance of payments. Exports fell off in 1893 and 1894 but not as much as imports, while in 1896 they spurted to a new high level. The result was that import contraction, reflecting lower income levels, eased a difficult balance-of-payments situation somewhat. The contraction of the value of exports, to be analyzed below, reflected special circumstances with many quantities remaining the same or increasing.

During the depression, imports did not decline cyclically until August, 1893. In other words, imports fell off after the panic when the contraction in economic activity was clearly being felt. The upturn in imports, coming in the fall of 1894, also lagged behind economic expansion. In the next downturn of the economy, imports fell off about three months after the reference

Table 24

United States Imports, by Groups, 1892–1900

(millions of dollars)

Year	Total	Food & Live Animals		Crude Articles		Manufactures Used in Manufacturing		Manufactured Articles		Luxury Articles	
		No.	Percent	No.	Percent	No.	Percent	No.	Percent	No.	Percent
1892	841	287	34.2	212	25.2	90	10.8	137	16.3	114	13.6
1893	776	276	35.5	184	23.7	86	11.1	126	16.2	104	13.5
1894	676	264	39.0	160	23.7	70	10.3	91	13.5	92	13.5
1895	802	232	28.9	220	27.4	103	12.8	151	18.8	97	12.1
1896	682	234	34.4	162	23.8	86	12.7	210	18.8	79	11.5
1897	743	220	29.7	239	32.1	81	10.9	119	16.0	83	11.2
1898	635	n.a.[a]		n.a.		n.a.		n.a.		n.a.	
1899	799	230	28.8	268	33.5	75	9.4	118	14.8	108	13.5
1900	829	219	26.5	280	33.8	85	10.2	132	16.0	112	13.5

Source: U.S., Bureau of Foreign and Domestic Commerce, *Monthly Summary of Imports and Exports,* 1893–1900.
(a) Not available.

downturn in January, 1896. Imports improved, however, starting in March, 1897, three months before the reference trough of the depression. Throughout most of the depression, imports of raw and partially manufactured materials did not decline as much as other imports. In the early recovery of imports in 1897, it was these items which gave buoyancy to the total. Apparently this early recovery in imports was related to the early recovery in domestic manufacturing.[13]

EXPORTS

While imports fluctuated cyclically during the depression, export trade, as Table 25 shows, had its trend growth retarded by depression contractions to a plateau below the 1892 peak. Growth was recorded in almost all categories of exports, reflecting both quantitative increases and favorable price changes. The contractions in value of exports, which occurred in three years of the depression, can be traced mainly to agriculture. The growth of industrial exports was merely slowed up by the depression; but the depression effected significant declines in the value of exports for agriculture.

In the cyclical contraction of exports during the years 1893, 1894, and 1895—the last one of domestic recovery—prices of agricultural products were a factor of very great significance. The prices of many agricultural products reached their low points after two decades of secular decline—in the period from 1894 to the early part of 1896. An analysis of quantities of agricultural products exported emphasizes the significance of price declines. Though 1894 and 1895 were years of low agricultural export value, many agricultural products—such as sheep, cotton, beef, hams, lard, and tobacco—were exported in greater quantities than in previous years. The foreign demand for certain important grain crops—such as wheat and oats—fell off at a time when prices were low; while corn exports for the two years

Table 25
United States Merchandise Exports, by Groups, 1892–1900
(millions of dollars)

Year	Total	Agriculture	Per-cent	Manufactures	Per-cent	Forest	Per-cent	Fisheries	Per-cent	Miscellaneous	Per-cent	Mining	Per-cent
1892	923	713	77.1	152	16.5	28.5	3.1	5.6	.6	3.6	.4	20.6	2.1
1893	855	619	72.5	177	20.7	27.6	3.2	4.5	.5	4.4	.5	21.7	2.5
1894	807	574	71.2	178	22.1	28.8	3.6	5.2	.6	4.2	.5	17.6	2.2
1895	808	546	67.6	201	24.9	30.7	3.8	6.2	.8	4.2	.5	19.8	2.4
1896	987	665	67.5	254	25.7	36.3	3.7	6.6	.7	3.9	.4	21.4	2.1
1897	1,080	730	67.6	280	25.9	40.8	3.8	5.6	.5	3.6	.3	19.8	1.8
1898	1,234	852	69.0	308	25.0	39.0	3.2	5.8	.5	3.0	.2	25.9	2.1
1899	1,253	782	62.4	381	30.4	47.6	3.8	5.6	.4	3.5	.3	33.3	2.7
1900	1,453	905	62.3	441	30.4	54.5	3.8	8.1	.6	5.2	.4	39.2	2.7

Source: U.S., Bureau of Foreign and Domestic Commerce, Monthly Summary of Imports and Exports; U.S., Bureau of Statistics, Quarterly Reports Showing Imports and Exports for the Four Quarters Ending June 30th, 1889–1893.

averaged somewhat lower than the preceding years, though in 1895 corn exports were fairly good. As a result, a low of $546 million in agricultural exports was reached in 1895, some $165 million less than the value of such exports in 1892. Not until 1897 was the level of 1892 reached and passed as both world prices and demand strengthened and buoyed up a rapidly expanding export trade.[14]

The overwhelming significance of agricultural products in total exports is revealed by a quick glance at the other export categories in Table 25. The relative and absolute growth of manufacturing exports was only slowed up by the depression, a fact emphasizing the tremendous impact of manufacturing development. Other exports followed this pattern roughly. Forest products were exported in increasing amounts, though during the depression years the rate of growth was either slowed considerably or, as in 1893, exports fell off slightly—about 3 percent. Exports of fisheries also displayed fairly continuous growth with retardations only in 1893 and 1897. These contractions are explained mainly by price changes. Throughout the decade, as total exports grew, fisheries exports maintained the same relative position in the total picture. Mining exports expanded through the decade in great strides, almost doubling from 1892 to 1900. Cyclical influences on these exports are more markedly visible than for manufacturing, forest, and fisheries exports. Mining exports fell off during the worst depression years—down by 16 percent in 1894 and by 9 percent in 1897. Obviously the export declines in mining and fisheries was of no great consequence for total exports. Once again, the importance of the decline in the agricultural sector of exports—reflecting worsened terms of trade for farm products—emerges in any analysis. If the value of agricultural exports had been maintained or even had not fallen off so much—13, 19, and 23 percent less than the 1892 levels for 1893, 1894, and 1895, respectively—the balance of trade would have been more active.

THE BALANCE OF TRADE

From 1875 to 1895, exports were usually greater in value than imports. This was true in a period when capital inflow was steady and large; the exports surplus reflected, in fact, the need of the economy to pay interest and dividends on the growing foreign capital holdings in the United States. During the depression, this surplus persisted but at a reduced level. Moreover, international capital movements into the United States were adversely affected by the world-wide depression as well as by the special domestic depression conditions. This complex of factors interacted unfavorably on the United States balance of payments and intensified, in some respects, the depression at home.[15]

Table 26 shows the changing surplus of exports for the nineties. The decline in the surplus for some of the depression years reflects mainly the failure of agricultural products to maintain their former high level; while the worsening of the terms of trade, especially for agricultural products, is reflected in the export-import relationship changes. The falling off in demand at home, however, meant lower imports so that in 1894 the export surplus actually grew. As indicated above, this result eased balance-of-payments difficulties somewhat, but not to the degree to which the economy was accustomed. From 1875 to 1895, years of almost uninterrupted active trade balance, passive or only slightly active trade balances occurred occasionally and usually in depressed periods. The decline in active trade balance in the early nineties was relatively more marked than these previous declines since the total of trade was so much greater and the payments drain for invisible accounts so much more significant. The export excess necessary to support the debtor position of the United States was much greater than the eventual surplus.

The balance of trade changed in different ways during the depression. While export surpluses continued, with only a sharp drop in 1895 when domestic recovery stimulated imports while exports only held their own, they did not grow in measure with the quantitative increase of some exports, such as manufactures. Undoubtedly, unfavorable terms of trade were responsible for this halt in general export growth. Nevertheless, in spite of these adverse developments, the change in the trade balance, especially in the second phase of the depression, reflected favorable stabilizing effects of a built-in nature. As the depression proceeded, cycle-sensitive imports declined while exports continued. Were it not for the unfavorable price developments of the period, the stabilizing effects probably would have been even greater.

Table 26
United States Balance of Trade, 1890–1900
(*millions of dollars*)

Year	Imports	Exports	Export Surplus
1890	$823	$857	$ 34
1891	828	970	142
1892	841	938	97
1893	776	876	99
1894	676	825	148
1895	802	826	23
1896	682	1,006	324
1897	743	1,100	357
1898	635	1,256	620
1899	799	1,276	476
1900	829	1,473	643

Source: U.S., National Monetary Commission, *Statistics for the United States* 21:10.
Note: Exports include reexports unlike total in Table 25.

Invisibles During the Depression

Table 27 shows the main items in the balance of payments and the following analysis is based on most of these data. The invisible account amounted to a significant sum whose impact on the total balance of payments is of signal importance in evaluating the interrelationships between the domestic and international economy during the depression. The favorable and unfavorable effects on the economy of changes in the different categories in the invisible account will be weighed.[16]

INTEREST AND DIVIDEND PAYMENTS

Chief item among invisibles is the claims of foreigners in the form of interest and dividend payments due on United States corporate bonds and stocks held abroad. For the period under review, these claims totaled about $100 million.[17] The decline in interest and dividend payments for the years 1894 and 1895, by about $5 million, must have been due to foreign disinvestment and lowered and defaulted payments. In any event, the amount was not of great moment. It did ease somewhat the strain on the economy for payments abroad, but only in a minor way.

Heidelbach's estimate, in 1895, of the annual claims against the United States for freight charges was about $100 million,[18] a figure probably wide of the mark. The United States figures, in Table 27, show net annual freight charges amounting to little over $20 million. Both of these estimates seem incorrect. Statistics on foreign tonnage entering and clearing United States ports for the same years seem to contradict these series. Our own estimates are used in Table 28.

Table 28 shows the total of imports in foreign ships and exports in United States ships. The net figures reflect the changes in the base against which any freight charges have to be measured; they show a cyclical decline for fiscal 1894 and 1895.

Table 27

United States Balance of Payments, 1890–1900

(millions of dollars)

Fiscal Year	Merchandise, Including Silver	Interest & Dividends	Freight	Tourist Expenditures	Immigrant Funds	Immigrant Remittances & Miscellaneous[a]	Insurance Commissions & Miscellaneous[b]	Gold	Total
1890	+ 82	−119	−22	− 45	+ 9	− 30	—	+ 4	−112
1891	+ 44	−105	−22	− 40	+11	− 35	—	+ 68	− 79
1892	+216	−100	−21	− 40	+12	− 35	—	+ 1	+ 33
1893	− 1	−100	−21	− 45	+ 9	− 35	—	+ 88	−105
1894	+274	− 95	−23	− 47	+ 6	− 40	—	+ 5	+ 80
1895	+103	− 95	−23	− 48	+ 5	− 40	—	+ 30	− 68
1896	+135	−100	−23	− 60	+ 7	− 40	−35	+ 79	− 37
1897	+318	−110	−25	− 75	+ 5	− 60	−35	− 45	− 27

Table 27 (Continued)
United States Balance of Payments, 1890–1900
(millions of dollars)

Fiscal Year	Merchandise, Including Silver	Interest & Dividends	Freight	Tourist Expenditures	Immigrant Funds	Immigrant Remittances & Miscellaneous[a]	Insurance Commissions & Miscellaneous[b]	Gold	Total
1898	+640	−115	−25	−100	+5	−80	−30	−105	+190
1899	+556	−110	−25	−120	+6	−90	−30	−51	+136
1900	+566	−105	−28	−125	+9	−100	−30	+3	+190

Source: United Nations, Department of Economic Affairs, Division of Economic Stability and Development, Research Memorandum no. 9, *Annual Figures for the Balance of Payments, 1850–1914*, prepared by Folke Hilgerdt (International Financial and Commercial Relations Section, January, 1951).

Note: "If errors and omissions are disregarded, the active or passive balance for all the items shown should thus correspond to the outward or inward net movement of capital (including changes in earmarked gold, which are not entered under gold)," p. 1. Plus (+) means entering, and minus (−) means leaving, the United States.

(a) Does not include 'Miscellaneous' starting in 1896.

(b) Classification, including 'Miscellaneous,' starts in 1896.

The fiscal 1893 level was the highest for the decade. From 1892 on, freight rates in ocean transportation declined; by 1895 and 1896, these rates were 15 percent lower than in 1892. Though the estimates in Table 28 for fluctuations in net freight charges may be wrong as to magnitude, it seems clear that net freight changes should reflect cyclical changes with declines for fiscal years 1894, 1895, and 1896.[19]

TOURIST EXPENDITURES

An invisible item of growing importance during the nineties was expenditures of United States tourists abroad. By the end of the decade, this item was the most important of all the invisibles, having almost tripled from $45 million to $125 million. Apparently the upward trend was slowed down somewhat by the depression. Despite the lowered income levels of the depression, expenditures by United States tourists grew. The net additions, amounting to several millions of dollars each year at first and then to greater sums, must be added to other invisibles, aggravating the balance of payments situation.

IMMIGRANT FUNDS AND MISCELLANEOUS

The amounts that immigrants brought with them to the New World increased United States claims against foreign economies, while the many new Americans remitted sums of money abroad, increasing foreign claims on the domestic economy. During the nineties, these two flows of money changed. The depression caused many recent immigrants to return abroad; in fact, emigration increased during the middle nineties.[20] This situation presents a prima facie case for remittances abroad, going with the emigrants, increasing. With the nature of immigration changing during the nineties, more immigrants were coming from eastern and southeastern Europe and did not bring as much money with them. Quantitatively, immigration abated during the depression so that on this score, too, the sums of money brought by immigrants declined.[21] From 1893 to the end of the century, immigration occurred at a slower pace than earlier, and in the worst depression years it fell to less than half the rate for the first years of the decade. The decline from the high of almost 580,000 in fiscal 1892 to the fiscal 1895 level of over 358,000 was a decline of about 55 percent.

Table 28
Estimated Net Freight Claims Against the United States, 1890–1900
(millions of dollars)

Fiscal Year	Imports in Foreign Vessels [a]	Exports in United States Vessels	Net	Estimated Net Freight Charges [b]
1890	$578	$78	$500	$40.0
1891	626	79	547	43.7
1892	601	81	520	41.6
1893	644	71	573	45.8
1894	466	74	392	31.3
1895	547	62	485	38.8
1896	579	70	509	40.7
1897	573	80	493	39.5
1898	455	68	387	31.0
1899	538	79	459	36.7
1900	648	91	557	44.5

Source: U.S., Bureau of the Census, *Historical Statistics*, p. 217.
(a) Value of imports has been deflated to take out freight costs.
(b) The estimate is based on the notion that freight costs averaged 8 percent of the value of the products shipped. This notion is to be found in *Merchant's Magazine and Commercial Review* 62 (March, 1870): 232–233. Other trade journals gave similar estimates. Early in the nineties, Secretary of the Treasury Windom in an address (quoted in the London *Economist*, February 14, 1891, pp. 209–210) gave a 10 percent figure. We use an 8 percent figure.

In these circumstances, it is not surprising that immigrant funds dropped to less than half the 1891–1892 levels or that remittances abroad increased during the depression. Ordinarily, one would expect that in a depression remittances abroad would decline, but in the context of the times an increase is logically consistent with the evidence at hand. This is especially so since the category includes remittances for insurance and commissions, a substantial amount.[22] The net differences were an added burden to the balance of payments. These differences fluctuated as illustrated in Table 29.

Table 29
Funds Entering and Leaving the United States, 1890–1898
(*millions of dollars*)

Fiscal Year	Immigrant Funds	Foreign Remittances & Miscellaneous[a]	Net Totals
1890	+ 9	−30	−21
1891	+11	−35	−24
1892	+12	−35	−23
1893	+ 9	−35	−24
1894	+ 6	−40	−34
1895	+ 5	−40	−35
1896	+ 7	−40	−33
1897	+ 5	−60	−55
1898	+ 5	−80	−75

Source: United Nations, *Annual Figures for the Balance of Payments, 1850–1914*, prepared by Folke Hilgerdt.
Note: Plus(+) means entering; minus(−) means leaving.
  (a) Does not include 'Miscellaneous' starting 1896.

The net impact of immigrant funds entering the country and funds being remitted abroad is measured in the last column of

Table 29. In the period from 1893 to 1896, the balance of payments was adversely affected in the amount of about $30 million annually.

Gold Flows

One item for which reliable data are available on a monthly basis is gold flows. This item is a key one for the nineties, reflecting disequilibrium or equilibrium in the flow of payments, and together with invisibles already analyzed makes possible some inferences on capital flows during the depression. These inferences will be treated at length below; now we analyze the flow of gold during the depression period.

Balance-of-payments difficulties preceded the advent of the depression and can be clearly traced to the end of 1890, with some evidence of earlier origin. The outflow of gold in large amounts persisted from then until the summer of 1896. Since gold outflows were characteristic of the balance of payments in the late spring and early summer, it is probably true that disequilibrium was ended by the beginning of 1896. Certainly the dispatch with which the United States government gold loan was taken up after February, 1896, seems to support this proposition. The figures below measure the net outflow of gold from the United States in the period under review, by fiscal years: [23]

Fiscal Year	Net Outflow
1890	$ 4.3 million
1891	68.1
1892	.5
1893	87.5
1894	4.5
1895	30.1
1896	78.9
1897	44.7 (inflow)

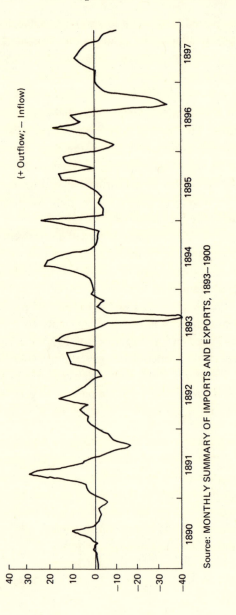

Source: MONTHLY SUMMARY OF IMPORTS AND EXPORTS, 1893—1900

Figure 9
Net Gold Flows, 1890-1897

A look at the monthly figures in Figure 9 indicates that there was a fairly continuous outflow of gold, with interruptions following the usual seasonal patterns. In fiscal 1893, there was a net outflow of gold every month, except October, 1892, which was seasonally a month of gold inflow in large amounts. During fiscal 1894, the gold outflow abated as the depression deepened and imports fell off sharply. In the first months of the fiscal year, gold flowed into the United States in response to the premium for cash and gold and the rising interest rates. After the summer, the inflow spent itself and from December, 1893, to June, 1894, there was a steady outflow of gold to Europe. This outflow persisted into fiscal 1895, though it was reversed in the autumn months of high agricultural exports when small inflows of gold were reported. The recurrence of gold outflows in December, 1894, and January, 1895, was followed by inflows in small amounts for the remainder of the fiscal year. In fiscal year 1896, total gold outflows were almost as great as those for fiscal 1893. From June, 1895, through January, 1896, gold flowed out of the United States despite the desperate efforts of bankers to forestall the movement. In February, 1896, another government gold loan was subscribed to in good order and the subsequent gold flows reflected a state of equilibrium despite the depression. By the middle of 1896, gold started flowing more steadily into the United States.[24]

Figure 9 reveals that except for large inflows during the summer of 1893—owing to special conditions—the balance of payments was characterized by large outflows with occasional small amounts of gold flowing in due to seasonal or random events—an almost constant drain on the economy's gold reserves. Such conditions weakened the Treasury, the currency, and bank reserves and contributed to economic instability.

Foreign Investments

In the period from 1892 to 1897, foreign investment in the United States increased as did investment abroad. The most cursory reading of the annals indicates that there were counter-flows in increasing and decreasing amounts during the depression, such movements representing responses to the many different stimuli during economic contraction and expansion. In order to see these changes in a meaningful perspective, the ranges of capital investment are listed below (billions of dollars):

Capital Investment	1892	1897	Net Changes
Foreign capital in the United States.	$2.8–$3.0	$3.3	.3–.5
United States capital abroad.	.350–.450	.600	.150–.250

Before analyzing the changes in net foreign investment during the depression, a brief survey of the condition of the international capital market is in order. From about the end of 1890 to the beginning of 1895, Europe was in the contractive phase of the business cycle. Since practically all of the foreign investment in the United States came from Europe, this depression abroad must be taken into account in any attempt to draw inferences about capital movements and the depression.[25] Even a glance at data on capital investments from Europe during the first half of the decade indicates a significant decline in such capital exports. During the depression, then, foreign investment did not continue to flow into the United States at the same rate. Moreover, many foreigners, reacting to conditions in the United States and abroad, liquidated their foreign investments. At certain times, foreigners responded to bargains or to other special circumstances to invest again in the United States. The net result was that total new investments in the United States declined, while

United States investment abroad continued to flow at the same or higher levels.

In the context of these circumstances, the data of residual capital movements can more meaningfully be analyzed. For the decade, these figures varied, as follows, in millions of dollars:[26]

Fiscal Year	Capital Movements
1890	− $112 million
1891	− 79
1892	+ 33
1893	− 105
1894	+ 80
1895	− 68
1896	− 37
1897	− 27
1898	+ 190
1899	+ 136
1900	+ 190

Looking at these net short- and long-term capital flows indicates that figures for fiscal years 1893–1897 are not so different from previous years. Nevertheless, when these figures are viewed against the other data in the balance of payments, especially the marked gold outflow over the period, qualitatively the figures take on a certain meaning. Since the gold outflow was very heavy for fiscal year 1893, while the net capital inflow was still relatively high, disequilibrium in the balance of payments seems clear. Especially when we trace evidence of foreign disinvestment, sharp decline in new foreign investment by European investors, and difficulties surrounding the United States government's four gold loans (two in 1894, one early in 1895, and the last one early in 1896) does the fact of disequilibrium emerge clearly.[27] See Table 30 for calendar year net flows.

The residual capital flow to the United States during the depression represents, then, several forces, acting either alone or in combination. Since the evidence on gold flows and the level of new foreign investment in the international capital market indicates that the disequilibrium was halted early in 1896, we can speculate on the nature of capital flows from 1893 to 1896. Our residual figures for fiscal 1894 show a net capital outflow of about $80 million. This can probably be explained by the following interaction of forces. Total net gold exports for the fiscal year 1894 were less than $5 million and in the first half of the fiscal year there was actually a large inflow of gold. There is evidence that once the panic broke and the depression took hold foreign short- and long-term investment rose. In the summer of 1893, short-term funds flowed to New York in response to the premium on cash. Furthermore, the sharp drop in the stock market together with the favorable exchange rate made United States securities very attractive.[28]

The first government gold loan of $50 million was floated early in 1894. Moreover, in the fiscal year 1894 there was a very large excess of merchandise exports, as the level of exports rose absolutely as well as relatively and imports fell off sharply to the lowest absolute level since 1886. In these circumstances, it is not unexpected that the residual claims in the balance of payments identified the United States as a net creditor—temporarily an exporter of capital.[29]

For the fiscal years 1893, 1895, and 1896, net capital inflows came again from Europe while there were large net gold outflows. During fiscal 1893, save for one month, there was a continuous outflow of gold, totaling over $87 million. In that year, there was a passive trade balance of about $18 million—the only one in the nineties. Our residual of capital imports totals $105 million. With new issues of capital falling off in the international capital market and some liquidation by foreign securities holders, the balance-of-payments deficit must have been met,

Table 30
Residual Estimates of the Net Changes in the International
Capital Position of the United States, 1890–1900
(*millions of dollars*)

Fiscal Years	Long-term Short-term Capital, Gold, Errors, Omissions	Long-term Short-term Capital, Errors, Omissions	Net Inflow (+) Outflow (−) of Funds on Gold Account	Kuznets' Calendar Year Long-term Short-term Capital, Gold, Errors, Omissions
1890	−116	−112	− 4	−115
1891	−147	− 79	− 68	− 26
1892	+ 32	+ 33	− 1	− 53
1893	−193	−105	− 88	− 41
1894	+ 75	+ 80	− 5	− 12
1895	− 98	− 68	− 30	−126
1896	−116	− 37	− 79	+ 86
1897	+ 18	− 27	+ 45	+116
1898	+295	+190	+105	+343
1899	+187	+136	+ 51	+201
1900	+187	+190	− 3	+315

Source: United Nations Research Memorandum no. 9, *Annual Figures for the Balance of Payments of the United States, 1850–1914,* prepared by Folke Hilgerdt.

Note: Except for merchandise and gold, the estimates are mainly interpolations of the estimates for 1850–1873, 1874–1895, and 1895–1914 by Bullock, Williams, and Tucker in *Review of Economic Statistics,* July, 1919. (Cited in National Bureau of Economic Research, Work Memorandum no. 31, *International Capital Movements,* Capital Requirements Study, pp. 60–64, 68–69.)

in a gross amount of much over $100 million, by foreign purchases of old United States securities, some purchases of new issues, and some degree of short-term loans.[30]

Whatever the source of foreign capital investment in the United States, it was not sufficient to meet all the claims on the economy arising from current transactions; hence the large unchecked flow of gold abroad. Probably there were large amounts of short-term capital flowing into the United States as interest rates here became more attractive. The period 1891–1895 in Great Britain was one of easy money with the bank rate around 2 percent, with the money market rates sometimes going below that. During the bank panic in 1893, British gold flowed to New York; perhaps changes in money rates here facilitated other flows of short-term funds which, in the context of the balance of payments, did not affect gold flows to the United States or if such flows were affected they were only sporadic and against the tide.[31]

In the fiscal year 1895, the net gold outflow was about $30 million, though in most months of the year there were small net inflows. The net outflows occurred in four months (July, August, December, and January) with the amount of outflow in January, 1895 ($24.4 million), almost totaling the net outflow for the entire year. The inflow after that month is partly related to the successful floating of the Morgan-Belmont syndicate project of a government gold loan of about $65 million. In the last half of 1894, as recovery made itself felt, imports increased while exports more or less held their own, this relationship increasing the pressure on the balance of payments and giving rise to large gold outflows. Over the entire fiscal year, net capital flows to the United States totaled almost $70 million, less than the total in fiscal 1893 but still a large sum which together with the totals on gold outflows indicated that there were severe balance-of-payments difficulties.[32]

The balance-of-payments situation, though eased somewhat in 1895, was still in disequilibrium. Gold flows from the United States and net capital flows into the country fell off a bit.

The British were not expanding capital exports, though they were beginning to expand capital issues as they started out of their depression. The lesser intensity in balance-of-payments difficulties for fiscal 1895, compared to fiscal 1893, was probably due more to the active trade balance of about $75 million than improved international capital flows.[33]

For the fiscal year 1896, there was, as in 1893, a large net outflow of gold, totaling almost $79 million. The net capital flow to the United States was, however, somewhat lower than in fiscal 1895, totaling only $87 million. Nevertheless, the fact of disequilibrium is clearly established. For the fiscal year, the gold flows occurred in concentrated amounts, almost equaling the year's total by the end of 1895. In only two months, February and March, 1896, was there a net inflow of gold.[34]

In the last half of 1895, difficulties arose regarding foreign capital movements. In the early autumn, there was a breakdown of speculation in London and Paris in African securities. This led to heavy selling by foreigners in the New York market to realize profits and use the funds abroad. From September, prices on the New York market eased considerably. In these circumstances, large amounts of gold had to flow abroad contra-seasonally.[35]

The last government gold loan of $100 million, floated in February, 1896, was easily oversubscribed and resulted in an easing of the outflow of gold. Europeans garnered some of this debt and despite the continuing contraction in the United States economy more of its securities were being purchased abroad during 1896.[36] It is quite likely that as the British capital market revived with expanded economic activity in 1895,[37] a parallel economic expansion in other European economies gave rise to expansions in their capital exports with possible favorable effects on the United States. Thus, while the domestic economy was going into the contractive phase of the business cycle in

1896, its balance-of-payments situation was becoming more favorable. And as the contraction spread, the situation was ameliorated: gold outflows first fell off and then a reverse inflow of gold developed; net capital inflows fell off somewhat in 1897, developing in 1898 into a capital outflow as manufacturing exports swelled the excess of merchandise exports.[38]

Our limits for capital movements showed a net increase in foreign investment of between $300 million and $500 million, with $400 million tentatively chosen as the estimate. Capital flowed from the United States in net amounts between $150 million and $250 million. The annual net flows analyzed showed that the net inflow from the end of 1892 to the end of 1897 was about $160 million. This amount falls about midway in our range of net capital inflows and outflows. The amount was not a large sum but was of strategic importance, reflecting depressed conditions throughout the world. This low level of net capital inflow perforce made more critical economic conditions in the contracting economy, especially as certain other items in the balance of payments increased our obligations abroad.[39]

Summary

During the depression, the balance of payments was in disequilibrium. The domestic economy was unable to pay for its merchandise and invisible imports with its merchandise exports and foreign funds made available by foreign investments in its enterprise. To make up the imbalance, the economy was forced, almost continuously from 1892 to 1896, to export gold. Important changes in the balance of payments, resulting from economic changes in the United States and abroad, led to these consequences. The excess of merchandise exports persisted throughout the depression, acting as a cycle stabilizer. Payments abroad for interest and dividends owed foreign creditors and for shipping services fell off, easing the payments situation. But this was more than offset by increased payments abroad due to tourist expenditures and an increase in net remittances abroad. Another crucial decline was in foreign investment in the economy, resulting from depressed conditions abroad and unfavorable expectations in the United States. In these circumstances, the flows abroad were a forced consequence.

NOTES

1. Attempts at such a reconstruction meet with difficulties. Reliable monthly data on exports and imports, broken down into significant classifications, make possible a thorough analysis of this part of the balance of payments. Data on the remainder of the balance of payments, however, are not as detailed or reliable. There are scattered statistics on foreign investment in the United States and some information on changes in investment as well as disinvestment. Other items in the invisible account can only be roughly estimated by years, let alone be set up in quarterly or monthly figures. Such important factors as short-term investment and tourist expenditures abroad must be very roughly guessed at. A recent project of the United Nations yields a series of annual data on the United States balance of payments broken down into major categories. They represent, in the main, interpolations based on more reliable data available for certain years. With Kuznets' data on residual estimates in the balance of payments and other scattered material on different aspects of the balance of payments, some reconstruction of the situation during the nineties is possible. The data must be used carefully since their assumptions may be questionable. For example, the United Nations estimate of freight payments seems off by a wide mark by this writer's calculations. See below. Cf. United Nations, Department of Economic Affairs, Division of Economic Stability and Development. Research Memorandum No. 9, *Annual Figures for the Balance of Payments, 1850–1914*, prepared by Folke Hilgerdt; National Bureau of Economic Research, *Capital Requirements Study*, Work Memo. No. 31, Vol. 1, *International Capital Movements*, Vol. 1, "Across United States Borders," Part 1, Solomon Fabricant, "Highlights and Questions;" Part 2, Robert E. Lipsey, "A Summary of Available Statistics," Capital Requirements Study, pp. 60–64, 68–69.

2. *Historical Statistics,* p. 244; U.S., Bureau of Foreign and Domestic Commerce, *Monthly Summary of Imports and Exports,* 1893–1900.

3. *Historical Statistics,* p. 244; U.S., Bureau of Domestic Commerce, *Monthly Summary of Imports and Exports,* 1893–1900.

4. Ibid.

5. Ibid.

6. R. S. Tucker, J. H. Williams, and C. J. Bullock, "The Balance of

Trade of The United States," *Review of Economic Statistics* 1 (July, 1919): 215 ff; Cleona Lewis, *America's Stake in International Investments,* pp. 76–113; Paul A. Dickens, "The Transition Period in American International Financing: 1897 to 1914," pp. 37–39.

7. Lewis, *America's Stake in Investments,* pp. 332–338; Dickens, "Transition Period," pp. 40–44.

8. Cf. Dickens, "Transition Period," pp. 37–44; N. Bacon, "American International Indebtedness," *Yale Review* (November, 1900); Lewis, *America's Stake in Investments.*

9. Cleona Lewis' estimates, made in the 1930s, are somewhat higher than those which Nathaniel Bacon made in 1899 and 1900. Looking at both estimates gives the analyst some notions as to the order of magnitude of foreign and United States investment after the depression. Lewis' estimates are for the end of 1897 and are the basis of our calculations though, in addition, we must take into account Bacon's figures for January 1, 1899. See Lewis, *America's Stake in International Investments,* pp. 184–200, 247, 249, 256, 266, 284, 301, 315–320.

10. The major difference in the estimates is to be found in the amount attributed to investment in Europe. Lewis' estimate is about $150 million while that of Bacon is only $10 million with a possible total of about $50 million if one of his categories, "Life Insurance guarantee investment," refers to Europe. See Bacon, "American International Indebtedness," p. 276.

11. Lewis, *America's Stake in International Investments,* p. 442.

12. U.S., Bureau of Foreign and Domestic Commerce, *Monthly Summary of Imports and Exports,* December, 1893, pp. 403–408; December, 1896, pp. 679–700; December, 1898, pp. 1321 ff.

13. U.S., Bureau of Foreign and Domestic Commerce, *Monthly Summary of Imports and Exports,* December, 1893, pp. 403–408; December, 1896, pp. 679–700; December, 1898, pp. 1321 ff.

14. Ibid.

15. Cf. Bullock, Williams, and Tucker, "Balance of Trade of the U.S." pp. 215 ff. *Economist* (London), Supplement, "Commercial History and Review," 1890–1897.

16. It is unfortunate that the available data are mainly interpolations between figures which are themselves not firmly established. Even assuming that these figures are correct, can the heroic assumption be made that the interpolations are close to the facts? Cyclical or random fluctuations are obscured by any interpolation. Nevertheless, in the absence of other, more reliable data, these data will have to be used. Where the data seem at variance with available evidence, our own estimates or qualifications are introduced.

17. A contemporary in a brief survey of the United States balance of payments estimated dividend and interest payments for 1893–1894 at a minimum of $75 million. His estimates, including the other major invisible items, totaled $350 million, an amount attacked as too high by other financial commentators, and one which according to Table 27 was too

high by a wide margin. See A. S. Heidelbach, "Why Gold Is Imported", *Forum* (February, 1895): 647–651.

18. Heidelbach, "Why Gold Is Imported," pp. 647–651.

19. See Erich W. Zimmerman, *Ocean Shipping*, p. 493, for changes in freight rates during the nineties. Table 28 indicates that net freight payments declined by a sizable amount in fiscal 1894 while the increases for fiscal 1894 left the net below the predepression level. It seems warranted to infer that as imports declined so did net freight payments, easing somewhat balance-of-payments difficulties.

20. The total number of passengers departing for foreign countries in other than cabin class increased for 1894 and 1895 by 40 percent and 60 percent, respectively, over 1893.

21. Walter F. Willcox, ed., *International Migrations* 1, 471; *Historical Statistics*, p. 33.

22. Though figures are not available for the period 1892–1896, some notion of foreign claims for insurance may be obtained. It is not likely that the figures for the period 1892–1896 were very much less than those in the subsequent years. One indication of insurance development is found in statistics on the conditions of branches of foreign marine, fire, life, and casualty companies. Their assets and liabilities (representing mainly insurance coverage) increased throughout the nineties. The depression did not cause any decline in assets and liabilities. While these data only cover a part of all foreign insurance, they give some idea of the trend among almost fifty companies. See New York State, Insurance Department, *Annual Report of the Superintendent*, 1893–99, Part II, Table X; 1893–96, Part I, Table IX, Table XI; 1897–98, Table V, Table VI.

23. *Historical Statistics*, p. 244.

24. U.S., Bureau of Foreign and Domestic Commerce, *Monthly Summary of Imports and Exports of the United States*, 1893–1899.

25. Seventy-five percent of foreign investment in the United States came from Great Britain, so that our task of tracing major changes in the international capital market may be safely limited to that country without distorting unduly the overall capital picture. See Lewis, *America's Stake in Investments*, pp. 78–113. The Appendix at the end of this chapter traces changes in British capital issue and export.

26. Kuznets's calendar-year net flows in Table 30 differ in detail from these United Nations figures. The totals, however, for revival years are about the same. See Table 30.

27. These gold loans represented, in effect, an underwriting by the government of foreign investment in the United States. Foreign investors apparently could only be induced to invest large amounts during the depression by having the government guarantee that there would be a steady return. European investors were wary of equity or security investments in United States enterprises, such as railroads and breweries, where "mismanagement" and bankruptcies threatened their capital. In a sense, the government loans "socialized" the risk of investing and thus

were a form of government intervention in the international capital market—an intervention necessary to maintain both the Treasury gold reserve and the flow of investment into United States industries.

28. For example, the number of foreign stockholders in the Union Pacific Railroad increased from the end of 1892 to the end of 1893 by over 86,000—most of the new stockholders being Dutch—to a total of over 287,000. It is hardly likely that this increase took place in the early months of 1893, when the stock market was at first cautious and then in a panic.

29. *Historical Statistics,* p. 244; *Chronicle,* April 28, 1894, pp. 700–701; U.S., Bureau of Foreign and Domestic Commerce, *Monthly Summary of Imports and Exports,* January, 1898, p. 1088; ibid., 1893–1898; A. D. Noyes, *Forty Years of American Finance,* pp. 210 ff.

30. *Historical Statistics,* p. 244; U.S., Bureau of Foreign and Domestic Commerce, *Monthly Summary of Imports and Exports,* January, 1898, p. 1088.

31. Cf. W. W. Rostow, "British Trade Fluctuations, 1868–1896," pp. 349–350.

32. This total of net capital inflow must be imputed partly to foreign purchases of United States government bonds issued early in 1895, short-term flows to the New York money market and other purchases by foreigners of new and old United States securities. In the last quarter of 1894, new capital issues in the British market totaled almost half as much as for the year while in the first half of 1895 such issues rose to a rate of over £104 a year—the actual amount issued in 1895. The net export of capital, however, does not seem to have increased: this was a period in which the low point was reached—£40 million in 1894 and again in 1895. Moreover, at this time British capital was being attracted to more highly profitable markets, such as gold mining in Africa.

33. *Historical Statistics,* p. 244; U.S., Bureau of Foreign and Domestic Commerce, *Monthly Summary of Imports* and *Exports,* January, 1898, p. 1088; *Economist* (London), Supplement: "Commercial History and Review of 1898," February 18, 1899, pp. 5–6; Noyes, *American Finance,* pp. 231 ff.; Albert H. Imlah, "British Balance of Payments and Export of Capital, 1816–1913," *Economic History Review,* 5 (1952):238.

34. The government gold loan of 1895 in which the Belmont-Morgan syndicate undertook to keep gold from flowing abroad had aided in the first half of 1895. But, in the summer, the exchange rates were too high to forestall further the outflow of gold and once merchants outside the syndicate used their commercial connections in Europe to facilitate the export of gold, the syndicate had to abandon its position.

35. Early in 1895, the New York stock market started upward and some foreign investors were attracted to it. As the market continued to rise, some foreigners realized profits.

36. Coincident with the large gold outflows at the end of 1895 there was a contraction, temporary in nature, in the amount of new capital

issues on the British market. But with the new year new British capital issues pushed forward again.

37. British net capital exports in 1896 rose 45 percent over the trough level of 1895 to almost £60 million.

38. *Historical Statistics,* p. 244; U.S., Bureau of Foreign and Domestic Commerce, *Monthly Summary of Imports and Exports,* January, 1898, p. 1088; Noyes, *American Finance,* pp. 231 ff; Imlah, "British Balance of Payments and Export of Capital," p. 238.

39. Foreign capital inflow had come mainly to be invested in railroads whose capital expansion generated investment in building, machine and iron and steel industries. The contractions in these areas during the depression were of great moment in the general stagnation of investment.

Appendix to Chapter 5
British Capital Issues

A brief survey of British capital issues in the period under review highlights important changes in this significant capital market. Below are listed the values of the new capital issues during the nineties:[1]

Year	Capital Issues
1890	£142.6 million
1891	104.6
1892	81.1
1893	49.1
1894	91.8
1895	104.7
1896	152.8
1897	157.3
1898	150.2

The severe contraction in British capital movements coincided with the balance-of-payments difficulties of the United States and the worst part of the depression period. An analysis

of the proportion of these capital issues going abroad emphasizes the retrenchment in British investment as it affected foreign
areas and the United States in particular. In 1891, a year of
moderately high capital issue, about one quarter of total British
capital investment went abroad with much of it going to the
United States. For 1893, the trough year in investment, about
one-fifth of the total went abroad—amounting to about 10 million pounds, only two-fifths of the 1891 investment abroad.

Although exact dates on amounts going to the different investment areas abroad have not been unearthed, the implications for investment in the United States are clear. If the great
concern on the part of British investors about the plight of
United States railroads during the depression and if the doubts
many foreign investors raised about our monetary policy are
seen in the context of the contraction in British foreign investment, contraction in foreign investment in the United States was
inevitable.[2] One foreign journal's comments reflect this syndrome:

> The year [1893] has been a disastrous one for American railroads.
> The industrial and monetary crisis which preceded the repeal
> of the Sherman Silver Act, by increasing the difficulty of carry-
> ing the heavy floating debts with which American railways are
> burdened, forced a number of them into the hands of receivers.
> And in connection with some of these receiverships there were
> proceedings which have demonstrated with renewed force . . .
> the unsuitability of these securities for investment purposes. . .[3]

Though the amount of new capital issues is a helpful indicator of fluctuations in the British capital market, a more useful
series is that of changes in net capital abroad. These changes represent new capital investment abroad, an aggregate which
more directly answers the question of what happened to the flow
of capital from one of the major sources in the international
capital market. Following is the net capital flowing abroad from
Britain from 1890 to 1898, in millions of pounds:

Year	Net Capital
1890	£98 million
1891	69
1892	60
1893	55
1894	40
1895	40
1896	58
1897	43
1898	25

These data trace the significant decline of capital flowing abroad from 1890 to 1895, the cumulative effect growing as the United States entered the depression. The decline was about 60 percent. This slackening in British foreign investment had its adverse effects on the United States economy.[4]

If these facts alone described the international capital market, they would support the inference that continuing investment in United States securities and enterprise declined markedly. There are additional facts which are consistent with significant decline in foreign capital investment during the depression. As British foreign investment contracted, proportionately less of what was invested abroad went to the United States. New and more attractive areas for investment such as South Africa were opening up while many British investors were evidencing dissatisfaction with the way United States management operated. The result probably was not only a decline in investment in the United States on cyclical grounds but also because of the greater attraction of South Africa where mining ventures were ripening.

Not only did British investment fall off in the United States, but there is also evidence that early in the nineties there was considerable disinvestment by Britons. The gloomy prediction in the *Statist* in the summer of 1892 that there would be a gold run and bank panic in the United States reflected a growing fear on the part of many British investors. In the summer of 1892, therefore, it is not surprising that the *Commercial and Financial Chronicle* reported the sellout by London of floating supplies of United States stocks.[5] A French observer, commenting on the international capital market for 1892, pointed to the disinvestment under way: "L'Europe a revendu d' énormes quantités de titres, qui ont servi à payer les céréales . . . mais . . . elle n'a pas montre de dispositions à rependre et à racheter. Le marché américain a besoin de l'appui de l'Europe et la reserve, l'abstention de celle-ci a contribué a l'inactivité du Stock-Exchange." [6]

In the United States, the impact of foreign disinvestment was recognized early and officially when the Chief of the Bureau of Statistics of the Treasury Department, Worthington C. Ford, pointed "to the withdrawal of large sums of foreign capital . . . while foreign investors have made limited purchases in our stock and investment markets, except . . . [under] special inducement." [7]

This development "was continued, even aggravated, in 1893." Taking into account foreign disinvestment, dividend payments to foreigners, and foreign investment in the United States, Ford estimated that the net capital flow amounted to over $100 million for the fiscal year 1893. This reduced capital inflow, starting before the depression began, continued into the depression, and though there were reverse flows under special conditions which stimulated investment disinvestment, it remained a principal factor in the balance-of-payments disequilibrium which plagued the economy during the depression.

NOTES

1. *Economist* (London), Supplement, "Commercial History and Review of 1893, February 17, 1894, p. 6; ibid., 1898, February 18, 1899, p. 506.
2. Ibid., February 17, 1894, p. 6.

3. Ibid.

4. Albert H. Imlah, "British Balance of Payments and Export of Capital, 1816–1913," *Economic History Review,* 5 (1952): 238.

5. *Bankers Magazine & Statistical Register,* November, 1892, p. 338; *Chronicle,* August 6, 1892, pp. 196–198.

6. Arthur Rafolovich, *Le Marché Financier 1892,* pp. 47–48.

7. U.S. Bureau of Statistics, *The Foreign Commerce and Navigation of the United States for the Year Ending June 30, 1893,* pp. xxiii–xxiv.

6

Monetary Policies and Government Fiscal Operations in the Depression

In most widely published contemporary evaluations of economic events including the depression, major emphasis has been placed on the monetary "causes." Sharp polemical battle was joined over the merits of bimetallism and monometallism and the therapeutic possibilities of either standard in curing the great malady of the day—declining prices or the crisis of lost confidence in the system, according to the polemicist's point of view. Once the panic was upon the country in 1893, the disagreements became more and more vitriolic and explanations of the events were usually trumpeted in more grossly oversimplified monetary terms. Both the panic itself and the depression which followed were blamed on the Sherman Silver Purchase Act of 1890 by leaders of many groups—from President Cleveland to a spokesman for the New York Chamber of Commerce.[1]

The more sophisticated opponents of the govenment's silver policy, as represented in statements of the New York Chamber of Commerce and the *Commercial and Financial Chronicle*, related the crisis to loss of confidence arising from fear that the gold standard would be repudiated. As a consequence, they averred, business was distressed, money was withdrawn from circulation, mills were closed, unemployment grew, interest rates became unfavorable for business—these were the dislocating effects blamed on the Sherman Act.[2] Much of the business community saw the financial and commercial troubles of the times as a direct result of the Sherman Act, and many other groups in the community agreed with this interpretation. In the silverite camp and among farmer groups, this view was vigorously rejected. They blamed poor economic conditions on an inadequate supply of money and heralded free silver as a panacea.[3]

While it goes without saying that to see the panic and depression as direct results of the Sherman Act is an oversimplification, one cannot reject out of hand implication that the silver purchase policy and its related monetary and financial effects might have been variables of importance in shaping the depression. It is necessary to review carefully the monetary forces at work in order to see just what the role of monetary factors was and to get a better perspective of how other important variables shaped the depression.

Some notion of the monetary and banking institutions is helpful in weighing the impact of monetary factors. The National Banking Act attempted to provide a sound commercial banking setup to meet the needs of an expanding industrial economy whose markets had broken through the narrow, localized, and regionalized framework characteristic of the early part of the century. Toward this end, reserves were funneled into the money centers—New York City in particular; the currency was in effect guaranteed and made uniform in form and value throughout the country; general standards of bank supervision and examination were made the responsibility of a federal officer, the Comptroller of the Currency; and so on. These banking reforms were a great advance over the uncoordinated type of banking prevailing from 1833 to 1862.[4]

Depsite these reforms, certain inadequacies in the banking system resulted: the system was characterized by instability and inelasticity of currency issue. The instability was reflected in the large number of bank suspensions whenever credit stringency was severe. Pyramiding of reserves in the money centers made such suspensions inevitable when demands for liquid funds in the interior became heavy. Interior banks, with reserves in faraway cities, often were forced to suspend before their reserves were returned. No reservior of funds for such emergencies existed. Moreover, a sudden sharp drain of funds from New York City banks which held reserves of interior banks usually resulted in a marked contraction in call loans with concomitant sharp declines in stock prices as shares were dumped to meet call-loan demands. This syndrome often reached proportions warranting the term "panic." [5]

As for inelasticity of currency issue, the expansion and contraction of national bank notes were not necessarily related to expanding and contracting needs of the business community for money. Since bank notes could only be issued when backed by government bonds, banks would only issue notes when government bond market conditions were favorable. The total of bank notes, moreover, was restricted by the total funded public debt. When the debt was reduced, the potential total issue of notes was contracted. Thus, because of profit considerations, notes were often issued at times when expansion of money was not required, and at other times, when such expansion was necessary for expanding business needs, the banks did not issue notes.[6]

The monetary mechanism's characteristic of instability was also affected by the government's currency policy. The purchase of silver through the issuance of full legal-tender Treasury notes neutralized, in some measure, the effects of gold outflows. Instead of such outflows forcing a contraction in credit and prices, legal reserves were maintained when the lost gold was replaced by the newly issued Treasury notes. For example, as gold flowed into the United States, the decline in reserves of the banks, they replenished those reserves by using newly issued Treasury notes to regain the gold lost through redemption at the Treasury, or by keeping the Treasury notes as part of their reserves. In the end, this process seriously depleted the Treasury's gold reserve. These interrelationships, then, did not make for an optimal or consistent set of banking and monetary conditions under the rules of the gold standard. To the extent that the Treasury's note issue upset the gold applecart, it postponed the deflationary effects of gold exports.[7]

Instability in the national banking system showed its extremes during periods of crisis, when bank suspensions and failures increased sharply in incidence. Such inherent instability in banking meant that the ordinary difficulties of economic contraction were aggravated by banking complications. Table 31 summarizes bank suspensions[8] during the decade of the nineties. From this table, we see that the average rate of suspensions during the nineties was about 15 per thousand banks in operation—midway between the rates of the seventies and eighties. The incidence during the depression years was very high, indicating the serious character of the contraction.

The Supply of Money

In the period, the economy was growing rapidly and credit and monetary needs perforce were also changing. Bank notes were being replaced in importance by demand deposits as the most widely used medium of exchange.[9] The more general ac-

Table 31
Bank Suspensions in the United States, 1890–1900

Year	Total Suspensions[a]	National Banks	State Banks	Private Banks	Total Number of banks[b]
1890	36	6	30	—	8,201
1891	60	16	44	—	8,641
1892	80	12	32	36	9,336
1893	491	69	228	194	9,492
1894	83	23	39	21	9,508
1895	110	34	51	25	9,818
1896	141	34	66	41	9,469
1897	139	28	64	47	9,457
1898	63	11	19	33	9,500
1899	32	10	8	14	9,732
1900	35	5	14	16	10,382

Source: U.S., Bureau of the Census, Historical Statistics, pp. 262, 273.

(a) Bank failures were sharply lower than suspensions. For example, in 1893, failures totaled about 65, and the total capital of failed banks amounted to $10.9 million.

(b) Figures for 1890 and 1891 are for fiscal years.

ceptance of checks reflected the changing nature of banking and monetary institutions; use of checks developed out of a more highly organized national market with more adequate clearing facilities being provided in cities.[10] In analyzing important changes which occurred during the depression, we trace fluctuations in the money supply in this framework of changing monetary and banking institutions, both in terms of the broad secular changes under way and the cyclical changes reflecting short-run interactions of the economy.

STOCK OF LEGAL MONEY

Changes in the stock of legal money in the United States are listed in Table 32. The increase in the total amount of money during the nineties was only slightly less, relatively, than that during the eighties when it was about 42 percent, compared to just under 40 percent for the nineties. In the seventies, the increase amounted to about 64 percent.

Table 32 also indicates that the supply of legal-tender money in the years immediately preceding the depression did not increase greatly, nor was there a sharp decline in the supply of money during the depression. The moderate increase in the total supply of legal money prior to the depression was followed by a slight ebb in that supply in the months immediately preceding the contraction in economic activity. Then there was a moderate

Table 32
Distribution of Stock of Money
in the United States, 1890–1900
(*millions of dollars*)

Year	Total Money	Money in Treasury	Money in Reporting Banks	Money Not in Treasury or Banks	Money Outside Treasury
1890	1,685	256	488	941	1,429
1891	1,678	180	498	999	1,497
1892	1,752	151	586	1,015	1,601
1893	1,739	142	516	1,081	1,597
1894	1,805	144	689	972	1,661
1895	1,819	217	631	972	1,602
1896	1,800	293	532	975	1,506
1897	1,906	266	628	1,012	1,640
1898	2,073	236	688	1,150	1,838
1899	2,190	286	723	1,181	1,904
1900	2,340	285	750	1,305	2,055

Source: U.S., National Monetary Commission, *Statistics for the United States, 1867–1909,* 21:155.
Note: The information given is for date closest to June 30 of each year.

increase until the trough of the depression was reached in June, 1894, when the total amounted to $1,805 million. For the next two years, the money supply remained relatively stable and then at the trough of the next cycle—June, 1897—there was another moderate increase. Once the economy began its recovery, the total money supply advanced at a steady rate.[11]

Money in circulation remained fairly stable as a total from 1890 until the middle of 1897 except for the last five months of 1893, when the amount increased moderately—probably due to hoarding. Monthly data show that the amount of money outside the Treasury and the banks increased seasonally at the end of 1892 and was stable for the first half of 1893. At the end of 1895, just prior to the downturn, the amount was stable; in 1896, there were slight declines. After the middle of 1897, the amount in circulation increased appreciably. It is difficult to find any basis in these data for supporting the notion that economic contraction resulted from an inadequate supply of legal money, as a short-term situation.[12]

DEMAND DEPOSITS, BANK NOTES, AND LOANS

Table 33 provides a more complete view of the variations in the supply of money by giving us data on demand deposits.[13] other deposits, national bank notes, and loans. Throughout the depression, fluctuations in the quantity of demand deposits were cyclical. The low point did not come at the cycle trough in June, 1894, but a year earlier.[14] This reflected the banking difficulties of the panic period when bank suspensions and pressures on reserves forced contraction in deposits so that new loans were not easily forthcoming. After the 1894 trough, demand deposits rose and, in the middle of 1895, while economic expansion was going on, demand deposits and loans reached levels approximating those of earlier prosperity periods. By the middle of 1896, with a new contraction in process, demand deposits slackened off again and a year later, at the 1897 trough, they were only slightly higher before their sharp increase in rhythm with the growing recovery of the economy. The June, 1897, level of demand deposits was about equal to that of June, 1892, while the level of loans in June, 1897, was only slightly below that of June, 1892.

Table 33
Bank Deposits, Loans, and National Bank Notes, 1890–1900
(*millions of dollars*)

Year	Total Deposits Adjusted	Demand Deposits Adjusted[a]	U.S. Government Deposits	Total	Commercial Banks[b]	Mutual Savings Banks	Loans	National Bank Notes in Circulation
1890	n.a.[c]	n.a.	n.a.	n.a.	n.a.	n.a.	3,854	182
1891	n.a.	n.a.	n.a.	n.a.	n.a.	n.a.	4,031	162
1892	4,823	2,880	14	1,929	470	1,459	4,337	167
1893	4,787	2,766	14	2,007	456	1,551	4,369	175
1894	4,815	2,807	14	1,994	456	1,538	4,085	200
1895	5,061	2,960	13	2,088	491	1,597	4,269	207
1896	5,074	2,839	15	2,220	532	1,688	4,251	215
1897	5,192	2,871	16	2,305	568	1,737	4,216	226
1898	5,882	3,432	53	2,397	572	1,825	4,652	223
1899	6,855	4,162	75	2,617	n.a.	n.a.	5,172	238
1900	7,534	4,420	99	3,015	n.a.	n.a.	5,658	300

Source: Historical Statistics, pp. 262, 275, 277; U.S., Board of Governors, Federal Reserve System, *Banking and Monetary Statistics*, p. 34.

Note: The amounts given are for dates closest to June 30 of each year.

(a) Includes demand deposits other than interbank deposits, government deposits, and cash items in collection.

(b) Except interbank time deposits.

(c) Not available.

National bank note circulation increased throughout the depression period, regardless of the variations in business activity. This was due in large measure to the note-issue provisions of the National Banking Act. Since national bank note issue was tied to the government bond market, expansion of bank notes usually reflected declining government bond prices which made bank note issue profitable. Therefore, despite the decreased need for money in the economy as business contracted and stagnated, the national banks expanded note issues. Savings banks, which needed more cash due to customers' withdrawals in the summer of 1893, were able to sell government bonds to the national commercial banks whose issuance of national bank notes replenished savings and commercial banks' supplies of cash. This acted as a counter-cyclical monetary force, but its impact was very limited.[15]

Time deposits were fairly stable during the first phase of the depression. With the recovery of 1895, however, there was a steady increase in total time deposits, ranging from 3.5 to 7.5 percent in the last years of the depression. These increases represented increased savings, which grew despite the depressed conditions of the economy in 1896 and 1897. The sharp increase after 1898 suggests that the tendency for savings to grow throughout the decade was retarded by the sharp economic contraction. Once the depression spent itself, savings increased sharply as greater economic activity enhanced income receipts.

During the depression, there was no sharp curtailment of the money forms used by business and consumers except during the banking panic. Fluctuations in that supply varied with the business cycle. When business activity expanded, the money supply did likewise, growing in moderate amounts; when business activity contracted, there was a tendency for the money supply to do likewise. National bank notes were an exception. Other things being equal, it seems that the supply of money was adequate prior to the depression. When depression conditions subsided, the amounts of money expanded readily.

BANK RESERVES

The basis of deposit expansion was the reserves held by the commercial banks. Under the National Banking Act, the fixed reserve requirement for banks other than "country banks" was 25 percent.[16] By examining the availability of reserves, we may be able to decide whether there was actually a shortage before or during the depression. To the extent that the absolute amount of reserves contracted appreciably, the supply of money was restricted.[17]

Table 34 records fluctuations in loans, deposits, and actual reserve ratios of the New York clearinghouse banks. The reserve ratios which they maintained throughout the nineties and during most of the depression met the requirements of the law. Actually, these ratios increased once the banking panic subsided, and during the trough periods of the depression—June, 1894, and June, 1897—they were over 30 percent.[18]

Although reserve ratios merely reflect proportions and do not indicate whether the monetary base was contracting, absolute amounts of reserves in specie and legal tender do give us data making possible an answer to that question. From Table 34, we see that the amount of reserves did decline during 1893 by almost 9 percent.[19] The decline during July and August, 1893, was much greater: the August reserve level was 46 percent below the average for 1892. Leaving out this period of extreme monetary stringency, during which cash was at a premium and gold flowed abroad from the reserves of the New York City New York City banks from 1892 to the second quarter of 1893 —a low point in reserves—amounted to 25 percent. This occurred after the general downturn in business conditions, though in the last quarter of 1892 reserves in the New York City banks were about $117 million—17 percent below the 1892 average. At the end of 1895—just before business began its downward movement again—reserves were about $128 million, or about 22 percent below the 1895 average. In the last quarter of 1892, the reserve ratio approached 25 percent in October and then rose over 26 percent. In the last quarter of 1895, the ratio was over 28 percent. Thus, in the period prior to the downturn

Table 34
**Reserve and Loan Positions of New York City
Clearing-House Banks, 1890–1900**

(*millions of dollars*)

Year	Loans	Net Deposits	Specie & Legal Tender	Reserve Ratio
1890	399.8	404.3	104.4	25.7
1891	400.9	409.3	114.5	28.0
1892	472.9	502.4	141.7	28.0
1893	419.4	433.4	130.1	29.7 [a]
1894	470.9	568.9	213.5	37.6
1895	497.6	543.3	164.1	30.2
1896	463.8	482.5	142.0	29.4
1897	528.6	591.1	189.1	31.5
1898	636.9	729.8	213.4	29.3
1899	739.9	844.6	227.9	26.9
1900	779.5	852.8	228.8	26.6

Source: U.S., National Monetary Commission, *Statistics for the U.S.,* 21:74, 98–108.

Note: The national banks in New York City held about 17 percent of all the loans made by national banks in the United States from 1893 to 1897. The amounts given are averages for each year.

(a) During 1893, for the period of July and August, reserves declined below the legal minimum, reaching a low of 20 percent during August when the banking panic was running its course.

starting in January, 1893, there was moderate monetary stringency, and in the period before the downturn in December, 1895, there was considerable stringency though the reserve ratio was above 25 percent.[20]

Loans and deposits paralleled variations in reserves. While specie and legal tender declined about 9 percent from 1892 to 1893, deposits decreased about 13.5 percent and loans contracted by almost 11 percent.[21] During the fourth quarter of 1892, just prior to the downturn in business, loans were at a level approximating $440 million, about 7 percent below the year's average. Deposits, in the same period, were about $445 million—about 9 percent below the 1892 average. These declines were counterseasonal and indicate that there was tightening of credit conditions just before the business downturn took place. At the trough of the depression—June, 1894—loans, deposits, and reserves were all at levels on a par with the year's average, levels above those prevailing at the end of 1892 by some 5 percent for loans, 25 percent for deposits, and 47 percent for reserves. This reflected, in some measure, the inflow of cash into banks as public confidence grew and more bank money was used. The failure of loans to respond is evidence of the widespread low level of business activity.[22]

In the economic contraction commencing at the end of 1895, the decline in specie and legal tender reserves, loans and deposits varied somewhat from that in 1893. Reserves declined most sharply, by about 13.5 percent, while deposits and loans decreased less sharply, by 11 and almost 7 percent, respectively. At the end of 1895, just before contraction commenced, loans were at a level approximating the average for the year, though off slightly from the midyear level. Deposits were off, for the same period, by about 5 percent from the year's average, likewise having declined from midyear levels. Reserves, in the fourth quarter of 1895, were off by about 8.5 percent from the yearly average, their decline from the midyear levels being similar to that of loans and deposits. Here, too, as in 1892, credit restriction preceded business contraction with reserves declining more sharply from 1895 to 1896 than they had from 1892 to 1893.[23]

GOLD FLOWS

Since specie and its representative forms—silver and gold certificates—were the major portion of bank reserves, some notion of the movement of gold—the preponderant part of specie and the only money form acceptable in Europe for clearing payments—is necessary to see fluctuations in the money supply more clearly. The period prior to the depression, we have seen, was one of large net outflows of gold, mainly to Europe. From 1890 to 1897, gold flowed out each year, except for 1896 when net imports amounted to almost $29 million. The net outflow for these years was:

Year	Net Outflow
1890	$ 9.0 million
1891	43.8
1892	62.1
1893	9.5
1894	78.9
1895	73.4
1897	16.1

Gold production in the United States during the nineties increased annually. In 1890, it totaled $32.8 million; by 1897, the total had increased to $57.4 million. For the years 1891, 1892, 1894, and 1895, net gold exports exceeded by an appreciable amount the total gold production of the economy. While this gold drain from the economy forced some contraction in bank reserves, the impact of gold production mitigated the full effects of the outflow.[24]

During 1892, gold outflows were concentrated in the second and third quarters, with $26.9 and $18.0 million flowing out, respectively. In the last quarter, $10.8 million flowed out. These large outflows affected both the reserves of New York City banks and the Treasury gold reserve. In the first two months of 1893, over $29 million in gold was shipped abroad in net terms. This outflow continued with $16.2 and $14.9 million in net exports for the months of March and April. In May, there was a net outflow of only $1.8 million. For the next five months, there were net imports in gold totaling over $54 million.[25] In December, there was a net outflow of $2.2 million. From July, 1892, through June, 1893, the total net outflow was over $90 million, affecting greatly both the Treasury gold reserve and banks' gold holdings and reserves. To meet the demand for gold necessary to satisfy claims abroad, the New York City banks obtained gold by presenting legal tenders for redemption in gold at the Treasury, continuing the drain on the dwindling gold reserve of the Treasury. One historian of the period observed that "from June, 1892, throughout the troubled years which followed, almost every dollar of gold exported from the United States was obtained on note redemption from the Treasury." [26]

While the heavy gold drain in fiscal year 1893 undoubtedly worked difficulties on domestic banks by drawing down their reserves and thus braking industrial and commercial activity, the outflow of gold in 1894 and 1895 did not adversely affect banks' reserves for any length of time. The adverse effect was mainly upon the Treasury, whose gold reserves were constantly impaired as banks replenished their exported gold by presenting Treasury notes, and as the Treasury paid for its deficits by drawing on gold holdings. This latter factor assumed more importance from the summer of 1893 on. By the end of the year, the Treasury's gold reserve was about $80 million—$20 million below the statutory limit. The main adverse impact on bank reserves had passed, but the gold outflow continued and disrupted Treasury financing.[27]

During the closing months of 1895, when bank reserves contracted, net gold exports were high, totaling over $60 million for the last six months of the year. As we have seen above, the decline in reserves was considerable, and it seems clear that the outflow had some adverse effect on availability of money. At the end of 1895, the Treasury's gold reserve once again declined below the $100 million level and reached $63 million by the end of the year. Continued deficits accounted mainly for the decline in gold holdings. The Morgan-Belmont bond syndicate's operations during the year brought some relief to the Treasury but, as it drew to a close, the old problem of gold outflow became serious again, complicating the monetary picture.[28]

INTEREST RATES

We have seen that loans, deposits, and reserves contracted in some measure late in 1892 and late in 1895. On the average, short-term interest rates (stock exchange renewal call loans, ninety-day time loans, and prime commercial paper, four to six months) were lower during 1892 than during the preceding years, while the average rates in 1895 were slightly higher than in 1894—a depression year. For our purposes, however, these annual rates are hardly of assistance. We must examine the rate schedules on a shorter period basis.[29]

A careful analysis of weekly loan and discount rates for the crucial periods is revealing. Even a glance at the data shows that starting in August and September, 1892, the entire rate schedule started to rise. Table 35 focuses on the changes in rates from August to December during which, for the most part, the increase was continuous. Even allowing for the seasonal factor wherein rates rose at the end of the year, the increases from

August to September and then to December represented significant changes in the cost of borrowing, which must have had an important bearing on some entrepreneurs' production decisions.

The high short-term interest rates at the end of 1892 persisted throughout most of 1893. During the banking crisis in the summer of 1893, many of the rates rose much higher, but thereafter they eased considerably and by the end of the year they were at moderately low levels. During 1894, the rate structure remained low with funds going unwanted. At the year's end,

Table 35
Weekly Loan and Discount Rates, New York Market, 1892

	Stock Exchange Call Loans	Time Loans			Commercial Paper Four to Six Months	
		30-Day	90-Day	6-Month	Double-Name	Single-Name
August low	1.5%	2%	2.5%	3.5%	3.75%	4.25%
December low	4.5	4	5	5.5	5.25	5.5
December high	10	6	6	6	6	6

Source: U.S., National Monetary Commission, *Statistics for the U.S.* 21:121.

there was a slight rise in rates, but the new level was no higher than for August, 1892. That level persisted through most of 1895, but by August there were signs of an upward movement and for the remainder of the year rates advanced, reaching highs on a par with the 1892 highs shown for December, 1892, in Table 35. Rates for call loans at the New York Stock exchange shot up in the near-panic atmosphere attending President Cleveland's message on the Venezuelan boundary dispute in mid-December. These increases in short-term interest rates occurred concomitantly with contractions in deposits, loans, and bank reserves.[30]

After the downturn in business of the new year, short-term interest rates remained at their December, 1895, high level for most of that year. This undoubtedly was a severe restricting factor, forcing further business contraction. It was only during November, 1896, after the election, that the rates eased somewhat and the decline continued through December, 1896. As 1897 progressed, the structure of short-term interest rates reached a moderately low level, reflecting an easy credit market. At the depression trough, in June, these rates were at their low point and deposits, loans, and bank reserves grew each week in the expansionary movement which took hold in the summer of 1897.[31] In both cycles, in the period immediately preceding the downturn, interest rates rose as credit contracted and at both troughs rates eased to low levels, enabling entrepreneurs to expand with no difficulty.

BANK CLEARINGS AND VELOCITY

Though we have seen how the amounts of the various money forms fluctuated during the depression, their interaction and total impact on the economy need further clarification. Toward that end, we undertake a brief analysis of the rate and total quantities of money used. One rough indicator of the velocity of demand deposits may be obtained by relating total demand deposits to total outside bank clearings. In the period from 1892 to 1900, the ratio of total clearings (outside New York City) to demand deposits varied (see table, p. 216).[32]

The change in velocity [33] reflects the falling off in business activity as mirrored in bank transactions. In the first year of the depression, when many banks suspended payments and transac-

Year	Ratio
1892	8.8
1893	8.3
1894	7.6
1895	7.9
1896	7.9
1897	8.3
1898	7.9
1899	8.0
1900	7.6

tions were thus disrupted, the velocity fell off markedly. During 1894 and 1895, velocity was greater, but at a lower level than during prosperity years. The increase in velocity during 1897 was the result, mainly, of the great increase in bank clearings during the latter part of the year when economic activity picked up sharply. The declines at the end of the decade must be evaluated in the light of an increased supply of money, so that while the velocity was relatively low the total spent was greater than during the depression when velocity was also low.

Table 36 shows the annual changes in bank clearings and interpolation of data on monthly changes completes the picture. The decline in clearings as a whole was about 28 percent from the 1892 high to the low of 1893. New York City bank clearings fell off much more in the period, while those of outside banks did not decline as much—33.5 percent for the former, 16 percent for the latter. This meant that the level of general economic activity fell off in money terms by about 16 percent. Considering the important price declines, this probably represented a drop in real terms of greater magnitude. In the commercial and industrial centers, the amount and rate of spending fell off greatly in the downward sweep of the depression. The decline from 1895 to 1896 was negligible by comparison with the 1892 to 1894 drop.

Table 36
Bank Clearings in the United States, 1890–1900
(*billions of dollars*)

Year	N.Y.C. Banks	Percent Change	Outside N.Y.C.	Percent Change	U.S. Total	Percent Change
1890	$37.5	4.4	$23.2	14.2	$60.6	7.9
1891	33.7	−9.9	23.0	−.8	56.7	−6.4
1892	36.7	8.6	25.3	10.8	62.0	9.5
1893	31.1	−14.7	23.0	−9.4	54.2	−12.5
1894	24.4	22.0	21.2	−7.6	45.5	−15.9
1895	29.8	22.3	23.4	10.1	53.3	16.6
1896	28.9	−3.3	22.5	−4.2	51.3	−3.7
1897	33.4	15.8	23.9	6.4	57.3	11.7
1898	42.0	25.6	27.0	12.6	68.9	20.2
1899	60.8	44.8	33.4	23.9	94.2	36.6
1900	52.6	−13.7	33.4	.3	86.2	−8.5

Source: *Financial Review,* 1901, p. 25.

In 1897, when business activity was again at a low, bank clearings actually increased. The mild nature of the decline in clearings parallels the declines in loans, deposits, and reserves from 1895 to 1896. While the annual figures tend to obscure troughs and turning points, the monthly data uphold the notion that the decline from 1892 to 1894 was a very sharp one, while that from 1895 to 1896 was less marked. In the summer of 1894 when the trough in clearings was reached, they were at a rate slightly below the yearly average. Thus, if anything, the monthly data accentuate the sharp decline. The decline from 1895 continued until a short-lived trough was reached in August and September, 1896, when the rate of clearings was almost as low as in the summer of 1894. The rate of clearings for the other months of the year was about the same as the yearly average. The sudden decline in the summer of 1896 represented a trough occurring one year before the reference-cycle trough.[34]

Government Fiscal Operations

The foregoing analysis of monetary factors would be incomplete without including the role of government fiscal operations. The federal government's receipts and expenditures, loan operations, and handling of the gold account and the general account were all factors of some significance in the depression. They were important not because of the magnitude of the sums involved but rather because of the impact such operations had on the effective functioning of the banking system under a gold standard and on GNP.[35]

RECEIPTS AND EXPENDITURES

Table 37 gives data on receipts, expenditures, net differences, and changes in the public debt. Expenditures on the average remained stable over the period of the depression, averaging about $368 million from 1893 through 1897. The maximum variation from the average was about $16 million in 1895—less than a 5 percent variation from the average. But in 1892 and 1893, expenditures rose by over 10 percent and about 4 percent, respectively, and in 1896 and 1897, the increases were roughly 3 and 4 percent, respectively. Although the magnitude of government expenditures was not very great, these increases in expenditures and continuous deficits had a multiplied effect on total income and increased the total money supply, including bank reserves, making possible a further expansion of the money supply. Given the contractionary forces in the economy, this pattern of expenditures and deficits was a positive countercyclical factor in the total situation.

While government expenditures remained fairly stable throughout the depression, receipts fluctuated much more—

Table 37
United States Government Receipts,
Expenditures, and Debt, 1890–1900
(*millions of dollars*)

Year	Receipts	Expenditures	Surplus or Deficit (−)	Public Debt
1890	$420.0	$325.6	$94.4	$890.8
1891	355.9	332.5	23.4	851.9
1892	374.5	368.4	6.1	841.5
1893	343.0	382.5	− 39.5	839.0
1894	306.0	365.1	− 59.1	899.3
1895	322.5	352.0	− 29.5	901.7
1896	315.3	364.8	− 49.5	955.3
1897	398.7	378.6	20.1	986.7
1898	442.3	564.7	− 122.4	1,027.1
1899	555.0	539.3	15.7	1,155.3
1900	574.4	497.0	77.4	1,107.7

Source: U.S., National Monetary Commission, *Statistics for the U.S.* 21:253–255.

from a low of $306 million to a high of about $400 million in the period from 1892 to 1897. The declines in 1893 and 1894 were roughly 8 and 11 percent, respectively; in 1896, the decline was about 2 percent. As one would expect, these fluctuations were mainly cyclical, though the changing schedules of the tariff did bear on the magnitude of receipts. The McKinley Tariff of 1890 revised schedules, the sugar duty in particular, and a decline in customs revenue resulted. The Wilson Tariff of 1894, aimed at remedying the revenue shortcomings of the McKinley Tariff, failed to bring revenue relief. Not until the Dingley Tariff of 1897 did revenue from customs grow; to what extent the increases in revenue were due to returning prosperity rather than the new tariff schedules it is difficult to say.[36]

Declining government receipts also had a countercyclical effect. Though the contraction in receipts occurred only in three years—1893, 1894, and 1896—and represented modest absolute and relative amounts, those who formerly paid duties and taxes were now paying less. Even if their total incomes were falling, the decrease in tax payments softened the blow and reduced somewhat the total negative impact of dwindling income.

With expenditures stable and receipts declining during the depression, there was a deficit in each year starting with 1893 and carrying through 1896. Even in 1897, there were deficits throughout the year, though the surplus in the last months led to a net surplus for the year. These deficits must be considered inflationary or expansionary since they added to the income stream. During 1893, when the deficit mounted, the Treasury had to draw upon all kinds of money in its vaults to make payments. First the legal tender funds were used, but since only $25 million of funds were left in the Treasury by the Harrison administration, this did not last long. Next, the Treasury drew upon its gold reserves. In the second half of 1893, the Treasury used $79 million in gold coin to meet debit balances of the New York Clearing-house. By the end of the year, the Treasury gold reserve was down to $80 million.[37]

As a result of the deficits, the public debt grew. At the beginning of the depression, the debt was at a minimum after years of continuous retirement. Then it mounted each year, approaching the $1 billion mark by the end of the depression.

The total effect of this situation, however, was probably not of very great moment, though its positive aspect should not be obscured. In the total income stream, government deficits were an inconsiderable amount; the reserves of the banks, as we have seen, were not generally low during the depression period but rather were swollen as business loans fell off. When bank reserves were diminished by gold outflows, then government deficits counteracted the deflationary effects. But since the government deficit never exceeded $15 million in any month from 1893 through 1897, it is clear how limited the inflationary or expansionary impact was. Over the four years of deficits, the total excess of expenditures over receipts was less than $180 million.[38]

TREASURY ACCOUNTS

The continuous deficits during the depression placed a heavy strain on the Treasury. Table 38 shows what happened to the Treasury's holdings of gold. The continuous decline from 1890 through 1895 testifies to the heavy pressures on the Treasury both in the form of redemption of legal tenders and in the outpouring of Treasury gold as monthly deficits persisted. Not only were legal tenders presented for redemption, but gold certificates also were redeemed throughout the depression period, reflecting in some measure the inclination to hold or use gold in its specie form.

Although Table 38 shows only December data, the general impression obtained from these data is supported by the monthly figures. The December, 1893, total was the minimum amount for the year. In 1894, the monthly data displayed a more depressed gold situation for August, when the total was $52.2 million. In only two months—March and April—did the net gold reserve exceed $100 million. In 1895, the low point for the year was $41.3 million, reached in February, but this did not fairly reflect the general picture of the year during which the year-end total was exceeded every month except three. In 1896, the first two months registered very low totals, under $50 million, but for the remainder of the year, except for July, the totals were all over $100 million. After March, 1896, the gold reserve of the Treasury was never again in jeopardy despite the continued deficits of the government into 1897. The govern-

Table 38
Total Gold in Treasury, 1890–1900
(*millions of dollars*)

End of Year	Total	Held for Certificates Outstanding	Net
1890	$293.0	$144.0	$149.0
1891	273.8	148.1	130.7
1892	238.4	117.1	121.3
1893	158.3	77.4	80.9
1894	139.6	53.4	86.2
1895	113.2	49.9	63.3
1896	175.2	37.9	137.3
1897	197.5	36.6	160.9
1898	281.7	35.2	246.5
1899	398.0	161.1	236.9
1900	479.3	232.8	246.6

Source: U.S., National Monetary Commission, *Statistics for the U.S.* 21:268–270.

ment's position was strengthened by the more favorable balance-of-payments situation, with the net inflow of gold into the United States persisting during 1896.

The overall Treasury position is summarized in Table 39. The difficulties revealed in our analysis of the Treasury gold reserve are less apparent in Treasury balance totals. The decline in totals parallels the gold-account decline from 1890 to 1895. Retirement of the public debt and deficits explain the contraction in Treasury balances. From 1890 to 1895, the depletion in Treasury holdings of gold and legal tenders meant that the economy and banking system kept adding to its stock of money in the form of reserves and currency and coin and specie. In a sense, the depletion of the Treasury's holdings bolstered the banks' reserves as gold flowed out of the country to satisfy for-eigners' claims on the United States; it enabled monetary and banking expansion or maintenance of some monetary stability despite the deflationary pressures of gold exports. The economy was not the complete captive of the gold standard.

After the repeal of the Sherman Silver Act, late in 1893, the Treasury accounts at first declined. Early in 1894, its balances grew as bond issues were floated and these balances were not thereafter impaired despite the government's deficits. The gold account fluctuated, as we saw above, in reaction to the deficits, but the accumulation of balances resulted from the new mone-tary and currency situation.

Table 39
Treasury Net Balances, 1890–1900
(*millions of dollars*)

End of Year	Total	In Treasury	In Depositary Banks
1890	$163.2	$137.8	$25.5
1891	134.6	119.1	15.4
1892	129.1	118.0	11.1
1893	90.4	78.8	11.6
1894	153.3	142.2	11.1
1895	178.0	167.6	10.5
1896	228.3	215.9	12.4
1897	235.5	190.5	45.0
1898	294.8	205.4	89.4
1899	383.6	202.7	80.9
1900	140.1	50.2	89.9

Source: U.S., National Monetary Commission, *Statistics for the U.S.* 21:261–263.
Note: The following lows were reached during the period: total—$84.1 million in January, 1894; In Treasury—$72.3 million in January, 1894; In depositary banks—almost $10 million in June, 1893.

GOVERNMENT LOANS

In order to strengthen both its gold-account position and its net balances, the Treasury was forced—in the face of continuous deficits—to resort to borrowing. The first bond issue came at the end of January, 1894, when the Treasury's gold and cash position was precarious; it held only $12 million in unimpaired funds. A $50 million gold bond issue was floated in a period of two weeks and when the issue appeared to be going very badly Secretary of the Treasury Carlisle was forced to appeal in person to New York bankers to support it. Carlisle's urgings did, however, turn the tide and the New York banks absorbed about 80 percent of the issue. [39]

With gold exports and government deficits continuing, the Treasury's position deteriorated so that as 1894 drew to a close it was again in a precarious state: by October, Treasury gold totaled only $61.4 million. The Treasury appealed once again to the New York banks to exchange gold for the Treasury's legal tenders, but the $15 million forthcoming was hardly adequate to meet drains on the gold reserve. Thus, in November, the Treasury was forced to make another loan, relying again on the support of a group of banks. The loan was for another $50 million at 5 percent and once again about half of the subscription gold came from the Treasury through legal tender redemption. These loans hardly solved the basic problem of gold drain; they merely provided the Treasury with the funds to carry on its deficit activities. The drain on gold could only be stopped by changes in basic domestic and international economic relationships—and not by loans or repeal of the Sherman Silver Act alone.[40]

The November gold loan bolstered the Treasury's gold and other balances only momentarily. By January, 1895, cash balances of the Treasury were down as the deficit continued and the gold reserve contracted again so that its total was below the

$100 million limit. A new technique was thought necessary to stop this gold outflow from the Treasury and the country since a bond issue such as the two of 1894 was likely to be as ineffectual. In these circumstances, the government turned to a syndicate—the Belmont-Morgan syndicate—to float a *gold* bond issue, and guarantee obtaining the gold outside the Treasury and preventing redemption of notes for gold export. The loan was to secure 3.5 million ounces of gold coin through the issue of 4 percent bonds redeemable after February 1, 1925. Half of the coin was to be obtained in Europe, where the Belmont group was allied with the House of Rothschild; the syndicate was to use all its power to prevent withdrawal of gold from the Treasury pending completion of the contract in October, 1895. The group got the bonds at a price equivalent to 3¾ percent for par whereas the earlier loans had been at prices equivalent to 3 percent at par. In this issue, the total amount received by the government exceeded $62.3 million. These very favorable terms for the syndicate occasioned much adverse comment among the general public.[41]

The syndicate's operation meant that the Treasury was to get assistance from abroad—a gold loan—to counteract the gold outflows stemming from an adverse balance of payments. They were in effect underwriting foreign investment in the United States economy. Foreign investors had been discouraged by the adverse effects of domestic bankruptcies and, as we have seen, were cautious about direct and portfolio investments in the United States at this time and in many instances were withdrawing their funds with consequent pressure on the balance of payments. The syndicate bound together New York financial institutions with important European connections, getting all members to promise not to withdraw gold from the Treasury while the contract was being executed. The syndicate hoped that the withdrawal of foreign capital from the United States would slow down and thus aid in the successful execution of the project.

Moderate success was achieved through the first part of 1895; in May, foreign purchases of domestic securities bolstered the syndicate's operations. In London, however, speculative buying in South African gold enterprises began at this time with subsequent withdrawal from the United States market, complicating the balance-of-payments situation once again. For a time, the syndicate was able to hold the line; but the boom of 1895 in the United States generated higher prices which impaired exports somewhat, and as demand grew imports responded. In these circumstances, the foreign exchange rate rose, the incentive to ship gold was heightened, and a New York coffee-importing house broke the syndicate's hold by selling drafts on London, covering with gold shipments acquired by presenting legal tenders for redemption at the Treasury. In the next five months, about $65 million in gold, most of it obtained from the Treasury, was shipped abroad and the syndicate's operations, which ended by contract in October, were no longer effective. In the autumn, foreign disinvestment due to breakdown of African speculation grew, aggravating balance-of-payments difficulties.[42]

By January, 1896, the Treasury's gold reserve was under $50 million and the Treasury was in straits again. Another loan was deemed necessary and in early January a 4 percent gold bond issue in the amount of $100 million was announced. The loan was offered, not through a syndicate this time, but rather at popular subscription under competitive bidding. The loan was very successful with applications oversubscribing by over $450 million. Over $111 million was received for the bond issue and after that the gold reserve remained unimpaired above $100 million. As economic conditions in Europe grew more favorable, balance-of-payment difficulties took a favorable turn and the gold "problem" ended, despite the continuing and growing depression in the United States.[43]

The difficulties attending these lending operations were related to a complexity of factors, the most important ones being reflected in the balance of payments. Table 40 recapitulates the outstanding funded debt of the United States government, showing changes occurring during the depression. In effect, the government's gold bond issues funded the Treasury's floating debt. This debt of the Treasury, in the form of notes, was a burden which in view of balance-of-payment difficulties necessarily led to gold drains—Gresham's Law took over.

While there were forces making for a gold drain from abroad, though, the floating of gold loans helped meet the problem. To the extent that the Treasury was forced to hold silver and paper money which others converted into gold, the Treasury had to

Table 40
Total Interest-Bearing United States
Bonds Outstanding, by Rate of Interest, 1890–1900
(*millions of dollars*)

Fiscal Year	Total	2 Percent	3 Percent	4 Percent	4.5 Percent	5 Percent	6 Percent
1890	$775.9	—	—	602.3	109.0	—	64.6
1891	675.2	—	—	559.7	50.9	—	64.6
1892	649.7	25.4	—	559.7	—	—	64.6
1893	649.7	25.4	—	559.7	—	—	64.6
1894	699.7	25.4	—	559.7	—	50.0	64.6
1895	780.8	25.4	—	590.8	—	100.0	64.6
1896	912.0	25.4	—	722.0	—	100.0	64.6
1897	912.0	25.4	—	722.0	—	100.0	64.6
1898	861.4	25.4	—	722.0	—	100.0	14.0
1899	1,046.9	25.4	198.7	722.0	—	100.0	
1900	1,023.5	329.1	128.8	517.9	—	47.7	

Source: U.S., National Monetary Commission, *Statistics for the U.S.* 21:277–278.

build up a working balance in gold beyond its silver and paper balance. Loans thus enabled the Treasury to exchange bonds instead of gold for the paper and silver offered in the money market. The pressures forcing paper and silver off the market were powerful since the gold standard ruled out devaluation and only gold served in international payments. With exchange rates thus weakened, the need to maintain confidence in the Treasury called for building up the gold reserve. The Morgan-Belmont syndicate did succeed partially by getting Europe to invest in the United States through the safer medium of government bonds, but in the face of capital repatriation the amounts secured in Europe were insufficient to forestall gold outflows for a prolonged period. Table 40 shows that from the middle of 1893 to the middle of 1897 the government's funded debt increased by over $262 million—an increase of over 40 percent effected at higher rates of interest.[44]

Summary

To explain the depression in terms of the Sherman Act or silver policy in general is to oversimplify the economic relationships of the time. It seems clear that the depression was not the result of an oversupply of money, of an inflation precipitated by monetary policies. Nor was it "caused" by too little money: the ratio of money to economic activity was not distorted before the depression. In the period 1880 to 1910, on the whole the quantity of money increased as greatly as did national wealth and manufacturing output. During the nineties and in the years preceding the depression, the supply of money grew proportional to growth in most parts of the economy. [45]

The money market tightened just prior to the downturns in 1893 and 1896, due to a complex of factors in which currency policy plays a role. Tighter credit conditions contributed to economic contraction but cannot be blamed for the downturn and depression. The money forms in use contracted, though not sharply, during the depression. There was less money and it was used less as economic activity contracted. The increased issue of Treasury notes under the Sherman Silver Act did not lead to a marked increase in money though it did postpone credit contraction by augmenting bank reserves as gold flowed out of the economy. Insofar as Treasury deficits were not funded, they complicated the monetary picture. Their inflationary or expansionary impact must be recognized, but as a relatively minor factor.

NOTES

1. The Sherman Act required the purchase, each month, of 4.5 million ounces of silver bullion, paid for by the issuance of Treasury notes of full legal tender. The Treasury had to redeem these notes in either gold or silver. Under the 1878 (Bland) Act, notes issued to pay for silver purchases were only partial legal tender. The Sherman Act, in effect, required the monthly domestic silver output to be bought by the Treasury. See D. R. Dewey, *Financial History of the United States,* pp. 437–438.

2. Senator Sherman himself traced the origin of the "present stringency" to the "apprehension of the mercantile and financial world that we will not meet our obligations in gold but will pay in cheap money." The *Chronicle* stated: "The Country is struggling with disturbed credit and the general derangement of commercial and financial affairs which a forced and over-valued currency has developed. . . . Nothing but . . . corrective legislation which shall remove the disturbing law, can afford any measure of real relief" (July 8, 1893, p. 42). In his message to a Congress specially convened to repeal the Sherman Act, President Cleveland asserted that the Act was a principal factor in the nation's financial plight. His strictures were considered "cogent" and his case "clear, succinct and comprehensive" by *Bradstreet's.*

3. *Bradstreet's,* July 8, 1893, p. 421; ibid., August 12, 1893, pp. 502–503.

4. See Margaret G. Myers, *The New York Money Market: Origins and Development,* vol. 1, passim.

5. Ibid.

6. Ibid., especially pp. 392–402.

7. Ibid.

8. Bank suspensions, of course, were more numerous than actual failures, but in terms of measuring the instability of banking and its dislocating effects the former category is more appropriate.

9. Besides bank deposits, bank notes, and national bank notes, other
kinds of money included United States notes. Treasury notes, currency
certificates, subsidiary silver coin, silver certificates, silver dollars, gold
coin, and gold certificates. Of the total supply of money—excluding
bank notes and demand deposits—at the beginning of 1893, gold coin
was the largest proportion (26 percent), United States notes (20 percent) and silver certificates next (20 percent), followed by national bank
notes (10 percent). The remaining kinds of money amounted to less
than 25 percent of the money supply. Demand deposits were almost
double the amount of other money in circulation. See U.S. National
Monetary Commission, *Statistics for the United States, 1867–1909*
21:161.

10. In this period, the role of demand deposits as a money form was
becoming more prominent and this development made possible an eco-
nomizing in the use of legal tender money, in general, and gold, in particular. By 1894, the percentage of checks used for payments in retail
trade was close to 60 percent for the entire country. By 1896, this percentage had risen greatly, averaging about 65 percent for the nation. In
the South, the percentage was lowest, while in the North it was highest
—61.5 percent and 69.2 percent, respectively. In 1896, the percentage of
checks used in payments of all kinds was close to 95 percent in the
North. See R. F. W. Whittemore, "The Gold Reserve and the Treasury
Crisis in 1894–1895", p. 111.

11. U.S., National Monetary Commission, *Statistics for the U.S.*
21:155, 161–162.

12. Ibid.

13. Other types of deposits, while not properly classified as money,
may give an indication as to what the general tendency of money and
near monies was.

14. In New York City, deposits were at a low of $370 million at the
end of August, 1893, while the currency premium was in effect. This
was at a time when reserves totaled only about 22 percent—below the
legal requirement. See U.S., National Monetary Commission, *Statistics
for the U.S.* 21:101.

15. *Bradstreet's*, August 5, 1893; *Financial Review*, 1901, pp. 61–63.

16. In the national banking system, reserves had to be met at all
times. When the reserves were less than the required proportion of deposits and notes, the banks were not allowed to increase their liabilities
through new loans or discounts.

17. U.S., National Monetary Commission, *Financial Laws of the
United States, 1778–1909* 2:345.

18. New York City banks, during the period under review, held over
30 percent of the reserves of all national banks, except for 1893 when
the proportion dropped to 26 percent. Their reserves represented, par-

tially, the reserves of many national banks throughout the country. They held between 21 and 25 percent of all the deposits of the national banks. We use New York City banks because weekly data are available only for them. See U.S., National Monetary Commission, *Statistics for the U.S.*, 21:74. At certain points during the depression, reserves of the New York City banks were more greatly in excess: the depression highs of 45 percent in February, 1894, and about 36 percent in February, 1897, occurred at seasonal high periods but reflected more than seasonal forces. Reserves fell below the legal requirements only during the months of July and August, 1893, when the banks were under their most severe pressures.

19. The decline for all national banks was over 20 percent.

20. U.S., National Monetary Commission, *Statistics for the U.S.* 21:98–108.

21. Loans for all national banks decreased 4 percent and deposits almost 17 percent.

22. U.S. National Monetary Commission, *Statistics for the U.S.* 21:98–108.

23. Ibid.

24. Ibid.

25. As we saw above, these imports are explained mainly by the premium on cash, attractive interest and exchange rates, and some foreign purchases of security "bargains."

26. A. D. Noyes, *Forty Years of American Finance*, p. 173, 168–173; U.S., National Monetary Commission, *Statistics for the U.S.* 21:169.

27. Noyes, *American Finance*, pp. 182–206; U.S., National Monetary Commission, *Statistics for the U.S.* 21:169, 269.

28. Noyes, *American Finance* chap. X; U.S., National Monetary Commission, *Statistics for the U.S.* 21: 103, 169, 269.

29. *Historical Statistics*, p. 276.

30. *New York Times*, December 18, 1895; U.S., National Monetary Commission, *Statistics for the U.S.* 21: 103, 122–124.

31. U.S., National Monetary Commission, *Statistics for the U.S.* 21: 104–106, 124–126.

32. *Historical Statistics*, p. 277; *Bradstreet's*, December 3, 1898, p. 770; *Financial Review*, 1901, p. 25. The total demand deposits were for June 30 of that year, while total clearings were for the calendar year.

33. In assessing changes in velocity, it is important to see the relative changes from one year to the next in order to gauge the degree of cyclical reaction.

34. *Bradstreet's*, December 3, 1898, p. 770.

35. Average federal government expenditures from 1890 to 1897 were about equal to the average value at the farm of the wheat crop in the same period, or a little more than half the value of the corn crop. They were about half the value of the average of imports in the period or about 40 percent of the average value of exports. They averaged about 20 percent of the realized production income of agriculture. As a per-

centage of total private production income, the money spent by the federal government was only about 3 percent. See U.S., National Monetary Commission, *Statistics for the U.S.* 21: 15; *Historical Statistics*, pp. 14, 244.

36. Noyes, *American Finance*, pp. 134–135, 227.

37. Ibid., pp. 204–206.

38. U.S., Bureau of Foreign and Domestic Commerce, *Monthly Summary of Imports and Exports*, 1893–1900.

39. The issue was a $50 million gold coin loan at 5 percent with the bonds selling at over 117.2, the equivalent of a 3 percent bond at par. The issue received over $58.6 million for the Treasury but since about $24 million in gold was redeemed by the Treasury prior to the consummation of the issue, the net gold take was much less. Noyes, *American Finance* pp. 209–215; U.S., Treasury Department, *Annual Report of the Secretary, 1894*, pp. xxxiii–iv.

40. Noyes, *American Finance*, pp. 230–233; U. S., Treasury Department, *Annual Report of the Secretary, 1895*, p. xxvii.

41. Noyes, *American Finance*, pp. 234–237; U.S., Treasury Department, *Annual Report of the Secretary, 1895*, p. xxvii.

42. Noyes, *American Finance*, pp. 237–250. See also U.S., National Monetary Commission, *Statistics for the U.S.* 21.

43. Noyes, *American Finance*, pp. 251–254; U.S., Treasury Department, *Annual Report of the Secretary, 1896*, p. xxix; U.S., National Monetary Commission, *Statistics for the U.S.* 21:269.

44. Noyes, *American Finance*, p. 252.

45. *Historical Statistics*, pp. 179, 262, 275, 277; U.S., National Monetary Commission, *Statistics for the U.S.*, 21:155; Simon Kuznets, *National Product Since 1889*, pp. 228, 231.

7
Prices During the Depression

Under perfectly competitive conditions, sharp declines in money demand precipitate downward price adjustments which allow output to be maintained at the level of employment prevailing before changes in demand occurred. In the abstract, then, full employment, once attained, is perpetuated by flexible price changes which keep all factors of production employed at new factor prices. Since levels of employment do fluctuate—we have throughout been discussing a major case history of such fluctuations—the nature of price changes must bear significantly on the degree and quality of such changes in output and employment. We look, therefore, at the patterns that prices traced during the depression to unravel their meaning and to see if further light can be thrown on the nature of that economic contraction.

Most prices reached the bottom of a long secular decline from the seventies during the depression. Farm wages, however, increased continuously starting in the seventies, rising over 10 percent by 1892. Series for industrial wages start in 1890, so that generalizations on them are not possible. For the years 1890 to 1892, however, wages in all industries remained fairly

stable. In some industries there were increases, in others declines—but in most instances not by large amounts. Bond
interest rates exhibited an insubstantial downward movement
from 1880, while dividend rates fluctuated sharply in a cyclical
manner displaying, nevertheless, a downward trend in the
eighties and a slight upward trend in the early nineties. Short-
term interest rates did not show any marked changes: their
responses were cyclical and random. There is some evidence
of a slight downward movement in commercial paper rates.[1]

Producer Prices

WHOLESALE PRICES

Basic commodity prices are an important element in entrepreneurs' decisions: plans of enterprises' levels of activity are
determined in part by the prices which must be paid or are expected to be paid for the materials going into the production of
the firms' goods. Even a cursory look at Table 41 indicates the
unusual nature of wholesale price fluctuations during the depression. Wholesale prices usually respond quickly and sharply
to depressed conditions. In most major depressions, wholesale
prices have fallen by at least 20 percent, while in very severe
depressions declines come closer to 30 percent. According to
Table 41, the index for wholesale prices of all commodities declined a maximum of about 15 percent from the high in 1893
to the trough in 1896 and 1897. The decrease in these prices
did not begin until the middle of 1893 and the low point was
not reached until the end of 1893. Interestingly, most of these
prices continued to decline during the 1895 recovery.[2]

Some price series were about as insensitive in responding to
contraction as was the All Commodities index. Others responded more quickly and more sharply. In no group was there
the usual depression sharp, downward drop in commodity and

Table 41
Index Numbers of Wholesale Prices, by Groups
of Commodities, 1890–1900

Year	All Commodities	Farm Products	Foods	Clothing Material	Fuels	Metals & Metal Products	Chemicals & Drugs	House furnishings	Miscellaneous
1890	107.6	101.9	108.8	104.1	109.3	125.2	98.1	103.6	109.7
1891	107.0	109.5	107.4	99.6	106.0	109.7	99.1	104.7	106.5
1892	100.0	100.0	100.0	100.0	100.0	100.0	100.0	100.0	100.0
1893	102.4	103.2	107.2	98.4	101.2	91.5	97.3	99.9	101.1
1894	91.8	89.6	94.6	87.0	98.4	78.2	87.8	94.3	97.5
1895	93.6	89.3	92.7	84.8	115.8	83.3	86.7	90.5	102.4
1896	89.2	80.3	86.5	83.1	113.4	84.8	87.1	90.0	101.1
1897	89.3	86.4	89.2	82.0	97.2	77.4	95.1	88.3	102.9
1898	93.0	91.7	93.6	84.4	98.9	77.7	103.8	91.3	105.4
1899	100.1	93.6	93.6	88.2	118.1	119.0	108.7	93.6	109.9
1900	107.6	102.8	99.5	96.3	132.7	116.6	110.0	101.6	114.3

Source: U.S., Bureau of Labor Statistics, Index Numbers of Wholesale Prices on Pre-war Base, 1890–1927, pp. 2–4.
Note: 1892=100.

raw-material prices. Even prices of farm products did not react at once to contraction; their decline commenced late in 1893. By 1896, when the trough was reached, these prices had declined over 20 percent from the 1893 high level. The drop was in two sharp steps, from 1893 to 1894 and from 1895 to 1896. Of all wholesale prices, those of farm products declined the most during the depression. Prices of metals and metal products and foods declined almost as much as those of farm products.

PRODUCER DURABLE PRICES

The prices of producer durable goods—a variable of significance in entrepreneurs' investment decisions—declined more sharply than those of wholesale prices though in some categories the decline was moderate. The overall decline, as seen in Table 42, was just over 17 percent—a decline 50 percent greater than that of wholesale prices. Most producer durable prices, however, declined more moderately.

Among those producer durable prices showing price fluctuations less marked than that for the total were miscellaneous subsidiary durable equipment prices, which fell almost as greatly as did the total—just over 16 percent. The decline in prices of farm equipment[3] was a gradual one over the period 1893 to 1897, totaling just under 13 percent; each year saw a decline of about 2.5 percent. Prices of locomotives and railroad cars declined in the same measure as those of ships and boats. Over the four-year period 1893 to 1896, the decline amounted to about 7.5 percent. Prices of carpenters' and mechanics' tools declined even less in the period from 1892 to 1896, totaling just over 4.5 percent.

The prices of some producer durable goods fluctuated more sharply than the total, conforming more closely to the usual,

Table 42

Producer Durable Goods Price Indices, 1890–1900

Year	Total	Industrial Machinery & Equipment	Electrical Equipment— Industrial & Commercial	Farm Equipment	Office & Store Furniture & Fixtures	Locomotives & RR Cars	Ships & Boats	Carpenters' & Mechanics' Tools	Miscellaneous Subsidiary Durable Equipment
1890	109.6	111.0	111.1	105.4	100.0	103.1	103.1	103.2	117.1
1891	101.4	101.0	101.1	101.4	100.0	101.2	101.2	103.3	101.5
1892	100.0	100.0	100.0	100.0	100.0	100.0	100.0	100.0	100.0
1893	98.0	100.1	100.1	98.5	92.7	97.9	97.9	99.6	92.8
1894	97.8	106.4	106.4	95.1	91.1	95.9	95.9	97.2	84.5
1895	90.3	87.0	87.7	92.5	83.4	93.1	93.2	95.6	98.7
1896	82.6	77.0	77.7	89.7	74.7	92.5	93.5	95.3	92.6
1897	94.9	106.5	106.6	87.2	74.2	93.9	93.9	95.6	83.6
1898	103.1	114.7	114.7	84.1	82.3	93.5	98.5	95.1	101.0
1899	110.1	122.9	128.0	86.6	83.3	103.4	103.3	101.2	114.2
1900	112.5	121.4	121.6	89.9	93.5	104.7	104.8	108.7	122.6

Source: W. H. Shaw, Value of Commodity Output Since 1869, pp. 294–295.
Note: 1892 = 100.

sharp decline during a depression. The decline in prices of industrial machinery and equipment and of electrical equipment (industrial and commercial) was exactly parallel, amounting to about 22 percent from 1892 to 1896.[4] Along with these prices, office and store furniture and fixtures prices dropped sharply. The trough level, reached in 1897, was about 26 percent below the 1892 level of prices. These groups of prices showed some of the sharpest declines of all prices during the depression.

CONSTRUCTION MATERIAL PRICES

During the nineties, the prices of building construction materials declined considerably. The decline was almost as sharp in the first three years of the decade as during the five-year depression period 1893 through 1897. The level of these prices during the nineties was at the lowest point since the period before the Civil War and not until 1900 and the years thereafter was the level of the eighties attained again. Construction material prices, thus, followed the general secular price decline trend but reflected certain special forces peculiar to the building industry.[5]

Following is an index of price fluctuations in the prices of construction materials:

Year	Index
1890	111.1
1891	105.7
1892	100.0
1893	99.3
1894	94.3
1895	93.1
1896	94.6
1897	88.4
1898	92.1
1899	106.3
1900	113.0

Though the 1890 level of prices was not a high one, the total decline from 1890 to 1897 was over 20 percent. The maximum decline from 1892 to the trough was only about 12 percent—a moderate decline compared to the fall in other prices such as producer durables, but on a par with the decline in all wholesale prices.[6]

Consumer Prices

Consumer prices posted varying declines during the depression too. Figure 10 and Table 43 trace these changes in major categories of consumer goods: general cost of living, perishables, semidurables, and durables. Hansen's Cost-of-Living Index based mainly on food costs shows that the general cost of living declined from 1892 to 1897 by almost 11 percent. The maximum decline during the depression of almost 12 percent occurred from 1893 to 1897. Figure 10 indicates, however, that there were sharper declines in most major classifications of consumer goods.

From 1893 to 1896, the prices of perishable consumer goods declined by about 16 percent while the decline from 1892 to 1896 was only 11 percent. The drop in semidurable and durable prices behaved during the nineties. Although all perishable semidurable prices, the decline from 1892 to 1897 was almost 19 percent, and the decline from 1890 to 1897 was almost 20 percent. As one would expect, consumer durable prices declined most of all. The decline from 1892 to 1897 was just over 20 percent and from 1890 to 1897 over 23 percent.[7]

PRICES OF PERISHABLES

Table 44 illustrates how different perishable commodity prices behaved during the nineties. Although all perishable prices declined about 11 percent from 1892 to the trough, most prices declined less. Prices of food and kindred products fell by

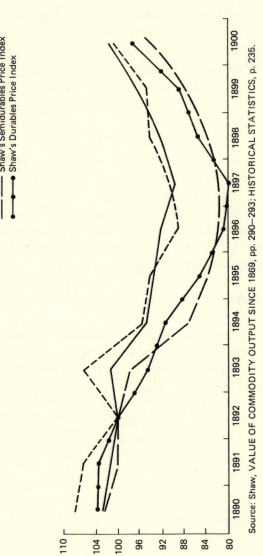

Hansen's Cost-of-Living Index
Shaw's Perishables Price Index
Shaw's Semidurables Price Index
Shaw's Durables Price Index

Source: Shaw, VALUE OF COMMODITY OUTPUT SINCE 1869, pp. 290–293; HISTORICAL STATISTICS, p. 235.

Figure 10
Consumer Prices, 1890-1900

Table 43
Consumer Price Indices, 1890–1900

Year	Cost of Living (Hansen)	Perishables (Shaw)	Semidurables (Shaw)	Durables (Shaw)
1890	102.7	107.9	102.5	103.9
1891	101.3	106.3	100.0	103.7
1892	100.0	100.0	100.0	100.0
1893	101.3	106.1	97.7	94.4
1894	94.7	95.6	86.9	91.3
1895	93.4	94.0	83.3	85.1
1896	92.1	88.8	81.5	80.6
1897	89.4	90.2	81.5	79.5
1898	92.1	93.9	83.5	85.2
1899	96.0	94.5	87.5	88.4
1900	101.3	100.5	93.6	97.2

Source: U.S., Bureau of the Census, *Historical Statistics*, p. 235; Shaw, *Value of Commodity Output*, pp. 290–93.
Note: 1892 = 100.

about 13.5 percent—more than that of all perishables. But prices of the other perishables did not react as sharply. Prices of fuel and lighting products increased quite sharply, except for the slight decline in 1893.[8] Prices of tobacco goods, toilet and drug preparations, and newspaper and paper supplies were fairly stable throughout the depression. The first group did not decline until 1896, the preceding years being ones of some price increases. The second group likewise did not decline until late in the depression, while the last group recorded a very slight decline in 1893. Measuring from 1892, the price decline did not reach 7 percent for any of these groups. Measuring from highs established during the depression, the maximum declines were greater.

PRICES OF SEMIDURABLES

The prices of semidurable consumer goods started declining before those of perishables and the degree of contraction was much greater, amounting to almost 19 percent. Table 45 lists the varying declines in prices for different groups of semidurable goods. In all the groups, except house furnishings, the decline in prices commenced early in the depression, usually at the begin-

Table 44
Price Indices of Perishable Consumer Goods
1890–1900

Year	Food & Kindred Products, Manufactured & Non-manufactured	Cigars, Cigarettes, & Tobacco	Drug, Toilet, & Household Preparations	Magazines, Newspapers, Stationery, & Supplies, Miscellaneous Paper Products	Fuel & Lighting Products, Manu-factured
1890	108.8	103.5	106.8	107.4	135.5
1891	107.4	103.3	106.6	101.6	113.0
1892	100.0	100.0	100.0	100.0	100.0
1893	107.2	102.7	114.6	98.9	98.9
1894	94.6	103.0	106.0	100.2	110.0
1895	92.7	101.7	92.8	98.2	156.4
1896	86.5	98.1	101.8	93.2	150.5
1897	89.2	96.7	97.7	93.8	117.3
1898	93.6	103.3	91.5	93.8	125.9
1899	93.6	105.6	89.4	70.5	159.3
1900	99.5	107.8	92.9	85.4	173.2

Source: Shaw, *Value of Commodity Output*, pp. 290–293.
Note: 1892 = 100.

Table 45
Price Indices of Semidurable Consumer Goods,
1890–1900

Year	Dry Goods & Notions	Clothing & Personal Furnishings	Shoes & Other Footwear	House- furnishings
1890	104.5	101.1	102.5	103.2
1891	95.9	101.1	100.8	105.1
1892	100.0	100.0	100.0	100.0
1893	98.7	96.1	98.8	102.9
1894	82.3	83.7	98.3	93.8
1895	80.3	77.4	98.8	91.0
1896	76.5	75.6	99.0	93.9
1897	77.3	76.7	95.4	91.9
1898	79.9	80.0	94.0	89.2
1899	88.9	83.7	93.1	95.0
1900	95.7	90.5	94.9	106.1

Source: Shaw, *Value of Commodity Output,* pp. 290–293.
Note: 1892 = 100.

ning of 1893. The prices of dry goods and notions, and clothing and personal furnishings declined more sharply than the average of all semidurables—approaching 25 percent—while those of footwear and housefurnishings declined much less than the average, not exceeding 9 percent.

PRICES OF DURABLES

The overall decline in the prices of consumer durable goods shown in Table 46 was slightly greater than that of semidurables, amounting to almost 20 percent. The variation and timing of fluctuations in this category differed among the categories. Except for floor coverings and miscellaneous house furnishings, durable prices started their descent in 1893 or earlier. At one extreme, prices of household furniture declined almost 26 percent; at the other extreme, prices of floor coverings declined only 15 percent. The prices of household furniture and jewelry and silverware dropped more than that of all durable prices, while those of the remaining categories fell by less than the overall decline.

Table 46
Price Indices of Durable Consumer Goods,
1890–1900

Year	Household Furniture	Floor Coverings	Miscellaneous House-furnishings	China & Household Utensils	Musical Instruments	Jewelry, Silverware, Clocks, Watches
1890	100.0	101.1	103.6	102.3	93.9	109.9
1891	100.0	107.9	101.6	102.7	91.8	109.9
1892	100.0	100.0	100.0	100.0	100.0	100.0
1893	92.7	101.5	101.7	99.8	97.3	89.8
1894	91.1	95.2	94.2	97.9	99.0	85.1
1895	83.4	86.1	86.3	94.4	80.7	85.1
1896	74.7	85.0	86.9	92.3	80.8	85.1
1897	74.1	88.5	83.9	84.0	81.5	78.2
1898	82.9	94.8	82.0	84.1	80.1	83.6
1899	85.6	93.7	82.1	86.6	86.6	86.4
1900	96.5	97.9	95.3	91.4	93.6	86.4

Source: Shaw, *Value of Commodity Output,* pp. 290–293.
Note: 1892=100.

Export and Import Prices

Although we have sketched the important changes in basic commodity, producer, and consumer prices, it is also necessary to see what changes occurred in relationships between export and import prices since balance-of-payment difficulties assumed importance in the depression. As we do not have price indices of actual import and export prices, we shall draw on price indices for those commodities comprising the bulk of our exports and on price indices of British exports which were a significant segment of total imports.[9]

EXPORT PRICES

Table 47 lists the relative fluctuations in prices of farm products, producer durable goods, and metals and metal products. The items included in these indices comprised an overwhelming portion of total exports so that some rough idea of fluctuations in prices of exported goods emerges. Farm product prices rose in 1893, but quantities of agricultural products exported fell off. Both the prices of wheat and corn—important segments of agricultural exports—fell in 1893 as world market conditions were unfavorable. From 1893 on, prices of farm products dropped sharply until 1896 after which recovery began. The maximum decline in farm product prices was about 20 percent from 1892 to 22 percent from 1893.[10]

The descent in the prices of metals and metal products was as sharp as those of farm products. From 1892 to 1894, these prices declined by almost 22 percent; the recovery in 1895 still left them 16 percent below the 1892 level.

The next decline was to a level almost 23 percent below that of 1892. Much of this price decline was due to technological improvements in metal refining and production rather than purely cyclical forces. The maximum decline for producer durable prices was almost 18 percent from 1892 to 1896—mainly a cyclical decline.[11]

IMPORT PRICES

Table 48 lists price indices for British exports during the

depression. Since the price indices for all exports and for raw materials and semimanufactures exported include prices of materials not imported, we shall concentrate on the prices of manufactured goods, noting the others mainly for direction and limits

Table 47
Selected Prices in the United States, 1892–1897

Year	Farm Products	Metals & Metal Products	Producer Durable Goods
1893	103.2	91.5	98.0
1894	89.6	78.2	97.5
1895	89.3	83.8	90.5
1896	80.3	84.8	82.5
1897	86.4	77.4	95.0

Sources: Shaw, *Value of Commodity Output,* p. 294; U.S., Bureau of Labor Statistics, *Index Numbers of Wholesale Prices,* pp. 2–4.
Note: 1892 = 100.

Table 48
British Export Price Indices, 1892–1897

Year	Weighted Average of All Exports	Manufactured Exports	Raw Material & Semi-manufactures Exports
1893	99	99	93
1894	95	94	96
1895	92	92	105
1896	93	94	84
1897	92	93	85

Source: Werner Schlote, *British Overseas Trade from 1700 to the 1930s,* p. 177.
Note: Schlote's indices were converted to an 1892 base. 1892 = 100.

of price changes. British export prices declined a maximum of about 8 percent during the depression and prices of manufactured exports followed a parallel movement. From 1892 to 1895, they declined about 9 percent. The decline in prices of raw-material and semimanufactured exports was greater, though not until late in the depression after the balance-of-payment difficulties were resolved. From 1892 to 1893, these prices declined about 7 percent while in the later period they were at a level 16 percent below that of 1892. The maximum decline was 20 percent after the sharp recovery in 1892.[12]

While the prices for these groups declined by moderate amounts, other British export prices also dropped. Prices of textile exports declined by about 11 percent from 1892 to 1897, while those of iron and steel declined about 12.5 percent from 1892 to 1895. Export prices of chemicals declined about 12 percent from 1892 to 1896 and prices of miscellaneous exports fell off 5 percent from 1892 to 1895. It is important to note that the major portion of these declines came toward the end of the period, not in the 1892–1893 period. In the years 1893 and 1894, prices of these exports had not yet declined their maximum amount.[13]

Relating British prices to those in the United States, it seems clear that prices of United States agricultural exports declined much more greatly than those of British manufactured exports. The decline in prices of United States manufactured exports was also greater than that of British goods.[14] The worsening terms of trade between the United States and England (and probably Europe) are underscored if we realize that much of the decline in British prices came after 1895 while most of the decline of United States export prices came before then. Price declines in agricultural and manufactured products in the United States totaled between 16 and 22 percent. The maximum decline for

British exports did not exceed 12.5 percent, while most export prices declined about 8 percent. The United States economy was undoubtedly exporting more goods per unit of imports than it had before the depression.

Security Prices and Yields

STOCK PRICES AND YIELDS

During the course of the depression, both stock prices and dividend yields fell off considerably. Figure 11 shows the fluctuations in stock prices. The deep valleys reflect the strong impact of the depression on stock investments. From the high of August, 1892, to the trough in August, 1893, there was a decline of almost 28 percent. The low point of the depression was reached in August, 1896, when stock prices were only 68 percent of the August, 1892, level. With the exception of the restricted recoveries in stock prices early in 1894 and late in 1895, the period from early 1893 to early 1897 was one in which stock prices were declining or at low levels. The depression was characterized, thus, by a fluctuating low level of stock prices at about 75 percent of the highs achieved in 1892 —a year of high stock prices.[15] Dividend yields varied with stock prices. Over the decade, dividend payments on all stocks fluctuated (see table, p. 249; 1892 = 100). From 1892 to 1897, dividend payments dropped by almost 25 percent, while in the same period stock prices declined by 28 percent. The decline in dividends was less sharp than that of stock prices. The decline in real yield was substantial: from 1893 to 1894, it amounted to about 15 percent, while from the high in 1893 to the low in 1897 the decline reached almost 23 percent. The decline in dividend payments approximated that in real yield, suggesting that payments declined in proportion to most other major prices.[16]

Year	Index of Payments	Real Yield
1890	91.5	5.8%
1891	93.0	5.9
1892	100.0	6.0
1893	103.8	6.6
1894	87.5	5.6
1895	78.0	5.3
1896	76.4	5.3
1897	75.4	5.1
1898	81.2	5.4
1899	87.2	5.5
1900	122.7	7.6

BOND PRICES AND YIELDS

Bond prices did not fluctuate greatly in the depression and this fact was also reflected in bond interest yield. Figure 11 traces the slight variations in bond prices (based on railroad bonds) while variations in bond yields are illustrated in Figure 12. From a peak in 1893, bond prices fell to a trough in 1894 —the total decline amounted to just over 2 percent. From that point on, bond prices rose to levels above those of the early nineties in an almost continuous pattern. During 1896, a depression year, there was a very slight drop in prices by about .5 percent, but the level of prices was higher than in any preceding year of the nineties except 1895.[17]

The real interest yield of bonds remained high throughout the depression. From 1893 to 1897, the real interest yield each year was higher than that before or after the depression. In money terms, bond interest declined only 3 percent from 1892 to 1897 in a gradual decline each year. In such circumstances of steady and rising bond prices with money yields declining only slightly, the increase in real yield reflected the sharp decline in other prices.

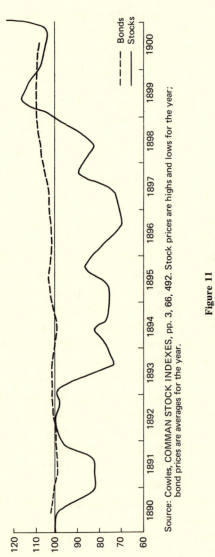

Figure 11

Stock and Bond Prices, 1890-1900

Source: Cowles, COMMAN STOCK INDEXES, pp. 3, 66, 492. Stock prices are highs and lows for the year; bond prices are averages for the year.

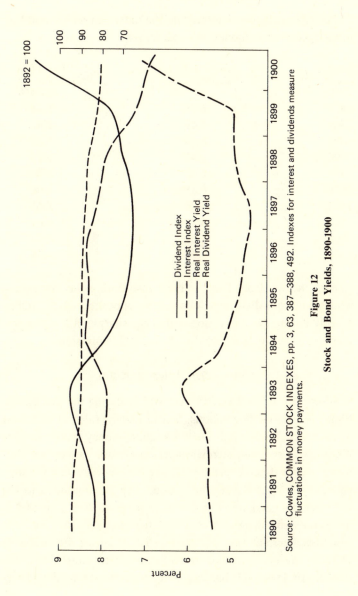

Source: Cowles, COMMON STOCK INDEXES, pp. 3, 63, 387–388, 492. Indexes for interest and dividends measure fluctuations in money payments.

Figure 12

Stock and Bond Yields, 1890-1900

The figures below demonstrate the extent to which bond interest fluctuated in money and real terms:[18]

Year	Money Yield	Real Yield
1890	6.57%	8.34%
1891	6.58	8.46
1892	6.49	8.45
1893	6.43	8.48
1894	6.41	8.94
1895	6.40	8.80
1896	6.38	8.90
1897	6.29	8.65
1898	6.26	8.41
1899	6.02	7.74
1900	5.90	7.40

Real income from bond interest rose during the depression, while that from dividends followed an opposite pattern, falling sharply during the depression and rising sharply in the prosperity periods before and after the 1893–1897 depression.[19]

Short-Term Interest Rates

Short-term interest rates varied widely during the depression. Figure 13 shows fluctuations in call-money rates at the New York Stock Exchange, ninety-day time-money rates in New York City, and commercial-paper rates (for choice sixty-to-ninety-day two-name paper). Though there were many differences in the rates during the period, they all responded to the same general economic conditions in the same directions and in much the same degree. Peaks and troughs coincided or came close together. The very high rates, such as during the middle of 1893 or the end of 1896, were responses to unusual circumstances. In 1893, the banking and stock-market panics gener-

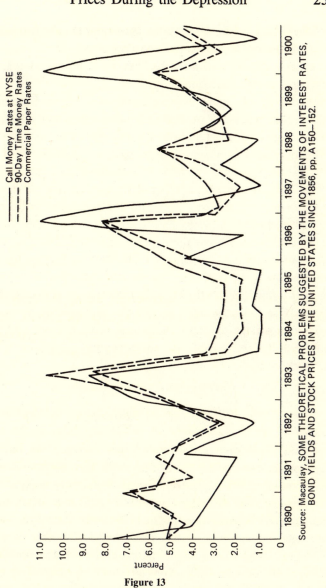

Call Money Rates at NYSE
90-Day Time Money Rates
Commercial Paper Rates

Source: Macaulay, SOME THEORETICAL PROBLEMS SUGGESTED BY THE MOVEMENTS OF INTEREST RATES, BOND YIELDS AND STOCK PRICES IN THE UNITED STATES SINCE 1856, pp. A150—152.

Figure 13
Money Rates in New York City, 1890-1900, Highs and Lows

ated the high rates for all types of short-term credit; at the end of 1896, the sudden impact of the President's message on the Venezuelan dispute had a marked effect on the money market carrying over to the election year 1896.

After the panic spent itself, interest rates fell to depression lows that were below 3 percent for commercial paper rates and below 2 percent for call loans and ninety-day time money. This easy-money condition continued during all of 1894 and much of 1895. At the beginning of 1896, only call-loan rates fell sharply, as the economy entered another depression period. Call-loan rates responded in this way again after the near panic in December, 1895, forced rates up sharply. During 1896, other short-term money rates rose as the depression deepened and election uncertainties spread, and call-loan rates followed in the second half of the year. In 1897, rates fell by midyear to levels approximating those of 1894—the earlier depression trough—and then increased as business activity expanded. In their many variations, money rates for short-term credit proved highly sensitive to general business conditions and sudden flurries and breaks in the stock markets.

Wage Rates and Earnings

As major determinants affecting important decisions and the levels of economic activity, wage rates and earnings, along with the other prices in the system, varied in differing degrees and patterns. Some rates and earnings were sensitive to changing economic conditions; others resisted the forces of change. Viewing wages and earnings in their cost as well as income context, we shall attempt to sketch the nature of their fluctuations and perhaps see how such fluctuations affected or reflected entrepreneurial decisions.

WAGE RATES

For the most part, wage rates did not decline as sharply during the depression as did other prices. Moreover, the declines in wage rates usually lagged behind the reference-cycle pattern by some time. Table 49 shows the extent to which wage rates varied in different industries. A closer scrutiny of the subclassifications included under the industries listed confirms the notion of moderate wage declines. In only a few instances did wage rates decline more than 5 percent during the depression. Wages were fairly stable and were a less uncertain factor from the employers' point of view than were other prices.[20]

Average hourly earnings in all industry declined after the onset of the depression. The maximum decline during the depression from .216 cents in 1893 to .21 cents in 1895 amounted to almost 3 percent. For the years 1894 through 1897, hourly earnings remained below the 1893 level by 1 to 3 percent. The moderate nature of the decline in wage earnings for those employed in all industry is clearly documented.

The daily earnings of workers in coal mining, however, did not follow the general pattern of wages: fluctuations in that industry were quite sharp. From 1893 to 1897—the trough year for coal miners' wages—daily earnings of coal miners declined by over 26 percent. Once the wages declined after the depression developed, daily earnings did not return to the 1893 level for the remainder of the decade. There was a steady decline from 1893 to the trough in 1897. For much of this period, coal miners were beset by unemployment problems arising either from a fall in demand for coal or strikes resulting from refusal of the miners to accept wage reductions. Output declined moderately with volume of output contracting more as prices declined.[21]

Hourly earnings of workers in manufacturing and building trades followed the general pattern. Rates in building trades

Table 49
Average Money Earnings in All Industry and
in Selected Industry, 1890–1900
(dollars)

Year	Hourly Earnings in all Industry		Hourly Earnings in All Manu-facturing Industry		Hourly Earnings in Building Trades		Daily Earnings in Coal Mining		Full-Time Weekly Earnings of Railway Workers	
1890	.211	98.2	.199	98.1	.341	98.0	1.80	100.5	11.38	99.4
1891	.213	99.1	.202	99.5	.341	98.0	1.69	94.4	11.27	98.4
1892	.215	100.0	.203	100.0	.348	100.0	1.79	100.0	11.46	100.0
1893	.216	100.4	.205	101.0	.347	99.7	1.88	105.1	11.37	99.2
1894	.211	98.2	.200	98.5	.339	97.5	1.71	95.5	11.25	98.2
1895	.210	97.7	.200	98.5	.341	98.0	1.58	88.3	11.22	98.0
1896	.213	99.1	.205	101.0	.343	98.5	1.47	82.2	11.22	98.0
1897	.212	98.6	.203	100.0	.346	99.5	1.38	77.2	11.25	98.2
1898	.215	100.0	.204	100.5	.348	100.0	1.50	83.8	11.31	98.8
1899	.220	102.3	.209	103.0	.361	103.7	1.62	90.5	11.37	99.2
1900	.228	106.0	.216	106.4	.374	107.4	1.79	100.0	11.43	99.8

Table 49 (Continued)
Average Money Earnings in All Industry and
in Selected Industry, 1890–1900
(*dollars*)

Year	Probable Hourly Wage of Unskilled Labor		Weekly Wage Rates of Farm Labor		Hourly Earnings of Government Employees	
1890	.148	99.4	4.49	98.0	.441	92.8
1891	.150	100.7	4.53	99.0	.448	99.5
1892	.149	100.0	4.58	100.0	.451	100.0
1893	.149	100.0	4.47	97.6	.452	100.2
1894	.147	98.7	4.12	89.9	.458	101.7
1895	.146	98.0	4.17	90.9	.460	102.2
1896	.147	98.7	4.24	92.6	.457	101.3
1897	.148	99.4	4.32	94.3	.451	100.0
1898	.149	100.0	4.39	96.0	.441	92.8
1899	.149	100.0	4.60	100.4	.436	96.6
1900	.151	101.3	4.75	103.7	.440	97.6

Source: Paul H. Douglas, *Real Wages in the United States, 1890–1926*, pp. 108, 135, 143, 168, 182, 197, 205.
Note: For Index Numbers, 1892=100.

started declining early, probably reflecting the falling off in building in 1892. The decline, however, never exceeded 2.5 percent during the depression. In manufacturing, rates started declining after the depression began; the decline from 1893 to the trough in 1894 and 1895 likewise amounted to about 2.5 percent. In manufacturing, however, wage earnings remained high and stable except for 1894 and 1895. Weekly earnings of railway workers started declining in the early part of the depression, but the declines were also quite modest reaching a maximum of 2 percent from 1892 to 1895 and 1896. The hourly rates of unskilled labor did not deviate from the general pattern, the total decline approximating 2 percent. Wage rates for farm labor reflected the more depressed conditions in agriculture. From 1892 to 1895, the maximum decline amounted to about 9 percent.

WAGE EARNINGS

Though wage rates did not generally decline sharply during the depression, there was a more marked contraction in average money earnings, as employment in hours ebbed with reduced production. However, in some industrial activities such as gas, electricity, and office work, there was an increase in earnings. Table 50 records these changes for all industries as well as for selected industries. The overall pattern, represented by all industries, including farm labor, shows a decline of over 10 percent from $445 in 1892 to $400 in 1894. The decline in earnings was almost as great as the decline in perishable consumer goods prices of about 11 percent. Naturally, these average figures obscure finer changes in income for different areas of the economy.

The general earnings decline for all industries excluding farm labor is slightly less than when farm labor is included. From 1892 to 1894, the decline totaled almost 9.5 percent, the maxi-

mum decline for the depression. In other industries the pattern
varied. In manufacturing, the maximum decline during the depression was almost 9 percent. In steam railroads, the extreme
decline of 3.5 percent was much less than the pattern just described. Earnings of workers on street railways showed a decline of almost 5 percent. The drop in annual earnings of coal
miners was significantly greater than that for any other industry
and was much greater than the decline in daily earning rates in
the coal mines. From 1892 to 1897, the average earnings of
coal miners declined by more than 31 percent. Farm laborers'
average earnings fell by almost 10 percent from 1892 to 1894.

In only two areas did average annual earnings actually increase during the depression. Earnings of clerical workers in
manufacturing and steam railroads and of workers in the gas
and electricity industry increased countercyclically and because
of lower costs of living this meant an appreciable rise in real income.[22] Clerical workers in manufacturing and steam railroads
increased their annual earnings by almost 10 percent in the period from 1892 to 1897. The increase for workers in the gas
and electricity industry was even greater, reaching almost 12.5
percent.

The decline in annual earnings for most workers was less
marked than the descent in the cost of living. Nevertheless, the
averages involved obscure what may have happened to many
groups of workers whose earnings are not covered or whose
earnings varied in differing patterns. The averages, of course, do
not take into account unemployment. Since the level of unemployment during the nineties, and especially during the depression, was quite high (over 10 percent from 1893 to 1898), it is
clear that money earnings declined sharply for most workers.
The 10 percent drop in annual average earnings in all industries
is only a first approximation of the contraction in income for
wage earners.[23]

Table 50

Average Annual Earnings in All Industries and in Selected Industries, 1890–1900

(dollars)

Year	All Industries Including Farm Labor		Excluding Farm Labor		Wage Earners Manufacturing		Wage Earners Steam Railroad		Street Railways		Gas & Electricity	
1890	$438	98.5	$486	98.2	$439	98.5	$560	99.5	$557	104.0	$687	110.0
1891	438	98.5	487	98.4	442	99.0	554	98.5	529	98.8	587	93.9
1892	435	100.0	495	100.0	446	100.0	563	100.0	535	100.0	625	100.0
1893	430	96.7	480	97.0	420	94.2	563	100.0	526	98.4	627	100.2
1894	400	89.8	448	90.6	386	86.5	546	97.0	508	95.1	670	107.2
1895	415	93.3	468	94.6	416	93.5	546	97.0	509	95.2	640	102.4
1896	411	92.3	462	93.4	406	91.2	544	96.6	531	99.4	665	106.4
1897	411	92.3	462	93.4	408	91.4	543	96.5	552	103.1	703	112.4
1898	417	93.7	468	94.6	412	92.4	542	96.4	558	104.5	698	111.8
1899	428	96.2	480	97.0	426	95.5	543	96.5	591	110.6	612	97.9
1900	438	98.5	490	99.0	435	97.5	548	97.4	604	112.9	620	99.2

Table 50 (Continued)

Average Annual Earnings in All Industries and in Selected Industries, 1890–1900

(dollars)

Year	Clerical Workers[a]		Coal Miners		Farm Labor	
1890	$ 848	96.9	$406	103.2	$233	97.9
1891	882	99.6	377	95.9	236	99.2
1892	885	100.0	393	100.0	238	100.0
1893	923	104.3	383	97.5	232	97.5
1894	928	104.9	292	94.3	214	90.0
1895	941	106.3	307	78.3	216	90.8
1896	954	107.8	282	71.9	220	92.4
1897	970	109.6	270	68.8	224	94.2
1898	1,010	114.3	316	80.5	228	95.7
1899	1,004	113.6	379	96.4	239	100.4
1900	1,011	114.3	416	106.8	247	103.9

Source: Historical Statistics, p. 68.
Note: For Index Numbers, 1892=100.
(a) In manufacturing and steam railroads.

To get a better approximation of the decline in wage earners' earnings, account must be taken of changes in earnings, unemployment, and cost of living. Using Douglas' data on unemployment, S. Lebergott constructed a series of fluctuations in real earnings of nonfarm employees.[24] Table 51 carries out the process of deriving real earnings fluctuations.

Table 51
Earnings of Nonfarm Employees in
the United States, 1890–1900

	Full-Time Equivalent Earnings	Percent Time Lost by Unemployment	Money Earnings	Cost-of-Living, 1910–1914 Base	Real Earnings in 1910–1914 Dollars
1890	$559	6.2	$524	81.4	$644
1891	560	6.7	522	79.0	661
1892	567	4.6	541	79.0	685
1893	553	10.6	494	78.5	629
1894	524	18.1	429	76.5	561
1895	542	13.3	470	76.5	614
1896	537	16.6	448	78.5	571
1897	537	15.8	452	78.5	576
1898	542	14.8	462	78.5	589
1899	553	8.4	507	80.1	633
1900	563	7.5	521	81.8	637

Source: S. Lebergott, "Earnings of Non-Farm Employees in the United States, 1890–1946," *Journal of the American Statistical Association,* 43 (March, 1948):74–93.

From these data, we see that from 1892 to the trough year, 1894, the real earnings of nonfarm workers declined over 18 percent. At no time in the period 1894–1897 did real earnings reach a level 90 percent of that of 1892. With the exception of a few years, the entire decade was one in which wage earnings, in real terms, remained below the levels at the bginning of the decade. Despite the favorable declines in prices, workers' real incomes were forced down as unemployment was widespread and sharp.

Summary

To recapitulate the fluctuations in prices, the maximum declines during the depression are listed:

Category	Decline
Wholesale prices	13.0%
Producer durables	17.0
Construction material	11.5
Cost of living	12.0
Perishable goods	16.0
Semidurable goods	18.5
Durable goods	20.5
Stock prices	32.0
Dividend yields	27.5
Bond prices	2.0
Wages	5.0
Wage income	10.0
Real wage earnings	18.0

The prices of consumer goods, as a whole, declined more than those of wholesale commodities and about as much as those of producer durables. The real incomes of most employed wage earners rose during the depression, since wages and wage income did not decline by as much as other prices. Of course, for many families real income declined due to partial or complete unemployment. It is likely that prices of wholesale commodities and producer durable goods did not decline cyclically as sharply as usual due to the fairly strong demand for many basic commodities and producer durable equipment as industrialization proceeded.[25] The levels of steel and iron production, for example, did not fall sharply during the depression. New ventures in iron and steel and allied basic industries were undertaken despite general economic contraction. Favorable prices of raw materials and equipment as well as availability of qualified manpower and construction at reasonable rates made capital growth in plant and equipment attractive during the period. On the other hand, the impact of the depression on consumer income was probably strong. The restraint of consumers, due to lower income, probably is reflected in the sharper fall in consumer, semidurable, and durable prices. Basic industries could expand even as consumer demand fell off, due to the ever growing markets abroad in which United States steel and machinery products were being sold on a favorable profit basis.

While prices for labor, commodities, and equipment were receding in various degrees, stocks and bonds were experiencing divergent price reactions. In circumstances of bank and stock-market panic, as well as prolonged depressed conditions, it is not surprising that stock prices fell as sharply as they did. The many failures of industrial corporations and railroads engendered deep pessimism in the market, and ownership of enterprises was not attractive. Consolidation and mergers were facilitated. On the other hand, bonds fared much more favorably. They offered a more certain source of income which, in a sound corporation, was not likely to be impaired despite severe depression conditions. Even in the bankrupt railroads, the bondholders' investment and income were safe. Bond prices fell only 2 percent during the depression and the yields of bonds in real terms actually increased. This contrasted sharply with stock dividend yields which dropped in money terms by 27.5 percent, while in real terms the decline was almost 25 percent. While long-term investment rates varied in this way, the short-term money market reflected the period's uncertainty, fluctuating violently with changing conditions. Responding readily to adverse events, these rates became prohibitive and, as circumstances became more favorable, rates were low as money was in abundant supply.

Clearly, the depression of the nineties was one of the most severe in this nation's annals. And yet, unlike practically all the other quite severe contractions, it did not record declines in prices as sharp as those of its analogues (the depressions of the 1870s, 1921, and 1929). What explains this deviation from the usual pattern?

The historical and institutional context in which this question has to be answered needs sketching. It must be recalled that the trough of the depression of the nineties was also the end of a secular price decline which started after the close of the Civil War. Thus, at the start of the contraction, many producers and traders had already been subject to a profit squeeze and where possible, in the market context, resisted further price reductions. If such resistance entailed larger inventories than contracting demand ordinarily would foreshadow, favorable interest rates made the cost of carrying swollen inventories for some businessmen less than the losses large-scale liquidation would generate. Of course, such a policy would mean, among other things, a sharper reduction in employment than if prices were allowed to yield to the pressures of greatly diminished demand.

The choice of whether or not to lower prices is not postulated in a competitive market, so the behavior described above could only be carried out in markets whose institutional arrangements deviated from the model. Actually, the eighties and nineties were periods of economic combination, so that in certain sectors of the economy administered prices were possible. The growth of trade unionism meant that wage rates would probably be resistant to economic contraction. (They declined only about 5 percent during the depression.) Thus, even if most of the economy remained competitive, the concentration in certain industries changed marketing and pricing patterns. Resistance to price declines was not only a possibility but a rational imperative under conditions of monopolistic competition.

The downward price rigidity during the depression undoubtedly contributed to the severity of this contraction. Since prices did not decline to their "natural" level, the consequence was greater unemployment and lower output and income than would otherwise have obtained. In those sectors where price did decline to the "natural" level, the decline may have continued to a still lower level commensurate with the greater economic contraction induced by the greater unemployment and reduction in output in sectors where administered prices were above the "natural" level.

NOTES

1. *Historical Statistics*, pp. 68–70, 231 ff.; Alfred Cowles 3rd et al., *Common Stock Indexes*, p. 63 and passim; Frederick Macaulay, *Some Theoretical Problems Suggested by the Movements of Interest Rates, Bond Yields and Stock Prices in the United States Since 1856*, pp. A141ff.

2. For an overall view of what happened to wholesale prices in prosperity and depression, see *Historical Statistics*, pp. 231–235 and U.S., Bureau of Labor Statistics, *Index Numbers of Wholesale Prices on Prewar Base, 1890–1927*, p. 2. This price decline in 1895 continuing into 1896 and 1897 confirms our feeling that the period 1893 to 1897 was one continuous depressed period.

3. Farm equipment prices roughly paralleled the decline in prices of farm products and foods, though starting earlier. The decline in prices of farm equipment came in response not only to generally depressed conditions but reflected the general depression in agriculture. These prices showed an almost steady decline throughout the nineties.

4. Both sets of prices increased during 1893 and 1894 after which they dropped sharply, as the first phase of the depression ended. The decline in these prices from 1894 to 1896 amounts to about 27 percent —a marked decrease. Purchase of these durable goods must have been very attractive in 1895 and 1896. In the next year, prices rebounded sharply to the higher levels of 1894. The abrupt decline in these prices probably had significant effects on growing heavy industries.

5. *Historical Statistics*, p. 231.

6. W. H. Shaw, *Value of Commodity Output*, p. 295. Shaw's index

figures were converted to a 1892 base for purposes of highlighting the fluctuations for the depression period.

7. Ibid., p. 20. Shaw's prices of consumer goods show greater amplitude than the actual fluctuations in consumer retail prices since they are prices for consumer goods at the factory.

8. This undoubtedly reflected an important change in consumer habits in which manufactured fuel products were being used instead of the nonmanufactured type. In the early period of use, such products had high prices which responded only mildly to cyclical forces.

9. Imports from Europe in the nineties totaled over 50 percent of general imports. Since the balance-of-payments problem resulted mainly from payments due in Europe and mainly in England, measurement of changes in terms of trade using price indices for British exports will give some indication of whether or not difficulties arose from our economic relationships with England. Since agricultural exports represented over 75 percent of all United States exports in 1892 and over two thirds of all exports in 1898, an index of farm products may be used as one measuring tool. Manufacturers were 16.5 and 25 percent of the totals for 1892 and 1898, respectively; for both years, manufacturers and agricultural products together were over 93 percent of total exports. Price indices of selected manufacturers, therefore, may also be used. Prices of imports as such are not available. Practically all manufactured imports came from Europe; imports from Europe usually amounted to slightly more than half the total of imports. Partly or wholly manufactured imports were 40 percent of total imports. To see what the price tendencies were, we shall look at selected British prices and compare their fluctuations with those of United States products exports in large quantities. See *Historical Statistics,* pp. 249–250; U.S. Bureau of Foreign and Domestic Commerce, *Monthly Summary of Imports and Exports,* 1893–1898.

10. With the exception of a recovery in the first few months of 1893, wheat prices declined steadily from 1892 to the end of 1894. From 1892 to 1894, the decline amounted to over 30 percent. The recovery in 1895 was short-lived and by the end of late 1892 to early 1894 wheat prices declined just about 30 percent; for the next year, there was a sharp recovery, then in 1896 the price of corn was down by 50 percent. These data on corn and wheat prices must be taken into account when examining the index of farm product prices since these two crops were an important element in agricultural exports. See Stanford University, Food Research Institute, *Wheat Studies* 10:316, 348–349.

11. There is evidence that United States steel producers sold in foreign markets at lower prices to beat British competition. Thus it is possible that this index overstates export prices.

12. The price indices used in A. G. Silverman, "Monthly Index Numbers of British Export and Import Prices, 1880–1913," *Review of Economic Statistics* 12 (1930): 147, parallel those of Schlote. Silverman's index for all groups shows a maximum decline in export prices of 10 percent from 1892 to 1897 compared with Schlote's 8 percent. In Table

48, the index for Raw Materials and Semi-manufactured Exports was a combined one. For purposes of comparison, of course, raw-material prices are not relevant but since semimanufactures were an important part of United States imports, the index is of some use.

13. Silverman, "Monthly Index Numbers," p. 147. See also U.S., Bureau of Statistics, *Movement of Prices, 1840–1899* [from Sauerback's Tables and *Economist* (London),] pp. 3132, 3144, where the price declines for specific items and groups parallel those cited above.

14. This decline was, of course, necessary in order for United States manufacturers to compete on world markets with the British, as at this time such competition was growing sharper. While part of this decline in United States manufactured prices was due to increased efficiency, some reflected cyclical forces.

15. Cowles et al., *Common-stock Indexes*, pp. 3, 66. In their decline, stock prices conformed to the reference-cycle pattern: the decline started early in 1893. The trough reached in August, however, anticipated by ten months the reference-cycle trough, but the nature of the panic was such as to precipitate a quick and early decline in stock prices. The trough in 1894 was a plateau which started at the reference-cycle trough and continued until early in 1895. The recovery in prices thus was delayed by nine months and the peak reached in September, 1895, anticipated by three months the reference peak. The next trough in prices was in August, 1896, ten months before the reference trough. But from August, 1896, to April, 1897, though there was an increase in stock prices of almost 6 percent, prices remained at a low level. The sharper recovery in prices early in 1897 led the reference cycle by a few months.

16. Ibid, p. 62.

17. Ibid., pp. 63, 492.

18. Ibid., pp. 62–63, 492.

19. Ibid. This decline was in line with the slight downward trend in bond interest yield over the years starting in 1880 and continuing until after the turn of the century.

20. Paul H. Douglas, *Real Wages in the United States, 1890–1926*, pp. 95–204. While wage rates did not, on the average, fluctuate much there were important instances where the rates were reduced appreciably with explosive consequences. For example, in May, 1894, the Pullman strike broke out as a result of eight months of wage cuts amounting to between 25 and 40 percent. Other instances of wage rate reductions exceeding 10 percent were in steel and coal mining. Another consideration to be kept in mind is that data on wage rates before 1890 are not available so that the relative level of wage rates prevalent in the early nineties may not be precisely set forth. Below we shall consider the impact of unemployment on wages to get a more meaningful view of the impact of the depression on workers.

21. *Historical Statistics*, p. 142.

22. Of course, these increases do not take into account the cost of

unemployment. See Table 51 and the analysis below for consideration of unemployment effects on earnings.

23. Douglas, *Real Wages in the U.S.,* pp. 430–439.

24. "Earnings of Non-Farm Employees in the United States, 1890–1946," *Journal of the American Statistical Association* 43 (March, 1948):74–93.

25. The moderate declines in prices may have been due to the mildness of monetary deflation during most of the depression. Money forms did not decline sharply. Moreover, as the depression proceeded domestic gold output increased (see Chapter 6) having an inflationary effect on the money supply.

8

Conclusion

The depression, we have seen, took place during a period of rapid industrial and manufacturing development. From 1880 to 1910, national wealth increased by about 275 percent, output of all finished commodities by almost 250 percent, and output of all consumer goods by roughly 220 percent. The rapid growth of manufacturing was made possible by parallel growth in mining, transportation, distribution, and financial activity, while the increased need for manpower was met by immigration and a diminution in the relative number of workers in agriculture. Agriculture grew with other industries but its growth was less rapid and its relation to other sectors of the economy changed qualitatively as overall economic growth forged new and modified relationships. These changes were reflected in the development of new techniques of production and business organization, increasing productivity, and changing market relationships.

The changes in technology and business organization were responses as well as stimuli to the rapid and widespread changes shaping mining, transportation, and manufacturing. These industries grew in a climate of declining prices, which reached a half-century low during the depression and affected different sectors of the economy favorably or adversely as their price-cost relationships mandated. The expanding industries in which technological changes were readily implemented were in a better position to prosper and grow rapidly than those in which such possibilities were more limited by slow technological advances. Such growth was enhanced by increasing availability of a relatively cheap labor supply of hundreds of thousands of immigrants arriving each year and as many from the more rapidly growing numbers of farm-family children migrating to the cities. Extended urbanization was a consequence of such developments but it also stimulated further expansion of industry. In these circumstances, technological advances and consolidation of economic units quickened as financial institutions coordinated the capital and management essential to the combinations being shaped in many economic areas.

Agriculture's less robust development affected the economy in several ways. In the marketplace, the products of America's farms did not enjoy the advantages of protection so that the more marked decline in farm prices meant worsening terms of trade with much of the economy during the depression. The worsening of the economy's terms of trade in the world markets was mainly a consequence of the preponderant position of agricultural exports in total exports and of the disinclination of foreigners to continue pouring as large amounts of capital into the United States as railroads became less lucrative investments vis-à-vis more attractive opportunities in Africa and elsewhere. Agriculture's difficulties led to softness in demand for farm equipment and other materials.

In this period of rapid economic growth and changed relationships, the depression of 1893–1897 was a jolting setback. From 1869 to 1913, only the seventies rivaled the depression of the nineties in severity. Even a cursory analysis of such indicators as clearings, strategic production series (such as pig iron), business failures, freight-car orders, stock prices, and the like sustains the view that the 1893–1897 depression was quite severe. Our judgement, however, is based on more than the mechanical consideration of such indices of economy activity. We have looked at the economy from different aspects to see the dynamic unfolding of the depression as different sectors of the economy responded to changing market and technological conditions. From 1869 to 1913, while significant changes underlined were occurring, only the depression of the seventies compared with that of the nineties.

By gauging the timing and assessing the degree of economic contraction in various sectors of the economy, the nature of the depression is partially revealed. Among the early, sharp contractions was that in overall building construction, starting after the spring of 1892 as part of a long building contraction. The falling off in immigration during the depression probably affected one segment of building construction. This early contraction in building construction was paralleled by an early decline in railroad construction late in 1891 or early in 1892. These declines reflected less sanguine profit expectations in major investment areas where a saturation level had been reached. The railroads had been through a period of tremendous construction activity in the eighties, stimulating much of the economy. In the nineties, railroad construction at the same levels was not feasible, both in terms of the limited areas for expansion and the financial consequences of overexpansion. The consolidations in the nineties were a result of overexpansion, overcapitalization, and mismanagement. Thus the downward revision of railroad plans for investment in rolling stock and steel rails late in 1892 was a harbinger of the general depression to come. Output of electrical and industrial machinery started to decline in 1892, adding to the downward pressure on the economy.

Among the economic indicators showing early contraction

were those tracing agricultural activity. At the outset of the nineties, agriculture was in a relatively depressed state from which it was temporarily aroused, during the 1890–1891 crop year, when European demand for agricultural products increased as the continent's granaries suffered drought. Thereafter the world grain markets were not favorable to the United States farmer and his income declined. The farmer's relative bargaining position both in the domestic and world markets was weakened. Output of farm equipment—an important indicator of agricultural investment—reflected these vicissitudes as it declined markedly during 1891.

While these forces were determining in important measure the nature of the depression-to-be, relationships between the domestic and international economies were also changing qualitatively. The international capital market was contracting since the industrial economies of Europe had entered the contraction phase of the business cycle in 1890 and 1891. Decreased total capital investment by the British, for example, meant a decline in foreign investment and especially in investment in the United States since a dim view was taken of the manner in which the railroads—the most significant investment area—were managed. Diminished British foreign investment was unlikely to go into risky United States railroad securities no longer attractively remunerative while more favorable opportunities existed in other parts of the world. To add to the balance-of-payments difficulties implicit in diminished foreign investment, many European investors liquidated their holdings in the United States as the depression reduced their income expectations sharply and threatened their equity claims.

The balance of payments was also upset by other factors as the depression proceeded. Immigration fell off so that foreign funds entering the economy with immigrants declined. At the same time, the depression stimulated emigration and the consequent transfer of funds abroad increased foreigners' claims on the United States. Payments for shipping services dropped as imports declined, but payments for other services such as tourist and insurance either held their own or increased. The decline in the value of imports after the depression began eased somewhat the payments problem, but the unfavorable terms of trade, developing early in the nineties, worsened as the depression proceeded and thus lessened the favorable effects of the import decline. The value of exports declined only slightly at a time when quantities of exports actually increased, illustrating clearly the unfavorable terms of trade. The net effect of these dynamic factors was disequilibrium in the balance of payments, a condition that had developed before the depression and was reflected in the almost continuous outflow of gold starting in 1891. This drain of gold had adverse effects on the banking and monetary system as well as on the fiscal operations of the Treasury. The dramatic gold-silver polemics culminating in the election of 1896 were symptomatic of the profound economic dislocations at home and in our economic relations with Europe.

As the depression continued, its cumulative effects mounted and most of the economy suffered contractions. Following the decline in construction, agricultural and railway investment, and electrical and machinery output, general investment decreased foreshadowing further contraction. Shipping output likewise declined as the depression spread. Other producer durables showed significant declines once the early impact of the contraction was spent. In the machinery industries, where output had increased greatly before the depression, the severe effects of the economic contraction were averted until its cumulative effects became more widespread in 1894. After that, very few industrial activities were able to avoid contraction; all categories of producer durables output showed important declines. The depression caused declines in industries which had been experiencing very sharp growth in size and output.

Total output dropped about 13 percent at a maximum, and this was partially reflected in the maximum decline in gross farm income (representing a fourth of total output) of about 15 percent and varying declines in the consumption of all types of goods, including food products. These declines brought the economy as a whole, in 1894, to levels almost 20 percent below capacity. While consumption of durables and semidurables contracted markedly in response to the decline in income, that of food was much less sharp, amounting to a few percentage points, though other perishables declined to a greater degree. Per-capita consumption of many food and clothing products declined significantly, underscoring the severe nature of the depression, for in most depressions consumption of foods is maintained. These declines in income and consumption, following upon contractions in investment, attested to the intensity of the decline in agricultural, railroad, and construction activity.

These decreases of real output of producer and consumer goods were a necessary consequence of income declines and they can be traced through the financial mechanisms. After the period of relatively tight money preceding the downturn in 1893, banks found idle balances building up as the velocity of payments declined. Except for the period of the panic, the banks had adequate reserves to meet all customers' needs despite the constant gold outflow. It was the drop in the use of money forms rather than in the quantity available which forced a series of relatively moderate price declines.

The decline of prices during the depression was less marked than usual for major depressions and undoubtedly was a major factor in forcing sharp contractions in output. Price declines, on the whole, were only slightly greater than the relative contraction in output. Prices of consumer goods, in an unusual behavior pattern, declined more sharply than wholesale prices and about as much as producer durable prices. The sharpest declines were in agricultural and metal prices, the latter reflecting in some degree technological improvements even during the depression period. With relatively inflexible price conditions such as these, some entrepreneurs able to produce with sharply reduced costs due either to innovations or a more favorable price complex were more strongly motivated. Some electrical and machinery industries were in such a position. In other activities, such as urban construction, less favorable price conditions were apparently overcome by the relatively strong demand for business buildings and multiple dwellings. In the complex of these price relationships, the conditions seemed to favor certain basic industries such as manufacturing and metal trades while agricultural and consumer goods were less fortunate.

As prices of commodities changed their relationships, other "prices" affected economic activity too. Ownership of corporate enterprise was made easy for many as stock prices fell sharply. Whether this facilitated combination is difficult to say. Creditors of corporations—bondholders—fared well throughout the period as bond prices remained fairly steady. Interest rates, except in crisis periods, were moderately low. Wage rates declined less than most prices, but unemployment was sharp and widespread. In some instances, however, wage reductions were sharp and occasioned violent reactions—as in the Pullman and coal strikes in 1894.

As the depression proceeded, economic activity recovering incompletely in 1895 and then relapsing again, some areas of the economy were not engulfed by cumulative ebbing forces. The process of urbanization, which was strongly evident throughout the nineties, was a source for continuing economic activity, despite the general contraction. Perhaps this continued expansion in residential building and electric street railway construction was partially a response to the depression, offering investment areas of relatively favorable expectations. At any rate, after an initial slump in 1893, construction of residential multiple-dwelling units increased sharply in succeeding years. Public building also increased to higher levels and skyscrapers, a growing fad, were built in every year of the depression. Paralleling these building activities was the boom in electric street railway construction, which coincided almost exactly with the depression period. The horse-drawn trolley was replaced with electric cars. Other technological advances in electrical machinery, steel products, and chemicals conspired to forge the metropolis with its skyscrapers, large factories, and apartment houses, spread over different parts of the city yet integrated spatially by new rapid transit units. This expansion in urban development occurred at a time when investment opportunities in the rest of the economy were mostly unattractive.

In mining also, investment and output failed to follow the general sharp contraction, though there were slight declines in output of some mineral products. Where such declines did occur, however, they were less marked than those in most sectors of the economy. The rapid growth of mining industries was slowed somewhat by the depression but not reversed. Here too technological advances most probably played an important role in attracting funds for investment.

As the depression continued, the value of exports declined by only 5 percent, while prices of exports probably fell off by more than 10 percent. Thus quantities of exports, especially manufactured goods, increased throughout the contraction period. The maintenance of net exports meant the declines in GNP were domestically generated. It is likely that many United States manufacturers advanced credit to foreign importers and that this type of investment proved especially attractive during a period of depression.

After the depression had run its course well into 1897, some of the countercyclical forces (such as the boom in electric street railways and exports of manufactured goods) were reinforced by other expansionary forces. Many sectors of the economy could no longer postpone replacement of equipment and materials. The railroads, for example, had allowed much rolling stock to deteriorate and their purchases of rails had been inadequate for proper maintenance. To maintain revenues, replacement was necessary. Likewise, industry had to increase investment outlays after the forced postponement of the depression years. These investment activities gained momentum and gathered with other forces to thrust the economy to higher levels of activity.

In the agricultural sector, favorable changes were also taking place in 1897. The previous year had marked the trough for farm income and prices but 1897 held out more favorable prospects. Europe's new prosperity, starting in 1896 after the long contraction from 1890 and 1891, led to increased demand for agricultural products and world conditions became more favorable as income and output rose. The result was a marked rise in farm prices and income as 1897 proceeded, this new prosperity giving rise to expanding farm demand for the products and services of the industrial sectors of the economy. Increased European demand also affected United States exports of mining and forest products, which paralleled the rise in manufacturing exports. Increased exports of manufactures were also made possible by the growth in United States capital exports, while increasing capital exports of European economies provided the wherewithal by which underdeveloped areas as well as other areas could raise the level of imports of manufactures from all industrial economies.

As these forces gathered momentum, they were aided by a moderate expansion in overall building construction. Throughout 1897, building construction maintained levels of activity at least 12 percent higher than in 1896 and considerably above the trough of the depression. The major investment areas—agriculture, railroads, construction, and manufacturing—were again expanding. Thus the impetus of expanding manufacturing—of increased agricultural income, of growing railroad investment and traffic, of greater construction activity in all areas—was intensified as the cumulative forces started by the countercyclical activities gathered strength. The result was a robust forward surge in output and income throughout the economy as economic activity reached historic peaks and as the clear imprint of an industrial-manufacturing economy was more widely felt.

The depression, thus, may be viewed as a profound economic dislocation arising from forces which were transforming an agricultural-industrial economy into an industrial-manufacturing economy with continuing large-scale agriculture. Disparate rates of economic growth of different parts of the economy affected their relative proportions of national product. Such new real relationships resulted from reorganization of technology and business and were transmitted through significantly changing market mechanisms. The 1893–1897 contraction was a contraction in which almost every sector of the economy experienced significant declines. Once these declines were reversed and the economy again resumed its upward movement, its industrial-manufacturing characteristics were most clearly discernible. The areas that were closely tied to manufacturing growth—mining, urban construction, rapid transit facilities, financial services, and public utilities—took on more important roles in economic activity.

The transformation of the economy was reflected in the change in agriculture's marketing position and its effect on the economy in its relationships with European economies. In the 1895–1896 period, agriculture was at its most depressed level. This resulted from worsening terms of trade with the rest of the economy and the world and lowered domestic demand. The markets in which agricultural products were sold, either at home or abroad, were unprotected, relatively competitive markets in which prices fluctuated quite readily. Moreover, supply conditions were not subject to control, due to the large numbers of independent farmers and the significant role of the weather in output. Therefore, domestically and internationally, the farmer's products were usually sold in a buyer's market. This was certainly true during the depression period. Just as the farmer's position was unfavorable vis-à-vis the rest of the economy, so was that of the entire economy which sold mostly agricultural goods and bought many manufactured goods abroad.

Although farmers sold in an unprotected market, many of the markets in which they bought were protected either by tariffs or monopolistic arrangements. The purchase of transportation, financial, and marketing services as well as manufacturing goods was under market conditions more favorable to the seller. While all prices were declining, those of goods and services bought by farmers did not decline as much as those of farm products. Such income and wealth redistribution through deflation also worked disadvantages for the economy as a whole. For, since most exports were products of agriculture and most imports were products of manufacturing and mining, the economy was forced to give more of the former for the latter as international terms of trade went against the United States.

The industrialization process modified these relationships and made the economy less exposed to outside forces. During the depression, technological, administrative, and economic changes hastened the development. Manufacturing and mining grew in importance and their exports persisted despite the general economic contraction. Their continued development made possible greater capital exports, increasing claims abroad. More significant, however, was the fact that the greater relative importance of manufacturing and mining in total exports meant that the economy was less vulnerable to the sharper price declines in agricultural products. Manufacturing exports, it is true, were being sold abroad in competition with the British and Germans, but in many areas, where capital was being exported, the market was protected. United States foreign policy attempted to strengthen its nationals' bargaining position. A large segment of exports was now sold under more favorable market conditions and this meant more imports received for a fixed amount of exports. Thus the significant advance of manufacturing and allied industries in the domestic economy enhanced the nation's economic wherewithal at home and abroad.

The depression thus emerges as a period of intense dislocation occasioned by the unhappy conjuncture of domestic and foreign economic forces shaped during the transformation of the economy. Depressions of varying severity occurred before and after the one under review and this depression was not unique because of the circumstances of economic transformation. Nevertheless, the depression must be seen as part of this process of transformation. Its most significant factors were elements in the interaction between agriculture, manufacturing, transportation, foreign economic relations, and the like as these areas changed their nature and the nature of their interrelationships. The details of the depression take on meaning only in the broader framework of economic development in which agriculture passed on to a new role in an economy more clearly bearing the mark of manufacturing and the tertiary activities of a modern industrial society.

The economic contraction from 1893 to 1897 was one that extended into most areas of the economy and its social and economic effects were felt among all the people. It sharpened conflicts among many social groups as its impact changed people's attitudes and ways of living. There were manifestations of conflicting interests as the economy's transformation led to new techniques and relationships, both domestically and in the world economy. The severity of the depression, borne by different social and economic groups in varying degree, was a partial measure of the real costs involved in shaping an industrial order with ramifying connections throughout the world and with a posture more adequate to support a vast population at higher levels of living. By the end of the century, it was undeniable that the United States was a world power with great economic influence. Its economic maturity pushed its economic relationships into new areas. In this development, the depression was an episode which reflected in microcosm the process and cost of economic maturation in an advancing capitalist economy.

Bibliography

Bibliographical Note

The Panic of 1893 and the ensuing depression period have long been viewed as economic events of signal importance in the annals of this country. Though many of the dimensions of the depressed period following the panic were left unrecorded or uncovered, most social and economic historians have accorded the panic and depression a rank of primary importance. The events following the panic were considered symptomatic of important changes in the development of the economy by some keen observers of the period.

In the contemporary explanations of the depression, oversimplifications abounded. One partisan observer, the Democratic governor of Massachusetts, projected his own answer to the question he asked: "Is our admitted distress due to existing Republican legislation which the country has condemned and ordered to be repealed, or the impending Democratic legislation which is to carry out the people's will?" Other explanations ran the gamut from this political reason to an opposite gold policy with emphasis on how widespread loss of confidence made economic health impossible. Whatever the putative key factor —silver, the tariff, iron prices— it was employed to explain in glib fashion the widespread economic contraction which had long been in the making and was not easily overcome—even when the "cause" was eliminated.

While economic and social historians gave a prominent position to the panic and depression, very few works are devoted exclusively to them. This dearth of material is surprising, considering the significance and relative recency of the period. One published work concerns itself with the panic and its causes: William J. Lauck, *The Causes of the Panic of 1893*. Published first in 1907, the work was awarded a Hart, Schaffner Marx first prize by a committee comprised of Professors J. L. Laughlin, J. B. Clark, and Henry C. Adams, Horace White, and Carroll D. Wright. The work, dealing unevenly and sometimes contradictorily with the background and course of the panic and its causes, does not analyze or describe the depressed period that followed the banking and market panic. Other works explain the forces giving rise to the panic and depression in different ways. In *The Mercantile Conditions of the Crisis of 1893,* a University of Nebraska study done in 1902, Frank S. Philbrick focuses mainly on the nature of business failures in 1893. Two doctoral dissertations are also concerned with the panic and depression. Frank P. Weberg traces the factors at work prior to the panic in "The Background of the Panic of 1893" (Catholic University, 1929). In Gerald T. White, "The United States and the Problem of Recovery after 1893" (University of California, 1938), the events following the panic are reviewed at length with discernment. This dissertation effectively traces the major events of the depression in a historical framework.

None of the works devoted to the description and analysis of the panic and depression measures the dimensions of either set of events. Lauck dealt only with the panic and attempted to make its explanation more complete by surveying the background of economic events in the United States and Europe. His emphasis was on currency policy and its repercussions, but there was no systematic connecting of statistical data to his hypothesis. Giving scholarly support to widely accepted popular explanations of the panic, he flatly identified the "causes" of the panic:

> This cause to which the crisis of 1893 is directly and wholly attributable consisted of a widespread fear, both home and abroad, that the United States would not be able to maintain a gold standard of payments . . . the precipitation of and recovery from the crisis furnished additional evidence to bear out the foregoing claim. The beginning of the crisis . . . was marked by the decline of the Treasury gold reserve, on April 22, below the $100,000,000 limit; the ending of the resultant industrial and financial chaos dated from the repeal, on August 28, of the Silver Law of 1890. [*sic*]

The antecedent forces at work—foreign investment, business conditions in the United States, silver acts, the panic of 1890, industrial and financial conditions abroad—were employed to dovetail with Lauck's "causes" of the panic. In effect, Lauck's work supports the widespread notion that the panic was directly related to unwise currency policy.

Lauck's work provides some useful background material for an understanding of the panic and subsequent events. Though his antisilver bias is evident, the early chapters, nevertheless, furnish helpful data on related economic developments in the United States and abroad. He surveyed the silver movement and its effects on the economy. The importance of the 1890 panic and depression are sketched, setting up the conditions preceding the 1893 panic. The major events of the panic are also set forth. In the concluding analysis, the "causes" of the panic indicated above are inferred. Yet, in the framework of his own analysis, his conclusions appear to be contradictory and unsubstantiated both in terms of the data he presents and all the data available to us today. His analysis is also punctuated with misstatements.

Some evidence to support these strictures is called for. In his final chapter, Lauck attributes British disinvestment and realization of gains from holdings in the United States to fear that the United States would leave the gold standard. Then he says: "The crisis of 1893 did not arise from any other causes which had their origin outside of the United States. This conclusion is incontrovertible, for the reason that financial and industrial conditions in other commercial nations during the three years, 1891–93, were not marked by any developments which could have possibly reacted disastrously upon this country. On the contrary, foreign countries during this period suffered severely from the state of affairs in the United States." He then goes on to trace the financial and industrial depression in England, France, and Germany. After this Lauck contradicts himself by saying that the crisis in the United States "could not have been due to any difficulties abroad. The general situation in Great Britain and Europe during these years [1890–1893] was marked by a steady upward movement from a condition of financial depression to one of prosperity." Actually, the period 1891 to 1895 was one of deep depression in England, France, Germany, and other European countries. Thus, in his haste to attribute the crisis to silver policy and make it domestic in origin, Lauck ignores his own evidence and tries to attribute difficulties abroad to the United States despite the timing inconsistencies. Aside from the logical discrepancies pointed out, Lauck does not present strong supportive evidence for the single "cause" which emerges from his analysis.

Weberg's work, a very short one, parallels much of what Lauck did by tracing the development of such factors as foreign influences, Populism, currency and tariff policy, the banking system, and so on. In no way is the impact of the panic measured quantitatively. Philbrick measured one dimension of the crisis—business failures—without drawing even in outline form the major forces at work during the crisis.

White's work is the most comprehensive of the group, tracing the major developments in the period ushered in by the panic of 1893. Essentially a history of the depression period, it marks the important events which shaped the economy. In chronological fashion, the author recounts what happened during the depression and gives scattered quantitative support to his story by quoting contemporary analysts and sources. Major issues such as the tariff, currency, and government intervention are carefully examined.

It seems clear that the works which deal directly with the panic and the depression do not make any significant contribution to an understanding of the depression. White's effort is an exception since it provides a useful, consistent set of descriptions and interrelationships. Weberg and Philbrick, as well as Lauck, furnish helpful background data and perspective. These works on the panic or the depression emphasize the need for a systematic treatment of the depression—one which would give a descriptive analysis of a major economic contraction.

Certain works aided the author in deciding what approach to take in analyzing the problem of the depression. We have indicated in our preface that the "historical-quantitative" approach of R. A. Gordon or the "descriptive analysis" of Mitchell inform the author's methodological approach. Other models were also helpful in developing the author's path:

W. W. Rostow's *British Economy of the Nineteenth Century* and his earlier work (Yale dissertation, 1940), "British Trade Fluctuations 1868–1896," provide models for descriptive analysis of a relatively long period of economic history. In both of these works, attempts are made to use current analytic tools to set up classifications useful in explaining important interrelationships in economic development.

For a shorter period of analysis, such as the one in this project, Arthur G. Auble's dissertation (Harvard, 1949), "The Depressions of 1873 and 1882 in the United States," serves as a useful model. He, too, uses modern tools of approaching the phenomena of the two depressions. His analysis follows quantification of important categories and he brings to bear many of the tools and the orientation of economic analysis.

In addition to these works, there are a number of other books which deal principally with other subjects the treatment of which necessitates some discussion of the panic and depression. These books cover such subjects as depressions, business cycles, financial developments, and the like—all of which impinge on the period under review. They are, in the main, studies interpreting developments with some quantitative data but more heavily qualitative and analytic in orientation. The generalizations from such works make possible a clearer view of the role of certain factors in the depression.

Some works review depressions in general and thus touch on the 1893–1897 contraction. Burton's work, written shortly after the depression, devotes a chapter to an account of crises in the United States. The outstanding features of each crisis are sketched very briefly; for the period following the panic, such factors as withdrawal of foreign investment, tariff legislation, change in political control, and so on are traced. In the main, the generalizations made are accurate but shallow. Two similar works in which monetary factors are stressed in superficial accounts of the 1893–1897 period are by Lightner and Juglar. In none of these works is the set of explanations for the period adequate.

A doctoral dissertation by Rendigs Fels, "History of American Business Cycles, 1865–1921" (Harvard, 1943), attempts to determine the extent to which economic historians and economists agree on the interpretation of the period. The author finds that substantial reconciliation between apparent divergent views can be effected. His generalizations about the major forces at work are rather sweeping and are not adequately corroborated by quantitative data. Moreover, the points which bear on the 1893–1897 period do not throw new light on it.

O. M. W. Sprague's work, *The History of Crises Under the National Banking System,* written for the National Monetary Commission and published in 1910, is an excellent treatment of the financial aspects of the depression. The scope of the work, of course, is wider than the subject under review here; nevertheless, the chapter on the 1893 crisis is a first-rate account and analysis of the monetary and banking factors at work.

Another financially oriented work is Alexander D. Noyes's *Forty Years of American Finance, 1865–1907.* Though the focus is financial, the author brings to bear an insightful grasp of economic events to give fuller meaning to the economic developments of the period. His three chapters on the panic and subsequent financial difficulties cover the period in our analysis. Without presenting a systematic and comprehensive statistical account of what happened in financial sectors of the economy, Noyes does nevertheless provide the quantitative and qualitative framework for a keener understanding of the period. His interpolations of nonfinancial data between his financial analysis are helpful guides to any attempt to reconstruct the main economic currents of the time.

D. D. Bremer's *American Bank Failures* offers valuable data on bank failures and suspensions during the depression.

In addition to the above works, there are many works and sources which have some bearing on the depression. Some of these works are on different facets of the business cycle or on the structure of the economy at that time. They provide data or understanding of an important phase of economic activity. Besides such works, there are others which present statistical series spanning many decades. The data for the years under review are very useful in piecing together the quantitative parts that help give a whole view of the depression of the nineties.

Scattered data of various sorts are also available for use.

Among the various reports of the state departments of labor, useful data on changes in economic activity within the states can be found. Some of these data are limited in value; other data are very useful. From them we are able to get information making possible substantiation of other sources, an independent estimate of unemployment, industrial activity, consumption, and so on. Such an approach has limited though specific value for the individual researcher. For those blessed with a research staff, construction of economic series would rely heavily on such sources, as well as others.

Federal government statistics are also a very useful source. The Census reports, as well as those of the Industrial Commission, are rich statistical mines. In addition, reports of the Commissioner of Labor as well as other publications of the Bureau of Labor are available. Also there are many helpful data to be found in certain congressional committee reports. Among the many volumes of reports of the National Monetary Commission, one section of one of the volumes provides invaluable data on financial and monetary activity. Other government publications of the Agriculture and Commerce departments helped to fill lacunae in quantitative data. To these publications may be added many similar ones, the listing of which we defer for the bibliography.

Several other works served to put the depression from 1893 to 1897 in perspective. Two articles related different phases of economic activity during the period to other periods in a simple, if mechanical, way. Hubbard measured business volumes in declines and recoveries and thus provided a rough gauge for placing the 1893–1897 decline high among the list of sharp declines. Eckler's measures showed the depression to be among the most severe in the period 1873–1932.

Frickey's work, *Economic Fluctuations in The United States,* provides a useful guide to economic change. Analysis of secular trend as a problem in economic theory leads to a detailed statistical-analytic framework in which developments during a depression can more easily be identified and measured. Mitchell's pioneer work, *Business Cycles,* served as an overall model for this author. It is the kind of institutional analysis which sees economic change in a dynamic frame of reference, subordinating broad deductive-theoretical analysis to empirically oriented analysis based on major theoretical propositions, the nature of which must change as empirical research informs theoreticians. Mitchell's analysis of the period of the nineties is a superior one in which he used data on hand to reconstruct, quantitatively, some of the major institutional changes of the period. His statistical tables span many years and are the basis of his generalizations about business cycles and development. His description of the 1893–1897 period is cast in this methodological framework. His explanations, while not complete, are supported by his data as well as subsequent analyses. The later statistical work undertaken with A. F. Burns, *Measuring Business Cycles,* provides a basis upon which to analyze and evaluate specific business cycles among the many which have occurred since the Civil War. Certain basic economic series are measured over the period, giving rise to an average cycle pattern for the series. From these, it is possible to assess the behavior of particular series in one cycle in terms of such average statistical behavior. The last Mitchell work, *What Happens During Business Cycles,* also provides data helpful in getting perspective as to where different cycles stood in the overall picture of economic fluctuations in the United States. The use of these approaches to business-cycle analysis as well as of the nine-phase framework used by the National Bureau of Economic Research helps greatly in raising important questions about quantitative change during the depression. Without using the same technique, the economic historian still benefits immeasurably from the Bureau's series and their analysis.

Certain works provide important data on major aspects of the structure of the economy. Two works which furnish helpful data and analysis on railroading during the period are S. Daggett, *Railroad Reorganization,* and Edward G. Campbell, *The Reorganization of the American Railroad System, 1893–1900.* The former provides the basic data and analysis behind each of the major railroad reorganizations and helps foster an understanding of the complex factors at work in that major area of the economy. Campbell's work is useful mainly in providing a meaningful analysis of the railroads' problems in this critical period of their operation. The bases for bankruptcies in past and contemporary policies are explored with keen insight into the nature of railroad investment and management.

In addition to the works cited above, which have a direct or indirect bearing on the period under review, there are a number of works which survey and measure changes in major sectors of the economy such as railroads, farm prices, and incomes. These works, for the most part, trace cyclical and secular development of certain economic activity without particular reference to one period or one depression. Such studies are important in providing significant measures of economic change, usually on an annual basis, so that the task of evaluating changes in consumption, prices, income, and so on is considerably simplified for the author. Many of these works are the product of research of the NBER in its continuing task of measuring business cycles. Other works represent individual studies analyzing a major facet of economic activity.

Aiding us in our attempt to delineate the changes in investment during the depression were several works: Partington's *Railroad Purchasing and the Business Cycle* is a pioneer study which provides valuable data on purchases of railroad equipment, while Hultgren's more recent work, *American Transportation in Prosperity and Depressions,* puts fluctuations in railroad activity in a useful framework. Building activity and investment are quantified in Long's *Building Cycles and the Theory of Investment,* while Hoyt's *One Hundred Years of Land Values in Chicago* provides useful data for one large city. In any attempt to trace important changes in agriculture, *Gross Farm Income and Indices of Farm Production in the United States, 1869–1937,* by Strauss and Bean, is an important source. Other aspects of farm activity are uncovered in *Wheat Studies of the Food Research Institute* (Stanford University). Change in agricultural equipment investment is traced in Shaw's *Value of Commodity Output Since 1869,* just as other series in this work provide a concrete basis for generalizing about fluctuations in manufacturing investment and consumption. Other works with series suggesting fluctuations in investment include Burns, *Production Trends in the United States Since 1870,* and G. H. Evans, *Business Incorporations in the United States, 1800–1943.*

In the area of international economic relations, several works provided useful series and analysis. H. Jerome's *Migration and Business Cycles* permits inferences on the impact of the depression on immigration and emigration. Series and qualitative analysis in several works permit generalization in regard to capital flows. Among these are Nathaniel T. Bacon's article "American International Indebtedness" in the *Yale Review* (November, 1900); the Bullock-Tucker-Williams article "The Balance of Trade of the United States" in the *Review of Economic Statistics,* 1919; C. Lewis' *America's Stake in International Investment;* Imlah's article "British Balance of Payments and Export of Capital, 1818–1913" in the *Economic History Review,* 1953; and Folke Hilgerdt's United Nations study on the United States balance of payments from 1850 to 1914, completed in 1952.

Other useful data are to be found in the London *Economist* during the period. A rather curious source is Raffalovich's *Le Marché Financier* which surveys, each year, conditions in the international money market. The author was actually a paid agent of the Czarist government working in France, so that his analysis must be used with extra care.

In tracing price changes during the depression, one finds many series and analyses available outside of government services cited. Douglas' works, *The Problem of Unemployment* and *Real Wages in the United States, 1890–1926,* offer data on wage fluctuations as well as unemployment. The Strauss-Bean work, cited above, provides valuable series on farm prices. Prices of stocks and bonds are traced in the series provided by Cowles in *Common-stock Indexes* and Macaulay in *Some Theoretical Problems Suggested by the Movements of Interest Rates, Bond Yields and Stock Prices in the United States Since 1856.* Shaw's work, cited above, offers a comprehensive set of price indices for consumer and producer goods which, in addition to government price series, makes it easier to get an overall view of important price fluctuations. In the area of export and import prices, in addition to government data, the work of A. G. Silverman in the *Review of Economic Statistics* (August, 1930 and 1931) helps avoid merely guessing at what happened to terms of trade during the depression.

Besides these many works, which have made possible the quantitative measurement of major forces in the depression, there are certain primary sources which have also provided valuable statistical data on consumption, foreign trade, and so on. Both the financial and commercial journals, as well as the reports of various government bureaus, have proved a rich source of such information. The bibliography immediately following catalogs such sources under the classifications "Government Publications" and "Periodicals and Journals." For example, the publications of the U.S. National Monetary Commission, especially Vol. 21 (*Statistics for the United States, 1867–1909*), made available statistical data on such varied factors as gold flows, population growth, foreign trade, and money in circulation. Such journals as *Bradstreet's* and the *Chronicle* have not only furnished useful statistical data but have also provided interesting comments on all phases of economic activity.

We can see from this analysis of material at hand that while complete data for a comprehensive descriptive analysis of the depression were not available in published form, there was enough published so that a meaningful description and analysis of the depression was possible. To see the depression with all of its major forces clearly measurable over its duration, we would have to add many important series, all of which would have to be at least on a quarterly basis. Given the sources available, this would mean the construction of new series. Instead of pursuing such a gigantic task, the historian, working alone, must use these sources to the fullest until additional significant series, such as Shaw's, are erected. Definitive analysis of the depression must await such development as well as improvement of statistical and analytic techniques.

I. Articles

BACON, NATHANIEL T. "American International Indebtedness." *Yale Review* 9 (November, 1900): 265–285.

BERNARD, JESSIE. "The Power of Science and the Science of Power." *American Sociological Review* 14 (October, 1949): 575–584.

BOCOCK, JOHN P. "How the Gold Reserve Was Saved." *Harper's Weekly* 44 (June 2, 1900): 501–502.

BULLOCK, C. J., WILLIAMS, J. H. and TUCKER, R. S. "The Balance of Trade of the United States." *Review of Economic Statistics* 1 (July, 1919): 215–266.

CLOSSON, CARLOS C., JR. "Unemployed in American Cities." *Quarterly Journal of Economics* 8 (January and July, 1894): 168–217, 257–260, 453–477, 499–502.

DAVID, HENRY. "Upheaval at Homestead." pp. 133–170. In *America in Crisis,* edited by Daniel Aron. New York: Alfred A. Knopf, 1952.

ECKLER, A. ROSS. "A Measure of the Severity of Depressions, 1873–1932." *Review of Economic Statistics* 15 (May, 1933): 75–81.

FELS, RENDIGS. "American Business Cycles, 1865–79." *American Economic Review* 41 (June, 1951): 325–349.

GORDON, ROBERT A. "Business Cycles in the Interwar Period: The 'Quantitative-Historical' Approach." *American Economic Review* 39 (May, 1949): 47–63.

————. "Cyclical Experience in the Interwar Period: The Investment Boom of the Twenties," pp. 163–215. In *Conference on Business Cycles.* New York: National Bureau of Economic Research, 1951.

HEIDELBACH, A. S. "Why Gold Is Imported." *Forum* 18 (February, 1895): 647–651.

HERBERT, HILARY A. "Why American Industry Languishes." *North American Review* 163 (October, 1896): 488–495.

HIDY, RALPH W. "The Standard Oil Company (New Jersey)." *Tasks of Economic History, Journal of Economic History* 12 (Fall, 1952): 411–424.

HUBBARD, JOSEPH B. "Business Volumes During Periods of Decline and Recovery." *Review of Economic Statistics* 12 (November, 1930): 181–185.

IMLAH, ALBERT H. "British Balance of Payments and Export of Capital, 1816–1913." *Economic History Review* 5 (1952): 208–239.

LEBERGOTT, STANLEY. "Earnings of Non-farm Employees in the United States, 1890–1946." *Journal of American Statistical Association* 43 (March, 1948): 74–93.

MITCHELL, WESLEY C. "Quantitative Analysis in Economic Theory." *American Economic Review* 15 (March, 1925): 1–12.

NOYES, ALEXANDER D. "Banks and the Panic of 1893." *Political Science Quarterly* 9 (March, 1894): 12–30.

PASSER, HAROLD C. "Electrical Manufacturing Around 1900." *Tasks of Economic History, Journal of Economic History* 12 (Fall, 1952): 378–395.

PERSONS, WARREN M., TUTTLE, P. M. and FRICKEY, E. "Business and Financial Conditions Following the Civil War in the United States." *Review of Economic Statistics,* Preliminary Volume 2 (December, 1920), Supplement, 1–55.

PERSONS, W. M. "Statistics and Economic Theory." *Review of Economic Statistics* 7 (July, 1925): 179–197.

PHILBRICK, FRANK S. "The Mercantile Conditions of the Crisis of 1893." University of Nebraska, *University Studies* 2 (October, 1902): 299–320.

PHINNEY, J. T. "Gold Production and the Price Level." *Quarterly Journal of Economics.* 47 (August, 1933): 647–679.

"The Relief of the Unemployed in the United States During the Winter of 1893–1894." *Journal of Social Science* 32 (November, 1894): 1–51.

REZNECK, SAMUEL. "Unemployment, Unrest, and Relief in the United States during the Depression of 1893–97." *Journal of Political Economy* 61 (August, 1953): 324–345.

RIGGLEMAN, JOHN R. "Building Cycles in the United States, 1875–1932." *Journal of the American Statistical Association* 28 (June, 1933): 174–183.

ROSE, ARNOLD M. "A Deductive Ideal-Type Method." *American Journal of Sociology* 56 (July, 1950): 35–42.

RUSSEL, WILLIAM E. "Political Causes of the Business Depression." *North American Review* 157 (December, 1893): 641–652.

SCHUMPETER, JOSEPH A. "Historical Approach to the Analysis of Business Cycles," pp. 149–155. In *Conference on Business Cycles.* New York: National Bureau of Economic Research, 1951.

SILVERMAN, A. G. "Monthly Index Numbers of British Export and

Import Prices, 1880–1913." *Review of Economic Statistics* 12 (August, 1930), 139–148.

STEVENS, ALBERT C. "Analysis of the Phenomena of the Panic in the United States in 1893." *Quarterly Journal of Economics* 8 (January, 1894): 117–145.

WELLS, DAVID A. "The Teaching of Our Recent Economic Experiences." *Forum* 16 (January, 1894): 527–543.

WRIGHT, CARROLL D. "Relation of Production to Productive Capacity." *Forum* 24 (November, 1897, and February, 1898): 290–302, 660–675.

YOUNG, ALLYN A. "An Analysis of Bank Statistics for the United States." *Review of Economic Statistics* 6 (July, 1924): 284–296.

II. Government Publications

A. FEDERAL GOVERNMENT
(GOVERNMENT PRINTING OFFICE)

U.S., Federal Reserve System, Board of Governors. *Banking and Monetary Statistics*, vol. 16. 1943.

U.S., Bureau of Agricultural Economics. *Gross Farm Income and Indices of Farm Production and Prices in the United States, 1869–1937.* Compiled by Frederick Strauss and Louis H. Bean. 1940.

U.S., Bureau of the Census. *Census Reports*, 1890 and 1900.

U.S., Bureau of the Census. *Historical Statistics of the United States, 1789–1945.* 1949.

U.S., Bureau of the Census. *Population: Comparative Occupations Statistics for the United States, 1870–1940.* Compiled by Alba M. Edwards. Sixteenth Census. 1943.

U.S., Bureau of the Census. *Special Reports: Mines and Quarries 1902.* 1905.

U.S., Bureau of Corporations, *Report of the Commissioner of Corporations on Transportation by Water in the United States.* Vol. 1. 1901.

U.S., Bureau of Foreign Commerce. *Commercial Relations of the United States with Foreign Countries*, 1890/1891–1896/1897.

U.S., Bureau of Foreign and Domestic Commerce. *Consumption Estimates*. Miscellaneous Series, No. 26. 1915.

U.S., Bureau of Foreign and Domestic Commerce. *Monthly Summary of Imports and Exports of the United States*, 1893–1901. (After 1898: *Monthly Summary of the Foreign Commerce of the United States*).

U.S., Bureau of Labor. *Annual Report of the Commissioner of Labor*, 1893–1897.

U.S., Bureau of Labor. *Third Special Report of the Commissioner of Labor*. 1893.

U.S., Bureau of Labor Statistics. *Index Numbers of Wholesale Prices on Pre-War Base, 1890–1927*. 1928.

U.S., Bureau of Labor Statistics. *History of Wages in the United States from Colonial Times to 1928*. Bulletin No. 499. 1929.

U.S., Bureau of Labor Statistics. *Statistics of Unemployment and the Work of Unemployment Offices*. Compiled by Frank B. Sargent. Bulletin no. 109. Miscellaneous Series, no. 1. 1913.

U.S., Bureau of Statistics. *The Foreign Commerce and Navigation of the United States for the Year Ending June 30, 1893*. 1893.

U.S., Bureau of Statistics. *Monthly Report*, 1893–1894.

U.S., Bureau of Statistics. *Movement of Prices, 1840–1899*. (From Sauerbeck's Tables, *Economist*, (London) and from Reports of the United States Senate and of the Department of Labor on Prices.) From *Summary of Commerce and Finance* for May, 1900, pp. 3129–3218.

U.S., Bureau of Statistics. *Quarterly Reports Showing Imports and Exports of the United States for the Four Quarters Ending June 30*. 1889/1890–1892/1893.

U.S., Commissioner of Labor. *Third Special Report of the Commissioner of Labor*. 1893.

U.S., Comptroller of the Currency. *Annual Report*, 1891–1898.

U.S., Congress. *Biographical Directory of the American Congress*. 81st Cong., 2nd sess., H.D. 607. 1950.

U.S., Congress, Senate. Committee on Agriculture and Forestry.

Report on Agricultural Depression. 53rd Cong., 3rd sess., S.R. 986, Serial no. 3290. 1895.

U.S., Department of Agriculture. *Yearbook.* 1894–1897.

U.S., Federal Electric Railways Commission. *Proceedings together with Final Report to the President.* Vol. 3. 1920.

U.S., Immigration Commission. *Report: Statistical Review of Immigration, 1820–1910.* 61st Cong., 3rd sess., S.D. 756. 1911.

U.S., Industrial Commission. *Reports.* Vols. 1–19. 1900–1902.

U.S., Interstate Commerce Commission. *Annual Report,* 1893–1897.

U.S., National Monetary Commission. *A History of Crises Under the National Banking System,* by O.M. W. Sprague. 61st Cong. 2nd sess. S.D. 538. 1910.

U.S., National Monetary Commission. *The History of National-Bank Currency,* by A. D. Noyes. 66th Cong., 2nd sess., S.D. 572. 1910.

U.S., National Monetary Commission, Publications. *Financial Laws of the United States, 1778–1909,* Vol. 2. 1910.

U.S., National Monetary Commission, Publications. *Statistics for the United States, 1867–1909,* by Abram P. Andrew, Vol. 21. 1910.

U.S., National Monetary Commission, Publications. *Seasonal Variations in the Relative Demand for Money and Capital in the United States, by* Edwin W. Kemmerer, Vol. 22. 1910.

U.S., National Resources Commission. *The Structure of the American Economy.* Part I, Basic Characteristics. 1939.

U.S., Strike Commission. *Report on the Chicago Strike of June-July 1894.* 1895.

U.S., Treasury Department. *Annual Report of the Secretary,* 1892–1898.

B. STATE GOVERNMENTS

Colorado, Bureau of Labor Statistics. *Biennial Report,* 1889/1890–1893/1894.

Connecticut, Bureau of Labor Statistics. *Report,* 1890–1897.

Iowa, Bureau of Labor Statistics. *Biennial Report,* 1890/1891–1897/1898.

Kansas, Bureau of Labor and Industry. *Annual Report,* 1890–1897.

Maine, Bureau of Industrial and Labor Statistics. *Annual Report,* 1890–1897.

Maryland, Bureau of Industrial Statistics. *Annual Report,* 1892–1897.

Massachusetts, Bureau of Statistics of Labor. *Annual Report,* 1890–1897.

Michigan, Bureau of Labor and Industrial Statistics. *Annual Report,* 1890–1897.

Minnesota, Bureau of Labor Statistics. *Biennial Report,* 1889/1890–1895/1896.

Missouri, Bureau of Labor Statistics. *Annual Report,* 1890–1897.

New Jersey, Bureau of Statistics of Labor and Industries. *Annual Report,* 1890–1897.

New York, Bureau of Statistics of Labor. *Annual Report,* 1890–1897.

New York, Insurance Department. *Annual Report of the Superintendent,* 1893–1899.

Ohio, Bureau of Labor Statistics. *Annual Report,* 1890–1897.

Pennsylvania, Secretary of Internal Affairs. *Annual Report of the Secretary of Internal Affairs,* Part III: Industrial Statistics, 1890–1897.

III. Books

A. BIBLIOGRAPHICAL WORKS

BOYD, ANNE MORRIS. *United States Government Publications.* 3rd ed., revised by Rae Elizabeth Rips. New York: H.W. Wilson Company, 1949.

HURT, PEYTON. *Bibliography and Footnotes.* Berkeley and Los Angeles: University of California Press, 1949.

RUSSELL, EDITH M., comp. *A List of Business Histories and Biographies in the Business Library.* New York: Dun and Bradstreet, 1949.

SCHMECKEBIER, LAURENCE F. *Government Publications and Their Use.* Washington: The Brookings Institution, 1936.

B. OTHER BOOKS

ABRAMOVITZ, MOSES. *Inventories and Business Cycles.* New York: National Bureau of Economic Research, 1950.

———. *The Role of Inventories in Business.* New York: National Bureau of Economic Research, 1949.

ACHINSTEIN, ASHER. *Introduction to Business Cycles.* New York: Crowell–Collier Publishing Co., 1950.

Arlington Mills (Lawrence, Massachusetts). *Tops: A Study in the Development of the American Worsted Manufacture.* Cambridge: Riverside Press, 1898.

AUBLE, ARTHUR G. *"The Depressions of 1873 and 1882 in the United States."* Ph.D. dissertation, Harvard University, 1949.

AYERS, LEONARD P. *Turning Points in Business Cycles.* New York: Macmillan Company, 1930.

BARR, ROBERT. *The Victors.* New York: Frederick A. Stokes, 1901.

BEACH, WALTER E. *British International Gold Movements and Banking Policy, 1881–1913.* Cambridge, Mass.: Harvard University Press, 1935.

BEVERIDGE, WILLIAM H. *Unemployment.* London: Longmans, Green and Co., 1930.

BREMER, CORNELIUS D. *American Bank Failures.* New York: Columbia University Press, 1935.

BRIDGE, JAMES H. *Inside History of the Carnegie Steel Company.* New York: Aldine Book Company, 1903.

BURNS, ARTHUR F. *Production Trends in the United States since 1870.* New York: National Bureau of Economic Research, 1934.

BURNS, A. F. and MITCHELL, W. C. *Measuring Business Cycles.* New York: National Bureau of Economic Research, 1946.

BURTON, THEODORE E. *A Century of Prices.* New York: Magazine of Wall Street, 1919.

———. *Financial Crises and Periods of Industrial and Commercial*

Depression. New York: D. Appleton & Company, 1902.

CAMPBELL, EDWARD G. *The Reorganization of the American Railroad System, 1893–1900.* New York: Columbia University Press, 1938.

CARNAP, RUDOLF. *Logical Foundations of Probability.* Chicago: University of Chicago Press, 1950.

CHAPIN, FRANCIS STUART. *Experimental Designs in Sociological Research.* New York: Harper, 1947.

CHAPMAN, SYDNEY JOHN. *The History of Trade Between the United Kingdom and the United States.* London: Swan Sonnenschein, 1899.

CLARK, VICTOR S. *History of Manufactures in the United States.* Vols. 2 and 3. Washington, D.C.: Carnegie Institution, 1929.

CLEWS, HENRY. *Fifty Years in Wall Street.* New York: Irving Publishing Co., 1908.

————. *Financial, Economic and Miscellaneous Speeches and Essays.* New York: Irving Publishing Co., 1910.

————. *The Wall Street Point of View.* New York: Silver, Burdett & Co., 1900.

COMMONS, JOHN, et. al. *History of Labour in the United States.* Vols. 2 and 3. New York: Macmillan Company, 1951.

Conference on Business Cycles. New York: National Bureau of Economic Research, 1951.

COWLES, ALFRED, 3RD, et. al. *Common-stock Indexes.* 2nd ed. Bloomington, Indiana: Principia Press, 1939.

DAGGETT, STUART. *Railroad Reorganization.* Boston: Houghton Mifflin Company, 1908.

DEARING, CHARLES L. *American Highway Policy.* Washington, D.C.: The Brookings Institution, 1941.

DEWEY, D. R. *Financial History of the United States.* 12th ed. New York: Longmans, Green, and Co., 1936.

————. *Irregularity of Employment.* Vol. 9. nos. 5–6. Baltimore: American Economic Association Publications, 1894.

DEWING, ARTHUR S. *Corporate Promotions and Reorganizations.* Cambridge, Mass.: Harvard University Press, 1914.

DICKENS, PAUL A. "The Transition Period in American International Financing: 1897 to 1914." Ph.D. dissertation, George Washington University, 1933.

DOANE, ROBERT R. *The Measurement of American Wealth.* New York: Harper, 1933.

DOUGLAS, PAUL H., and DIRECTOR, AARON. *The Problem of Unemployment.* New York: Macmillan Company, 1931.

DOUGLAS, PAUL H. *Real Wages in the United States, 1890–1926.* New York: Houghton Mifflin Company, 1930.

EDWARDS, ALBA M. *Comparative Occupation Statistics for the United States, 1870–1940.* Sixteenth Census: Population. Washington, D.C.: Government Printing Office, 1943.

ESPINOSA DE LOS REYES, JORGE. *Relaciones Economicas Entre Mexico y Estados Unidas, 1870–1910.* Mexico, D.F.: Nacional Financiera S. S., 1951.

EVANS, GEORGE H. *Business Incorporations in the United States, 1800–1943.* New York: National Bureau of Economic Research, 1948.

EVEREST, ALLAN S. *Morgenthau, the New Deal and Silver.* New York: King's Crown Press, 1950.

FAULKNER, HAROLD U. *The Decline of Laissez-Faire.* Economic History of the United States, edited by Henry David, et al., vol. 7. New York: Rinehart, 1951.

FEDER, LEAH H. *Unemployment Relief in Periods of Depression.* New York: Russell Sage Foundation, 1936.

FEIS, HERBERT. *Europe, The World's Banker, 1870–1914.* New Haven, Conn.: Yale University Press, 1930.

FELS, RENDIGS. "History of American Business Cycles, 1865–1921." Ph.D. dissertation, Harvard University, 1948.

FORD, HOWARD G. "The Wilson-Gorman Tariff of 1894." Master's thesis, Columbia University 1933.

FRICKEY, EDWIN. *Economic Fluctuations in the United States; a Systematic Analysis of Long-run Trends and Business Cycles, 1866–1914.* Cambridge, Mass.: Harvard University Press, 1942.

GARVY, GEORGE. *The Development of Bank Debits and Clearings and Their Use in Economic Analysis.* Washington, D.C.: Board of Governors, Federal Reserve System, 1952.

GALBRAITH, JOHN K. *The Great Crash.* Boston: Houghton Mifflin Company, 1955.

GINZBERG, ELI. *The Illusion of Economic Stability.* New York: Harper, 1939.

GOODRICH, CARTER, et al. *Migration and Economic Opportunity.* Philadelphia: University of Pennsylvania Press, 1936.

GORDON, ROBERT A. *Business Fluctuations.* New York: Harper, 1952.

HACKER, LOUIS M. *The Triumph of American Capitalism.* New York: Columbia University Press, 1946.

HALL, LINCOLN W. *Banking Cycles.* Philadelphia: University of Pennsylvania Press, 1927.

HANSEN, ALVIN H. *Business Cycles and National Income.* New York: W. W. Norton & Co., 1951.

————*Monetary Theory and Fiscal Policy.* New York: McGraw-Hill, 1949.

HART, ALBERT G. *Money, Debt and Economic Activity.* New York: Prentice-Hall, 1948.

HEPBURN, A. B. *Artificial Waterways of the World.* New York: Macmillan Company, 1914.

HOWER, RALPH M. *History of Macy's of New York.* Cambridge, Mass.: Harvard University Press, 1943.

HOYT, HOMER. *One Hundred Years of Land Values in Chicago.* Chicago: University of Chicago Press, 1933.

HULL, GEORGE H. *Industrial Depressions.* New York: Frederick A. Stokes, 1911.

HULTGREN, THOR. *American Transportation in Prosperity and Depression.* New York: National Bureau of Economic Research, 1948.

HUTCHINS, JOHN G. B. *The American Maritime Industries and Public Policy, 1789–1914.* Cambridge, Mass.: Harvard University Press, 1941.

JAFFE, ABRAM J. and STEWART, CHARLES D. *Manpower Resources and Utilization.* New York: John Wiley & Sons, 1951.

JAMES, FRANK C. *Cyclical Fluctuations in the Shipping and Shipbuilding Industries*. Philadelphia: University of Pennsylvania Press, 1927.

JEROME, HARRY. *Migration and Business Cycles*. New York: National Bureau of Economic Research, 1926.

JONAS, ALEXANDER. *Why Workmen are Unemployed!* New York: N.Y. Labor News Co., 1898.

JOSEPHSON, MATTHEW. *The Politicos, 1865–1896*. New York: Harcourt, Brace & Co., 1938.

————.*The Robber Barons*. New York: Harcourt, Brace & Co., 1934.

JUGLAR, CLEMENT. *A Brief History of Panics and Their Periodical Occurrence in the United States*. New York: G. P. Putnam's Sons, 1916.

KAUFMANN, FELIX. *Methodology of the Social Sciences*. New York: Oxford University Press, 1944.

KEYNES, J. M. *A Treatise on Probability*. London: Macmillan Company, 1929.

KUZNETS, SIMON. *National Income: A Summary of Findings*. New York: National Bureau of Economic Research, 1946.

————.*National Product Since 1869*. New York: National Bureau of Economic Research, 1946.

————."Annual Estimates of National Product, 1869–1949." Capital Requirements Study. Unpublished preliminary memorandum of the National Bureau of Economic Research, March, 1951.

LANDIS, PAUL HENRY. *Population Problems: A Cultural Interpretation*. New York: American Book Co., 1943.

LAUCK, WILLIAM J. *The Causes of the Panic of 1893*. Boston and New York: Houghton Mifflin Company, 1907.

LEIBOWITZ, H. "Unemployment Relief During the Depression of 1893–1984." Master's thesis, Columbia University, 1936.

LEONTIEF, WASSILY W. *The Structure of American Economy, 1919–1939*. New York: Oxford University Press, 1951.

LEWIS, CLEONA. *America's Stake in International Investments*.

Washington, D.C.: The Brookings Institution, 1938.

LIGHTNER, OTTO C. *The History of Business Depressions.* New York: Northeastern, 1922.

LONG, CLARENCE D. *Building Cycles and the Theory of Investment.* Princeton: Princeton University Press, 1940.

LUNDBERG, GEORGE A. *Foundations of Sociology.* New York: Macmillan Company, 1939.

MACAULAY, FREDERICK E. *Some Theoretical Problems Suggested by the Movements of Interest Rates, Bond Yields and Stock Prices in the United States Since 1856.* New York: National Bureau of Economic Research, 1938.

MACIVER, ROBERT M. *Social Causation.* New York: Ginn & Co., 1942.

MCGRANE, REGINALD C. *The Economic Development of the American Nation.* New York: Ginn & Co., 1942.

MCMURRY, DONALD L. *Coxey's Army.* Boston: Little, Brown & Co., 1929.

MARTIN, ROBERT F. *National Income in the United States, 1799–1938.* New York: National Industrial Conference Board, 1939.

MILLIS, H. A., and MONTGOMERY, R. E. *Organized Labor.* Vol. 3. In *Economics of Labor.* New York: McGraw-Hill, 1945.

MILLS, FREDERICK C. *The Behavior of Prices.* New York: National Bureau of Economic Research, 1927.

MITCHELL, WESLEY C. *Business Cycles.* Berkeley: University of California Press, 1913.

———. *Business Cycles and Their Causes.* Berkeley, Los Angeles: University of California Press, 1941.

———.*What Happens During Business Cycles.* New York: National Bureau of Economic Research, 1951.

MYERS, MARGARET G. *The New York Money Market: Origins and Development.* Vol. 1. New York: Columbia University Press, 1931.

National Bureau of Economic Research. Work Memorandum Number 31, *International Capital Movements.* Vol. 1, *Across United States Borders.* Part 1, Solomon Fabricant, "Highlights and

Questions." Part 2, Robert E. Lipsey, "A Summary of Available Statistics." Capital Requirements Study. New York: National Bureau of Economic Research, 1951.

NEVINS, ALLAN. *Grover Cleveland*. New York: Dodd, Mead & Co., 1933.

NORTON, JOHN P. *Statistical Studies in the New York Money Market*. New York: Macmillan Company, 1902.

NOYES, ALEXANDER D. *Forty Years of American Finance*. New York: G. P. Putnam's Sons, 1909.

————.*The History of National-Bank Currency*. 66th Cong. 2nd Office, sess., S.D. 572. Washington, D.C.: Government Printing 1910.

OGBURN, WILLIAM F., and GOLDENWEISER, A., eds. *The Social Sciences and Their Interrelations*. New York: Houghton Mifflin Company, 1927.

PARTINGTON, JOHN E. *Railroad Purchasing and the Business Cycle*. Washington: The Brookings Institution, 1929.

PATTEN, SIMON N. *The Consumption of Wealth*. Boston: Ginn & Co., 1901.

RAFOLOVICH, ARTHUR G. (Raffalovich, Arthur), ed. *Le Marché Financier*, 1890/1891–1897/1898. Paris: Guillaumin, 1891–1898.

RICE, STUART A., ed. *Methods in Social Science: A Case Book*. Compiled under the direction of the Committee on Scientific Method in the Social Sciences of the Social Science Research Council. Chicago: University of Chicago Press, 1937.

RIGGLEMAN, JOHN R. "Variations in Building Activity." Ph.D. dissertation, Johns Hopkins University, 1934.

RIPLEY, WILLIAM Z. *Railroads: Finance and Organization*. Vol. 2. New York: Longmans, Green & Co., 1927.

————., ed. *Trusts, Pools and Corporations*. New York: Ginn & Co., 1916.

ROGIN, LEO. *The Introduction of Farm Machinery in Its Relation to the Productivity of Labor in the Agriculture of the United States During the Nineteenth Century*. Berkeley: University of California Press, 1931.

ROSENBLATT, AARON. "United States Foreign Investment, 1880–1914." Master's thesis, Columbia University, 1948.

ROSHWALB, IRVING. "The Baring Crisis and Its Effect on the Panic of 1893 in the United States." 2 Vols. Master's thesis, Columbia University, 1947.

ROSTOW, WALT W. *British Economy of the Nineteenth Century*. Oxford: Clarendon Press, 1943.

————."British Trade Fluctuations, 1868–1896." Ph.D. dissertation, Yale University, 1940.

————.*The Process of Economic Growth*. New York: W. W. Norton & Co., 1952.

RUSSELL, BERTRAND. *An Inquiry into Meaning and Truth*. New York: W. W. Norton & Co., 1940.

SARGENT, FRANK B. *Statistics of Unemployment and the Work of Employment Offices*. Bulletin 109, U.S. Bureau of Labor Statistics. Miscellaneous Series, no. 1. Washington, D.C.: Government Printing Office, 1913.

SCHLOTE, WERNER. *British Overseas Trade from 1700 to the 1930's*. Translated by W. O. Henderson and W. H. Chalomer. Oxford: Blackwell, 1952.

SCHLUTER, WILLIAM C. *The Pre-war Business Cycle, 1907 to 1914*. New York: Columbia University Press, 1923.

SCHUMPETER, JOSEPH A. *Business Cycles*. 2 vols. New York: McGraw-Hill, 1939.

SHANNON, FRED A. *The Farmer's Last Frontier*. The Economic History of the United States, edited by Henry David, et al., vol. 5. New York: Rinehart, 1945.

SHAW, WILLIAM H. *Finished Commodities Since 1879: Output and its Composition*. National Bureau of Economic Research Occasional Paper 3. New York: National Bureau of Economic Research, 1941.

————.*Value of Commodity Output Since 1869*. New York: National Bureau of Economic Research, 1947.

SILBERLING, NORMAN J. *The Dynamics of Business*. New York: McGraw-Hill, 1943.

SMITH, WALTER BUCKINGHAM, and COLE, A. H. *Fluctuations in American Business, 1790–1860*. Cambridge, Mass.: Harvard University Press, 1935.

SMUTS, ROBERT. "Miscellaneous Memoranda on the Labor Force." Conservation of Human Resources Project, Graduate School of Business, Columbia University, 1951–1952.

SPRAGUE, O. M. W. *Banking Reform in the United States*. Cambridge, Mass.: Harvard University Press, 1913.

———.*A History of Crises Under the National Banking System*. 61st Cong., 2nd Sess., S. D. 538. Washington, D.C.: Government Printing Office, 1910.

STRAUSS, FREDERICK, and BEAN, LOUIS. *Gross Farm Income and Indices of Farm Products and Prices in the United States, 1869–1937*. Prepared through the cooperation of the Department of Agriculture and the National Bureau of Economic Research. Technical Bulletin 703, Bureau of Agricultural Economics. Washington, D.C.: Government Printing Office, 1940.

STRAUSS, FREDERICK. *The Composition of Gross Farm Income Since the Civil War*. National Bureau of Economic Research Bulletin no. 78. New York: National Bureau of Economic Research, 1940.

TARBELL, IDA M. *The Nationalizing of Business, 1878–1893*. A History of American Life, edited by A. M. Schlesinger and D. R. Fox, vol. 9. New York: Macmillan Company, 1936.

TAUSSIG, F. W. *The Silver Situation in the United States*. New York: G. P. Putnam's Sons, 1894.

———.*Some Aspects of the Tariff Question*. Cambridge, Mass.: Harvard University Press, 1934.

———.*Tariff History of the United States*. 6th ed. New York: G. P. Putnam's Sons, 1914.

TEBBUTT, ARTHUR R. *The Behavior of Consumption in Business Depression*. Business Research Studies, vol. 20, no. 3. Cambridge, Mass.: Division of Research, Graduate School of Business Administration, Harvard University, 1933.

TEGGART, RICHARD V. *Thorstein Veblen: A Chapter in American Economic Thought.* University of California Publications. Economics, Vol. 11, 1932. Berkeley: University of California Press, 1942.

United Nations, Department of Economic Affairs, Division of Economic Stability and Development. Research Memorandum no. 9. *Annual Figures for the Balance of Payments, 1850–1914.* Prepared by Folke Hilgerdt. New York: United Nations, Division of Economic Stability and Development, 1952.

WALLACE, D. H. *Market Control in the Aluminum Industry.* Cambridge, Mass.: Harvard University Press, 1937.

WATSON, FRANK D. *The Charity Organization Movement in the United States.* New York: Macmillan Company, 1922.

WEBERG, FRANK P. "The Background of the Panic of 1893." Ph.D. dissertation. Washington, D.C.: Catholic University, 1929.

WHITE, GERALD T. "The United States and the Problem of Recovery After 1893." Ph.D. dissertation, University of California, 1938.

WHITTEMORE, RICHARD F. W. "The Gold Reserve and the Treasury Crisis in 1894–1895." Master's thesis, Columbia University, 1949.

WILCOX, DELOS F. *Analysis of the Electric Railway Problem.* (Report to the Federal Electric Railways Commission.) New York: Delos F. Wilcox, 1921.

WILLCOX, WALTER F., ed. *International Migrations.* 2 Vols. New York: National Bureau of Economic Research, 1929, 1931.

WILLIAMSON, HAROLD F., ed. *The Growth of the American Economy.* New York: Prentice-Hall, 1944.

WILSON, THOMAS. *Fluctuations in Income and Employment.* 3rd ed. New York: Pitman Publishing Corp., 1948.

WINKLER, JOHN K. *Five and Ten: The Fabulous Life of F. W. Woolworth.* New York: McBride, 1940.

WOLMAN, LEO. *Ebb and Flow in Trade Unionism.* New York: National Bureau of Economic Research, 1936.

WOOTON, BARBARA. *Testament for Social Science.* London: G. Allen & Unwin, 1950.

YELLEN, SAMUEL. *American Labor Struggles.* New York: Harcourt, Brace & Co., 1936.

ZIMMERMANN, ERICH W. *Ocean Shipping.* New York: Prentice-Hall, 1921.

IV. Yearbooks, Directories, Proceedings, Reports

American Federation of Labor. *Report of Proceedings of the Annual Convention.* New York: 1893, 1894.

American Iron and Steel Association. *Annual Statistical Report.* Philadelphia: 1894–1896.

American Street Railway Investments. A Supplement to the *Street Railway Journal.* New York: 1894–1898.

Appleton's Annual Cyclopedia and Register of Important Events. New York: 1893–1898.

Atchison, Topeka & Santa Fe Railroad Company. *Annual Report.* New York: 1892–1896.

Banker's Directory. Chicago: 1894–1897.

Banking Almanac, Directory, Year Book and Diary. London: 1894.

Chicago Board of Trade. *Annual Report of the Trade and Commerce of Chicago.* Chicago: 1892–1897.

Commercial Yearbook. Edited by W. Dodsworth. New York: 1896, 1897.

Dictionary of American Biography. Edited by Allen Johnson, Duman Malone, Harris E. Starr. 21 vols. and index. New York: 1928–1944.

Erie Railroad Company. *Annual Report.* New York: 1897.

Financial Review. (Published by *Commercial and Financial Chronicle.*) New York: 1893–1899.

New York, New Haven & Hartford Railroad. *Annual Report.* New Haven: 1891–1896.

New York State, Chamber of Commerce. *Annual Report.* New York: 1891–1897.

Poor's Manual of Railroads. New York: 1893–1899.

Le Marché Financier. Edited by Arthur G. Rafolovich (Arthur Raffalovich). Paris: Guillaumin, 1890/1891–1897/1898.

Stock Exchange Official Intelligence. (Burdett's Official Intelligence.) London: 1893–1897.

Union Pacific Railway Company. *Annual Report.* Boston: 1892–1896.

United States Investor and Promoter of American Enterprises. Boston, New York, Philadelphia: 1891–1897.

V. Periodicals and Journals

American Banker. (weekly). New York. 1893–1897.

American Federationist. (monthly) New York: 1892–1897.

American Iron and Steel Institute. *Bulletin.* (weekly until February, 1895; three times monthly until December, 1897) Philadelphia: 1893–1897.

Bankers' Insurance Managers' and Agents' Magazine. (monthly) London: 1893–1896.

Banker's Magazine. (monthly) New York. 1893–1897.

Bradstreet's (weekly) New York: 1892–1898.

Commercial and Financial Chronicle. (weekly) New York: 1892–1897.

Dun's Review. (weekly) New York: 1893–1897.

Economist and Annual Supplements. (weekly) London: 1892–1898.

Knights of Labor. *Journal of the Knights of Labor.* (weekly) Philadelphia. 1893–1894.

New York Times. (daily) New York: 1892–1898.

Railroad Gazette. (weekly) Chicago: 1894–1898.

Stanford University, Food Research Institute. *Wheat Studies of The Food Research Institute.* Vols. 1–20. Stanford University, California: December, 1924–July, 1944.

Street Railway Journal. (monthly) New York: 1894–1898.

Index

Adams, Henry C., 286
Agricultural economy, change from, 10, 280
Agricultural equipment, rise in value of, 116
Agricultural investment, 125–127
Agricultural products
  expansion in, 30–31, 35, 88
  exports of, 166–168
Agricultural workers, increase in, 16
Agriculture
  changed marketing position of, 280–281
  countercyclical forces in, 279
  depression and, 272–274
  expansion of, 30–31, 35, 88
  low point in, 280–281
  mechanization of, 116
  recovery of, 75
  unemployment in, 86
  see also Farming; Farm prices
Allison, William Boyd, 52
American Federation of Labor, 37, 97
American Railway Union, 70
Auble, Arthur G., 289

Bacon, Nathaniel T., 162, 295
Balance of payments xxii, 78, 157–187
  for 1890–1900 (table), xli

export-import prices and, 244–248
fluctuations in, 274
foreign investments and, 180–186
gold flows and, 177–179
gold reserve and, 226
Great Britain and, 185, 193–196, 226
new data on, xxvi, xxxviii, liii
Treasury debt and, 227
see also Gold; Gold flows
Balance of trade, improvement in, 88–89, 169–170
Bank clearings and velocity, 72, 215–218
Bank deposits, changes in, 1890–1900, xliv–xlvi
Bank failures, 57–59, 62, 203
Bank loans
  fluctuations in, 205–208
  reserves and, 210
Bank notes, supply of, xlvi, 205–208
Bank of Amsterdam, failure of, 57
Bank reserves, xliv, 60, 208
Banks, suspension of cash payments by, 62
Baring crisis, England, 48–49
Bean, Louis, 295–296